ADVANCING PEACE

Urban and Industrial Environments

Series editors: Robert Gottlieb, Professor of Urban and Environmental Policy, Emeritus, Occidental College

Bhavna Shamasunder, Mellichamp Chair in Racially Just, Resilient and Sustainable City Futures, University of California, Santa Barbara

A full list of titles in this series is included at the end of this book.

ADVANCING PEACE

ENDING URBAN GUN VIOLENCE THROUGH
THE POWER OF REDEMPTIVE LOVE

JASON CORBURN AND DEVONE BOGGAN

THE MIT PRESS   CAMBRIDGE, MASSACHUSETTS   LONDON, ENGLAND

The MIT Press
Massachusetts Institute of Technology
77 Massachusetts Avenue, Cambridge, MA 02139
mitpress.mit.edu

This publication has been supported by the MIT Press Grant Program for Diverse Voices.

The MIT Press would like to thank the anonymous peer reviewers who provided comments on drafts of this book. The generous work of academic experts is essential for establishing the authority and quality of our publications. We acknowledge with gratitude the contributions of these otherwise uncredited readers.

This book was set in Stone Sans and Stone Serif by Westchester Publishing Services. Printed and bound in the United States of America.

Library of Congress Cataloging-in-Publication Data is available.

ISBN: 978-0-262-55221-9

10 9 8 7 6 5 4 3 2 1

EU Authorised Representative: Easy Access System Europe, Mustamäe tee 50, 10621 Tallinn, Estonia | Email: gpsr.requests@easproject.com

CONTENTS

ILLUSTRATIONS AND TABLES

TABLE

PREFACE

Each year during my nearly nine-year tenure as neighborhood safety director and director of the Office of Neighborhood Safety (ONS) for the city of Richmond, California, the city manager hosted a retreat with all the city's department directors. Attendance was mandatory. This was unpopular among some of the directors, as they saw it as a waste of a full day's work or perhaps it created anxiety for them. Others approached it with a mild spirit, accepting it as part of the job of a city director. For me, it was my job to be there, and I was always prepared with my departments completed "preretreat" assignment as instructed by the city manager. The retreat served as an internal "citywide" annual strategic planning, review, and learning session. The discussions were mostly deliberate, intentionally focused on where we were as a city government, where we were going, and how each department head's leadership and departmental team was to help us arrive at a destination healthiest for our residents. The daylong agenda was always packed, and portions often included discussions and presentations by external "experts" from a variety of fields. In a room full of seasoned government leaders with sizable egos, this part of the retreat was always of interest to me because it invariably created an environment for an extraordinary conversation.

It was at one of these retreats that I first was introduced to Dr. Jason Corburn. We were both much younger, and I remember thinking, Who is this young, bold, dude talking about "the people" of Richmond as if he was one with them? He presented as if he was deeply ingrained into the Richmond community. I just knew he had to have been from Richmond the way he talked about the city. It was as if it was his hometown. Jason had been introduced to us as a public health, urban planning social scientist working to support our integration of Health in All Policies into everything city government. The initiative was the city manager's big play, and we were all required to run this play as perfect as possible. Jason talked about urban planning and public health in ways unlike I had ever heard before. He was resolute, fresh, and even daring as he challenged us directors to think differently about how we saw the "playing field" of urban planning and public health. He was speaking my language. It was as if I had an advocate in the room. My head nods were pronounced, and I hoped they'd communicate to him that he had support in the room to take us deeper. For my peers, well, it was a mixed bag in terms of how they received Jason's presentation and guidance.

Jason believed in the power and authority of community in providing leadership to address the harms people were negotiating structurally, environmentally, socially, and physically. Like me, he believed that the solutions must come from those most impacted. He stressed that "healthy communities are guided by community-driven decision-making" and would challenge us not only to listen to what our most vulnerable communities were saying but also work with them. He emphasized how we as city leaders needed to lead by creating safe spaces that welcomed community members to speak for themselves. Jason would challenge us to not ignore, be impatient about, or sidestep input from our neighborhoods most impacted by a laundry list of social ills. "Be willing to really be accountable to them, not just in word, but in service," he would urge. And Doc (one of the names he is affectionately referred to by both the ONS and Advance Peace staff) had the data to back up everything that he was pushing.

I walked away from Jason's visit and presentation knowing that he was a true believer in community. He was sincere about the work of being an ally, and doing whatever he could to see that those indigenous to our most impacted communities were empowered with good data to hold power and help shape what as well as how the city would implement policies, programs, and practices focused on improving health equity.

He was speaking my language. I knew that we would become friends and collaborators. I was going to make sure of it.

Four years after meeting Jason, I would leave the city to create Advance Peace. One of the first calls I would make was to Jason. We set up a time to meet, have coffee, and discuss life and what I was diving into regarding my new venture. I wasn't leaving the meet without a "yes" to the primary purpose for my call. Jason agreed to lead the learning and evaluation work associated with Advance Peace efforts to support city replication of the Peacemaker Fellowship. For seven years now, Jason and his team at the University of California at Berkeley have been instrumental in helping us maintain and improve Peacemaker Fellowship fidelity by supporting our teams nationwide. Their learning and evaluation work is comprehensive and demanding. It has helped to demonstrate the effectiveness of our work specifically, and more generally, the viability and importance of community violence intervention (CVI) as a necessary part of the public safety ecosystem in cities most impacted by firearm violence.

Over the course of our relationship, Jason has invited me into university-sponsored Fellowships and supported my becoming a visiting scholar at the University of California. I hope you will find what I found in his words, spirit, and person: a sincerely committed soldier tenaciously working to improve opportunities for creating healthier, safer, and more just communities around the globe.

—D. B.

*   *   *

For the past twenty years, I have been working with (not for or on) communities to eliminate the sources of health inequities they face and support healing. Whether I was in Brooklyn or the Bay Area, Nairobi, Rio, or Medellín, or somewhere in between, I kept hearing the same concerns: fear of violence constrains our opportunities and choices to be healthy as well as heal.

When I was invited to work with activists in Richmond, California, in 2005, I heard the same concerns. While I was a partner with the environmental and human rights group Communities for a Better Environment, residents kept saying, "There is no environment for us if we live in fear, if gun violence keeps us inside, if the violence keeps opportunity beyond our reach."

Yet these same community members had ideas about what to do to eliminate the violence and believed they should be leaders in this effort. I was and remain committed to listening to and learning from those closest to an issue, whether it be the health of one's child, the air one is breathing, or how to improve safety in one's neighborhood. I listened to Richmond residents, and learned that they knew very well what was adversely impacting their health and had ideas for solutions.

As DeVone noted in his preface, I was asked to present some data to city leaders about how they could best support a community-driven, health equity strategy—what we called Health in All Policies. I too remember that while I was presenting, most city leaders were nodding off or looking out the window totally uninterested. I remember one leader, though, feverishly taking notes and nodding his head. That was DeVone. As he recalled, we spoke after, met for coffee a few days later, and have been collaborating ever since.

As we spent more time together, I learned how passionate D (what most people call DeVone) was about peace and racial justice. Peacemaking and peacekeeping wasn't just a city job for DeVone. It was a calling; he was willing to sacrifice time with his family, working long hours, and putting himself into personally and professionally vulnerable spaces to ensure the communities suffering the most got what they deserved. He was always ready to "dig in" and be a student of his craft while seeking greater success. D would describe his vision to me as moving from being "recreational" to transformational; he was a next-level guy. What I also learned from him was that to do this required investing more than our brains and bodies into peacemaking; it demanded a commitment from our hearts, souls, and full authentic selves. Another thing I learned from D was that when you build a strategy that involves authentic people, brave yet humble enough in their unyielding commitment to loving themselves and others, community transformation is inevitable.

It is this common dedication to the healing and transformation of people as well as places that I believe sustains our deep friendship and partnership. As DeVone mentioned above, this commitment demands valuing, respecting, and lifting up the voices, expertise, and experiences of those at the center of an urban (health) challenge. We see those at the center of gun violence along with those who have spent time in prison because of it as leaders, experts, and solution implementers.

When D and I started collaborating around his expansion of Advance Peace, I had already spent tens of hours doing ride-alongs with the outreach workers of the ONS in Richmond. I learned intimate details about their life stories told during hours together in the car, standing on street corners, and taking Fellows to get a bite to eat. The same outreach workers had introduced me to Fellows as "the professor" (which clearly didn't impress them), and for some reason they too shared intimate details about their lives, families, and dreams with me.

The Fellows and outreach workers—from Richmond and later Sacramento, Stockton, Fresno, and other cities—taught me how much we all had to learn from those closest to the issue of gun violence. Yet when I read reports or journal articles about this work, I was hard-pressed to find any mention of the participants or hear their voices. So D and I committed to make our Advance Peace partnership about how to build a learning organization. Part of what that meant was to continually listen, revise, and improve as we go. I committed to help the teams capture all that they do, and feed it back to them in a useful and timely way. The hope was to learn what was and was not working in each city—in the streets, in the office, with Fellows, and with service providers.

In order to help capture the details and nuances of this everyday work along with the unique characteristics, including assets, of the Peacemaker Fellows—or participants—I built a data collection system with the outreach workers. When I started, D and Sam from Richmond shared their data collection system—paper forms that they faxed to me! I worked with my team at the University of California at Berkeley to build an app that outreach workers could use to enter data on their phones out in the field. We designed it to capture voice memos and notes, so we wouldn't lose the nuance and stories behind the work. Together with the outreach workers, we designed an intake questionnaire, which captured each Fellow's strengths and challenges as they entered the Peacemaker Fellowship. Again, the commitment was to listen to, learn with, and lift up the expertise of those "in the life" and doing the work.

This book is much more than data. It is about a way to "ingest love into public policy" and help create true peace, not just end gun violence. I am grateful to DeVone for inviting me into this journey he launched and being willing to coauthor this book. I know he could have written most of this himself, but together we offer snapshots from years of relationship building as well as hundreds of hours of listening, watching, and learn-ing with the outreach workers and Fellows. We share a glimpse of this complex work of what we believe it takes to authentically advance urban peace. I think of it as an unfinished symphony, but hopefully you will hear in the music the urgency for action and our love for the people.

—J. C.

ACKNOWLEDGMENTS

This book wouldn't have been possible without my coauthor, DeVone. I am so grateful for your brotherhood, friendship, and every day inspiration. You are not only a leader but also a great teacher and mentor, and I truly enjoyed our collaborative writing and creative processes. I know we have more to do together. I am equally grateful to the people who lead and participate in Advance Peace and Richmond's Office of Neighborhood Safety. Your passion and commitment has taught me so much not just about this work but about myself too. I appreciate you, who you are, and all that you do, daily, to keep the peace, love 'em up, and see the humanity in us all. Many of you trusted me enough to share intimate details about your life and experiences, and I thank you for that. I hope this book does some justice to your stories. There is much more to tell, and I look forward to continuing to be your trusted partner in this work and life.

Some of my time, the data collection, and the writing of this book were supported by a grant from Arnold Ventures.

Of course, none of this happens without the support and love of my family, Judea, Azure, and Satya. You push me to just "find my voice" among all the noise. You know how much this work and the people mean to me, and even when you don't, you support me.—J. C.

* * *

Acknowledgments . . . this is the most challenging part of writing this book for me. Why? Because there are so many people to acknowledge who are in part responsible for making coauthoring a book possible. I never want to forget or leave anyone out. Let me just say, you know who you are, and I am grateful for your influence and impact on my personal and professional development. You are my family, close friends, teachers, elders, board and staff members, peers; private, philanthropic, community, and public sector supporters; researchers; evaluators; the City of Richmond, California; the Office of Neighborhood Safety team; and to all of my Peacemaker Fellows, and my Partners in Peace: Thank you.

I must provide a special shout out to my coauthor, Jason. Brother, this doesn't happen without you. Thank you for showing me how to do this. Because of your help, I will indeed do it again. I have so much more to communicate to the world.

To my parents, Daniel and Jacqueline Boggan, your unwavering support, encouragement, and belief in your son have guided him in the right direction. To my children, Imani and Caleb, my world would be empty without you. And finally, to my wife, Nerissa, thank you for your unending support and love, but most importantly, for your persistent nudges to do this and get it done! You are the best!

I am truly grateful.—D. B.

1

ENDING THE EPIDEMIC OF URBAN
GUN VIOLENCE

We are all called to make a difference in our generation. The kind of difference we make can be unfocused or powerful, oversold, or indispensable, recreational or transformational. We get to decide whether or not we accomplish the level of significance we were purposed here to contribute.

—DeVone Boggan

Imagine that two rival street groups are at war with one another in your city. There has been a long history of retaliation over unchecked violence and at least three generations of young people have been caught up in this seemingly never-ending street war. The neighborhoods at war are the most segregated, impoverished, and neglected in your city, and no one seems to have a solution for the decades-long gun violence. Few in the neighborhood feel safe there, and those with enough means have left. The neighborhood and its youths aren't being served by any supportive institutions since they are too afraid of the violence. Marches, volunteer initiatives, and take-back-the-streets campaigns have produced fleeting results, and increased, heavy-handed law enforcement has only locked up more people, angering their friends and families.

Now imagine that the rage has boiled over onto social media. A video was posted insulting one group and making threats. It has gone viral. The decades-long dispute was just inflamed by the rapid spread of the insult. The streets are hot.

This time, a small group of respected OGs from the neighborhood respond to the insults. They are people who know something about responding violently to an insult; most have been to prison for perpetuating this or a similar war in your city. These OGs, however, gained valuable insights while locked up and as adults—namely, that their anger was mostly a result of unaddressed traumas that weren't their fault. The traumas were everything from abuse, neglect, and seeing violence, to struggling for food, shelter, and clothing. They not only learned to identify their own traumas but also are in the process of healing from them through individual and expansive group supports, new friendships, extensive professional trainings, and other life opportunities.

Now imagine these OGs put their lives on the line and go talk to those young people about to continue the street war. They know them because the OGs were once part of it, and likely still know some cousins, friends, and others in that life. They know too the drivers of the anger, desperation, and disconnections those in the confused war are feeling.

These OGs reach out to both sides of the conflict. They talk to the "shot callers" in each group. They encounter mostly "get the f*ck outta my face" reactions. The OGs not only don't give up but they also don't leave. They stay at it. Maybe order some food. Other OGs join in, and one convinces a few in the group to get in the car and take a ride. Another OG takes a few in the group to play some video games. Late into the night, the OGs are still with the groups.

By the next day, over twenty-four hours after the social media post went viral, there is no retaliation. No gunfire. No one at the hospital needing lifesaving surgery. No parent visiting the morgue to identify a body.

A week goes by, and the same OGs have visited the group and their shot caller three times each day. They know them and their daily movements so well they start showing up with their favorite foods and playing their favorite music, and know all of their family and friends on a first name basis.

Another week goes by, and the most influential ones in the group, the leaders who are likely calling the shots to retaliate, are the OGs' mentees. One mentor takes a mentee to a music studio where they make music together. The mentor takes them to dinner at an out-of-town restaurant. A few more weeks go by, and the mentor and mentee are on a "double date" with their partners. The mentee meets other OGs as part of their mentor's team. They now have a new "family" of healthy adults around them, interested in their well-being, survival, and success. Its intensive, everyday relationship building. It's about authentic, trusting communication. It's about seeing the common humanity in this shot caller, whose environment and past traumas never allowed them to be a kid, cry, be afraid, and sometimes, even feel love. It's not easy, but every day they aren't shooting, together they are advancing peace.

WHY ADVANCING PEACE?

The story we just told isn't fiction. It's based on real events, real people, and a real place. It is a place-based initiative called Advance Peace that is now operating in more than a dozen cities nationwide. Its signature mentorship and violence interruption strategy is called the Peacemaker Fellowship, and it is part of the public safety field of community violence intervention (CVI) that together is working to end the US urban epidemic of gun violence.

What's unique about Advance Peace, which we will highlight more of in this book? First, you almost never hear about this incredibly hard but lifesaving/changing work being done in neighborhoods across the United States. The conflict mediation and peacekeeping work isn't a nightly news story like the shooting might have been or a police data point. Urban gun violence mediation and mentorship of those caught in the center of gun violence is happening, successfully, thus saving lives and transforming entire communities. We are here to tell you more about it.

Second, the OG mentors we mention, those formerly incarcerated "wounded healers," are also poorly understood, rarely recognized for how hard their work is, and vastly underappreciated. These OGs are what we call neighborhood change agents (NCAs). They are NCAs because they are interrupting imminent gun conflict, mediating the disputes that erupt on social media, mentoring those at the center of this violence, and improving public safety as they work all sides of community gun violence conflicts. They are changing neighborhoods and cities locally as well as nationally by building a continental network of professional practitioners who are sharing strategies, forging alliances, and supporting their collective healing.

Third, the NCAs recognize that most of what is driving the gun violence in their communities is unaddressed trauma. Using a trauma-informed approach, the NCAs work with their mentees to identify the sources of pain, anger, anxiety, and shame that are contributing to their anger. The NCAs use tools like cognitive behavioral therapy, culturally responsive counseling, social emotional learning, life coaching, and others to support the healing of their mentees. Yet there is no one-size-fits-all approach to Advance Peace. Each participant's experiences, traumas, and healing needs are unique, so their supports are tailored to their needs.

Fourth, the healing work doesn't happen through the NCA and mentee—now called a Fellow—working alone or only one-on-one. As in the situation we explained above, the NCA connects with others, and brings Fellows together to find supports and change their lives. The participants are called "Fellows" because the program is called the Peacemaker Fellowship. In the spirit of the word "Fellowship," the participants come together in group healing sessions, called life skills classes, and restorative justice circles, and get opportunities to travel out of town together. We show that traveling is an essential component of individual and group therapy as well as a pathway toward peace.

Fifth, this is an approach that is explicitly antiracist and informed by movements for Black liberation in the United States. We show that urban gun violence is a racialized epidemic disproportionately harming young Black (and some Brown) men (and fewer women). This means that any strategies working to end this racialized epidemic must be informed by and build on the successes of previous racial justice movements. Advance Peace incorporates much from and owes its Peacemaker Fellowship to such underappreciated urban peace builders, such as the Black Settlement House movement, Ida B. Wells, the Black Panthers, and others. We demonstrate that urban peacekeeping and peacemaking is fundamentally about racial justice and liberation, for it is hard to imagine something more important to be free from than violence. True peace, as civil rights leader Dr. Martin Luther King Jr. reminded us, is not the absence of violence but instead the presence of justice.

Sixth, a key reflection of how Advance Peace aims to embody racial justice is that it views today's active firearm offenders as part of the solution—in fact, leaders—in ending this epidemic. We should also mention here that Advance Peace engages those who are actively using guns to resolve conflicts and likely the next victim of a gunshot in their communities. Advance Peace does not engage every potential at-risk youth, every angry kid in the ghetto, or every gang member. Why? Because not all of these folks are using guns, and we are after a solution to ending urban gun violence. To do this, we are committed to seeing the humanity in these firearm "offenders." We aim to see and understand their traumas by asking, as our colleague Shawn Ginwright underscores, "What happened to you?" not, "What's wrong with you?" We value them as experts and capable leaders in generating solutions for their own healing and transformation as well as that of their communities.[1] For us, by us. This is part of Black liberation.

A seventh aspect of this story is another aspect of Black liberation and incorporated in the Advance Peace Peacemaker Fellowship: money. We are committed to a form of reparative justice for Back communities ravaged by gun violence. This means delivering the necessary supports and services to stabilize our Fellows, from finding them stable housing and getting them clothed to ensuring they are eating properly and regularly. It also means connecting them to other social services, education, and possibly employment, when they are ready physically and psychologically, and the environment is deemed safe. Furthermore, we invest in the Fellows for making progress toward peace and transformation. Just like a graduate student gets paid for their Fellowship, our Fellows are eligible for a monthly stipend if they are committed to their own healing and resolving conflicts with rivals peacefully. Gun violence is interrupting economic progress in Black communities and entire cities, and we view the stipends as an investment that can benefit everyone.

While we discuss the racial justice motivations of financial compensation for Advance Peace Fellows in more depth later in the book, we want to be provocative here because this strategy is controversial and has been labeled "paying shooters not to shoot." There is no doubt that urban gun violence has an economic cost to us all, by some estimates $200 to $500 billion a year.[2] These are costs for emergency response, policing, health care, the criminal justice system, and the lost wages and lifetime of productivity of the victim. Incarcerating someone costs $130,000 per year in California.[3] Economists at the Urban Institute found that surges in gun violence slowed neighborhood home values by 4%, and decreased credit scores and homeownership in affected communities. A single gun homicide in a census tract in a year resulted in decreases in home values the following year of $24,621 in Oakland, California, and decreases in homeownership by 3% in Washington, DC.[4] The costs of a gun injury can be immeasurable in terms of trauma as well as mental and physical disabilities. The costs to a family or loved one from losing someone are far beyond monetary. If we count the costs, however, we must also acknowledge the economic savings from preventing a nonfatal or fatal shooting. By some estimates, the costs of one nonfatal shooting are about $700,000 and about $1.2 million per firearm homicide. When Advance Peace NCAs and Fellows prevent shootings like the scenario above—and we will demonstrate they do this frequently—they are saving us all money. In fact, Advance Peace is saving cities tens of millions of dollars each year when it interrupts gun violence and mentors a shooter toward peacefully resolving conflicts. When we provide up to $1,000 a month to Fellows who are actively engaged in the Peacemaker Fellowship and preventing gun violence in their communities, we will show you that is not only a good investment but a form of reparations too.

We should all have an interest in ending the epidemic of urban gun violence. When gun violence—shootings and homicides—are commonplace, schools cannot properly educate children who are living in fear, parents keep their children inside due to fears for their safety, and medical professionals and health care systems can be overwhelmed. Gun violence puts a cloud over public life for those within its storm; civic life and business tends to decline, and residents in gun violent neighborhoods who can leave, flee. This exit leads to further decline in often already segregated and impoverished neighborhoods. So many of us feel the effects of gun violence, even those who are not direct victims. This is not just an epidemic in urban Black communities but rather a national emergency.

AN ENDURING EPIDEMIC IN PLAIN SITE

In 2024, the US surgeon general declared, "Firearm violence . . . an urgent public health crisis that has led to loss of life, unimaginable pain, and profound grief for far too many Americans."[5]

It was a declaration that was a long time coming for most Black and Brown communities in the United States. Shifting our understanding of and approaches to ending urban gun violence from those almost exclusively focused on punishment and incarceration, to those revolving around healing from trauma and creating alternative life opportunities, has been a demand made by those experiencing this epidemic for decades. African American communities have long generated a counternarrative to the white-dominated, criminal-justice-only approach to public safety.[6]

The urban gun violence epidemic that Advance Peace addresses is the cyclic and retaliatory violence we described in the opening to this chapter. It frequently involves beefs over perceived disrespect or identities among a small group of people in an even smaller area of our cities. Community gun violence happens on the streets and front porches as well as in the parks and back alleyways of urban neighborhoods. While we are concerned with gun suicides, school-based shootings, and so-called mass shootings (these happen far too often in urban areas, but aren't labeled as such), these are not the type of community gun violence we are focused on.

RACE AND PLACE STILL MATTER

We are focused on urban gun violence because for far too long its victims have been systematically ignored and dehumanized. We know that Black Americans are 60% of gun homicide victims and were fourteen times more likely than whites to die by a gunshot in 2021. Young Black males fifteen to thirty-four years old accounted for 36% of all gun homicides in 2021, but are only 2% of the total US population. In 2021, guns were responsible for 51% of all deaths of Black teens ages fifteen to nineteen.[7] As the US Centers for Disease Control and Prevention's web-based Injury Statistics Query and Reporting System reveals, the firearm homicide rate for young Black men has remained stubbornly high for over two decades, with a mean of about 74/100,000 from 2000 through 2023. Firearm homicides are only part of this racialized epidemic: over the past twenty years, for every gun homicide there were four to five Black men injured by a firearm, all of whom suffer lasting physical and emotional damage, as do their families and entire communities.[8] From

2009 to 2018, the rate of gun-related assaults against Black Americans was 208.9 per 100,000, compared with 90.5 per 100,000 for whites.[9]

This is also an urban community epidemic. In 2020, 71% of the nation's 35 largest cities had gun homicide rates higher than the national rate of about 12/100,000. From 2000 to 2019, the number of gun homicide deaths has remained relatively stable, but they increased by almost 30% from 2019 to 2020. Baltimore, Memphis, Detroit, Kansas City, and Cleveland were the five most gun violent cities in the United States in 2020.[10] According to a UK *Guardian* analysis, 127 cities in the United States contained 50% of the gun homicides and virtually all the gun homicides in 2019 happened in 1,200 census tracts (an area estimated to be 42 square miles).[11] In Oakland, 50% of the gun homicides were linked to about 1,300 people, or about 0.3% of the city's population.[12] In Chicago between 2012 and 2016, 70% of all nonfatal gunshot victims and 46% of gun homicides were linked to less than 6% of the city's population.[13] Over a thirty-year period in Boston from 1980 through 2008, almost 75% of all firearm incidents happened on fewer than 5% of the city's streets.[14] Urban neighborhoods that experience racial residential segregation, historic redlining, and other racially motivated disinvestments have thirteen times the rates of shootings compared to predominantly white and other areas.[15]

The impacts and costs of gun violence go well beyond the people most directly involved in it. Fear of gun violence along with the law enforcement response to shootings result in enormous psychological, physical, and economic costs to individuals, communities, and local governments. Those living in neighborhoods with frequent gun violence, even just hearing gunshots on a regular basis, experience unhealthy acute stress and anxiety and are at higher risk of post-traumatic stress disorder (PTSD).[16] As we will show in chapter 9, reducing gun violence over a sustained period, as has happened in Richmond, California, has a cascading set of positive community economic development and population health benefits.

STARTING WITH HEALING

Behind every difficult, seemingly intractable problem are people—frequently groups of people who don't get along together. Advance Peace is an intentional approach to healing the pain, grief, and often unaddressed traumas that are behind most of today's urban gun violence. Absent an explicit healing strategy, which transforms both lives and the neighborhoods where violence is concentrated, we will not end the epidemic. In fact, even when we reduce firearm homicides and nonfatal shootings—which we can and must do—only part of the public health work is done. This is so because we have not prevented the future "outbreaks" nor made whole the folks—mostly Black and Brown—and communities at the center of the violence.

As we discuss throughout this book, at the heart of the Advance Peace strategy is the Peacemaker Fellowship. This Fellowship voluntarily enrolls active firearm offenders in an attention intensive system of 24/7 mentorship from formerly incarcerated, now healthy adult healers called, as mentioned in the preface, neighborhood change agents (NCAs). The care provided by NCAs is grounded in an established protective relationship, and includes one-on-one coaching, cognitive behavioral supports, life skills training, and a myriad of other customized supports based on the unique needs of each Fellow. Instructed by Fellowship engagement and analysis, the NCAs also perform community violence interruption, getting in the middle of conflicts in the streets and on social media before guns might be used. In these related ways, Advance Peace is promoting healing within traumatized people and communities as well as helping secure a lasting public peace. When those in cities who are caught up in violence work to transform their trauma into positive growth, and commit to healing themselves and their places, we call this a form of neurourbanism.

NEUROURBANISM: HEALING-CENTERED
COMMUNITY DEVELOPMENT

Advance Peace in cities should be viewed as "neurourbanism" because it emphasizes understanding how trauma has adversely impacted our brains and decision-making, while also creating supports that can positively change our brains, bodies, and built environments toward peace and prosperity.[17] The "neuro" part of neurourbanism demands that we all—practitioners, community residents, decision-makers, service providers, and others—understand gun violence as a response to unaddressed traumas that aren't the fault of the people exposed to trauma.[18] These traumas include the adverse childhood experiences (ACEs) that too many people encounter early in life. ACEs include physical and psychological abuse, chronic deprivation, and frequently witnessing violence and the adverse behaviors of addiction. The greater the number of ACEs one experiences, the greater the likelihood of later in life adversity, including a propensity for violence.[19] Exposure to gun violence—hearing it, seeing it, knowing people killed, or being shot yourself—which disproportionately afflicts African American communities, is not considered an ACE but can also be a brain-damaging set of traumas, often contributing to post-traumatic stress disorder and the likelihood of using a firearm later in life.[20]

Our brains are adversely impacted by these traumas early in life, releasing too many "fight-or-flight" hormones to counteract these stressors. These hormones, like cortisol and adrenaline, deteriorate the brain's hippocampus, which is the part that helps us learn and control our moods. The trauma-induced fight-or-flight hormones also damage the brain's amygdala, which helps regulate emotions, aggression and processes how the body responds to a potential threat, and our prefrontal cortex is adversely impacted, which helps with impulse control, concentration, and decision-making.

As psychiatrist Bessel van der Kolk says in his book *The Body Keeps the Score*, "Trauma robs you of the feeling that you are in charge of yourself" and "changes not only how we think and what we think about, but also our very capacity to think."[21] Chronic exposure to trauma creates toxic stress in the absence of positive social supports. Our response to stress can be lifesaving—think of the fight-or-flight response—but constant stress that is out of our control can be toxic to our brains and bodies. Toxic stress leads to emotional distress, poor impulse regulation, learning difficulties, and other physical and mental health problems.[22] The impact of chronic trauma can damage our sense of self-worth and lead to dissociative challenges, including our inability to trust others and create affectionate social bonds. When we are in constant "fight-or-flight" survival mode, there is no room for nurture, care or love and little ability to imagine, plan, play, learn, or pay attention to the needs of others. These are often compounded when the stressors, particularly gun violence, remain in our lives and communities, as we adopt a hypervigilance to avoid reliving the trauma, causing further damage to our brains and bodies.[23]

All of this happens in the streets and is shaped by our surroundings. Yet our living conditions, housing affordability, quality of schools, presence of parks, and whether there are more liquor stores than libraries in our neighborhoods does not happen by accident. These are the result of specific urban policies, plans, and practices, or often a lack thereof. The classic example of an urban policy that created more trauma was when Daniel P. Moynihan advised President Richard Nixon in 1970 to institute a period of "benign neglect," by which he meant not addressing the poverty, inequities, and violence already plaguing Black communities.[24] This wholesale abandonment by the federal government at a time of great need let many predominantly Black urban neighborhoods fall into further decline. This was exacerbated by another government practice that took hold in the 1970s called "planned shrinkage," where cities closed fire stations and hospitals, and stopped collecting the trash in Black and Brown neighborhoods, under the guise of saving money.[25] These are just two examples of how public policies and practices shaped the presence as well as persistence of traumas in Black urban neighborhoods—many of which are still with us today.[26]

Advance Peace is neurourbanism because it doesn't just recognize that traumas are behind much urban gun violence but also understands that by investing in healing, we can reverse many of the adverse impacts of these traumas. Given the right conditions, particularly supportive social relationships and positive community environments, we can change our brains and bodies in positive ways. This is the idea of "neuroplasticity."[27] Neuroplasticity refers to the capacity of neural systems to adapt and change in response to experiences, and in the context of altering the impacts of ACEs and gun violence exposures, depends heavily on the presence of healthy interpersonal relationships, material resources, and what has been called positive community environments.[28] Thus safe, stable, and nurturing relationships and environments are known to reverse the negative impacts of trauma and adversity.[29] This is exactly what the National Academies Press described in its landmark report *From Neurons to Neighborhoods*, recognizing that healing must include interpersonal social supports and safe, nurturing communities.[30] In the presence of these healing supports, those suffering from PTSD and other forms of trauma can have an increased sense of self-awareness, recognition of personal strengths, improvements in intimate relationships, greater appreciation of life, and openness to discovering new possibilities.[31] The greatest contributor to neuroplasticity is moving from a sense of despair to hope through healthy social connections and unconditional love.[32] The processes that contribute to neuroplasticity are what shape the Peacemaker Fellowship.

BUILDING SAFER COMMUNITIES

Advance Peace, then, is about ending gun violence through investing in healthy human and community development. When those at the center of gun violence in our cities start to heal—through the social bonds and unconditional love of their NCAs—entire neighborhoods and cities are transformed. We will offer evidence that suggests that when the few yet influential shooters start committing to peace, the benefits reverberate throughout their neighborhoods. Fewer resources are spent on surveillance and policing, and instead go to schools and parks as well as keeping businesses open, and street life becomes a source of safety rather than fear. Whole neighborhoods can benefit from long-term investments in Advance Peace.

What role do police have in all of this? Advance Peace and the Peacemaker Fellowship do not work with the police, unlike other CVI strategies. We give more detail about why this is so later in the book, but the short responses are that too many police departments have dehumanized Black and Brown folks, thereby creating trauma and mistrust, and their role is often responding to, not preventing, gun violence. We do acknowledge that ending US urban gun violence will require law enforcement to do better at solving and prosecuting the firearm crimes that occur in Black and Brown urban neighborhoods as well as getting illegal firearms off our streets, but we will not and cannot arrest our way toward greater urban peace. Currently, seven out of ten gun homicides in Black communities go unsolved nationally. In Chicago in 2021, the clearance rate by prosecution was 21.7% in predominantly Black neighborhoods, but it was 45.6% in mainly white ones.[33] Gun possession arrests have not stemmed the tide of urban bloodshed; on the contrary, strict gun possession laws were incarcerating Chicago's African American men in 2022 at rates similar to the mass incarceration era of the 1980s and 1990s. According to a 2023 Marshall Project review of Chicago Police Department data,

82% of gun possession arrests between 2010 and 2022 were of African Americans, and 79% of those were Black men.[34]

BUT DOES IT (REALLY) WORK?

As of June 2024, the Peacemaker Fellowship was operating in a dozen cities with 98 NCAs (almost a dozen of which are women) and over 627 Fellows.[35] Of these Fellows, 90% are male and 10% female; 73% are Black, 20% are Latino, and 6% are others, primarily Asian. The average age of a Fellow is twenty-three, but Fellows' ages range from fourteen to fifty-five.

What we also know is that when these Fellows volunteered to join the Peacemaker Fellowship (which as we will show, takes months of trust and relationship building), 71% told us they wanted to change, over half had marketable skills, 59% were characterized as critical thinkers, and 71% were viewed as charismatic leaders. In other words, the active firearm offenders in these cities have assets that they can build on. Moreover, we know from our intake data that 57% of the Fellows reported having four or more ACEs, those traumatic early life experiences that adversely impact our brains, ability to decipher right from wrong, impulse control, and other mental and physical health issues; 30% have seven or more ACEs. We also know that about half of the Fellows, 47%, have *both* four or more ACEs along with two or more gun violence exposures, such as a gun injury, witnessing a gun homicide, being shot at, or having a family member killed by a firearm. Yet only 16% were receiving any social services when they enrolled. Most want out and are grappling with unaddressed trauma, but aren't getting any supports to leave the game.

During the Peacemaker Fellowship period from July 2021 through December 2023 (thirty months), NCAs interrupted and mediated 2,005 community conflicts, 361 of which involved firearms and 142 of which were on social media. This means, as we will describe later in the book, that NCAs likely prevented at least 361 firearm homicides or injury shootings during this period.

One important but overlooked measure of a successful CVI program is what happens to the participants. Of the 627 Fellows, 95% are still alive (tragically 31 were killed); of those alive, only 1 was injured by a gun, and 97.6% were not arrested on a gun charge during the program period. At the conclusion of their Peacemaker Fellowship, 83% reported an improved mental health outlook on life, 73% reported improved anger management skills, 68% felt safer in their communities, 50% reported being employed or having new job skills, 84% reported no longer using a gun to resolve conflicts, 82% reported peacefully resolving a conflict that previously might have resulted in gun use, and 92% reported having a trusted adult in their lives to talk to in times of crisis or to solve everyday challenges.

Gun violence is also declining in the Advance Peace cities and neighborhoods where it is operating. We provide more detailed data later in the book, but in Richmond, the Peacemaker Fellowship has contributed to a 55% reduction in fatal and nonfatal shootings since its launch.[36] The Fellowship in Fresno, California, has contributed to a 30% reduction in firearm homicides and assaults. In the Sacramento neighborhoods targeted for the Advance Peace intervention, there was an 18.2% reduction in gun homicides and assaults during the Peacemaker Fellowship.[37] The Peacemaker Fellowship in Rochester, New York, contributed to an almost 30% reduction in firearm homicides, 30% reduction in nonfatal shootings in Orlando, and 14% reduction in both firearm homicides and nonfatal shootings in Lansing, Michigan.

*   *   *

This book reveals that Advance Peace is an essential strategy for ending the urban epidemic of gun violence. Yet little is known about how the strategy came to be, the details of its Peacemaker Fellowship, who the Fellows and NCAs are, and what influences it is having in the specific cities where it operates. We also know that ending the urban gun violence epidemic will not happen on the backs of volunteers, faith-based groups, or nonprofits alone. The long-term sustainability of urban peacemaking demands that it become integrated into the everyday management responsibilities of local government, albeit not in the police department. We offer suggestions for how to integrate the Advance Peace commitment to humanizing and loving our Fellows into public policy.

A POSITIVE GOOD

King told us in 1956 that peace is not only the presence of justice but the presence of a positive good too.[38] Just like health is not simply the absence of disease, we need to end the United States' gun violence epidemic by bringing positive goods to dehumanized, disinvested in, and decimated urban neighborhoods. Advance Peace is about ending the bloodshed by investing positively in people. Justice is served when those currently traumatized become leaders in transforming communities. We show here how we can heal some of our deepest wounds and achieve a lasting public peace.

2

THE ADVANCE PEACE APPROACH

You can't separate peace from freedom because no one can be at peace unless he has his freedom.

—Malcolm X

The Fourth Street Market sits kitty-corner to the Nevin Community Center and its surrounding park. The park has a playground, ball field, and benches under old-growth redwood trees. It appears bucolic but almost eerily quiet. As James Houston, a street outreach worker with the ONS in Richmond, would describe it, the walk across this park and playground could easily get you killed. Four days before we joined James on a ride along through Richmond's neighborhoods, two young men had been shot in front of the community center. "It seemed like a random drive-by shooting, but we have a suspicion who was in that car based on who was in the park. Shootings around here are rarely random," James explained.

The phone rang while we were in the car and the caller ID said "Joe." James picked up and put it on speaker phone. It was Joe McCoy, another street outreach worker, and the two started discussing what they were hearing on the streets in their respective neighborhoods about the previous days' shooting. Joe exclaimed, "I seen the car. Fourteen rounds in it. His lil partner was murdered, and word is cats from the 'crescents' [a housing project] were behind it." James paused. He had a frustrated look on his face like a parent who finds out their child made a mistake but hadn't owned up to it yet. James grew up in the neighborhood where the crescents is located and was the lead outreach worker focused on preventing shootings from that area. "I heard that too," James responded on the phone. "He just called me for a ride sayin' certain people from North [neighborhood] were around Fourth Street and it wasn't safe for him no more. He said he was just tryin' to stay out the way, but I'll see."

James pulled the car over in front of the market and a tall, lean young man walked out who couldn't have been older than fifteen or sixteen. He got into the back seat. There was an awkward silence at first and then James asked him, "What's good with it?" The young man, chewing on some Sour Patch Kids candy, reached his hand into the front seat to give James a dap. "Aight. What up unc'?" the young man replied.

We drove three blocks to where he was staying, passing the Nevin Center. It took longer to drive than it would have been to walk the same distance. As James stopped the car and before letting the young man get out, he broke the silence again. "I'll come get you later for the life skills class. OK?"

"I don't know. You know I got to take care of that," he replied with his hand on the door handle.

"Hey. Forget later," James interrupted before the young man opened the car door. "I know those gummy bears aren't enough. Let's go get something real to eat. But first, go put that pistol away."

Surprised, the young man looked at James, who had a concerned smile on his face. The youngster nodded his head, looked both ways as if he was crossing the street, lifted his hoodie over his head, and ran from the car into the house's garage. In less than twenty seconds, he was back in the car, and with one eye on the road and the other on the kid in the back seat, James drove us to a restaurant in the Point Richmond neighborhood, an area with shops, cafés, and a hotel that seems a world away from the neighborhood we just left. Joe was waiting for us as we entered the restaurant. We were seated at a wooden table toward the back. We all scanned the menu until Joe broke the silence. "I like the burger, but let's talk about what you been up to."

*　　*　　*

James and Joe are NCAs with Richmond's Office of Neighborhood Safety (ONS). The ONS was the first organization to launch the Peacemaker

Fellowship, and gave birth to the Advance Peace model of healing and gun violence prevention.

The Peacemaker Fellowship is a unique "opportunity" for those at the center of and perpetuating the urban gun violence epidemic in the United States. The approach starts with building a team of credible messengers, like James and Joe, who seek out active firearm offenders and court them into the Fellowship.

THE NCA AS CREDIBLE MESSENGER

Advance Peace calls its street outreach workers and mentors NCAs. This is because the model of change is not only focused on supporting individuals but helping to transform entire communities by promoting and maintaining peace too. All the NCAs must be viewed as "credible messengers," which is someone who has "lived that life," yet often returned home from long prison sentences with a new awareness of their behavior and its causes, and with nonviolent communication and conflict resolution skills.[1]

The clients or participants in the Peacemaker Fellowship are intentionally called Fellows because Advance Peace views them as "a group of equals with a common interest," and the Fellowship as a "prestigious opportunity." The Peacemaker Fellowship is a countermeasure to the danger of isolation. It identifies an isolated, active firearm offender and invites them into a family as well as a healthy community. Advance Peace believes that each Fellow's destiny is defined by their relationships. Most of the future Fellows have long rap sheets, which keep them out of school and formal employment, and even from accessing basic services. Before inviting someone into the Fellowship, the NCA team spends at least six months or more identifying, recruiting, and courting these potentially lethal, highly influential individuals. As one Advance Peace outreach worker described the recruitment process,

It ain't like these people are easy to find, want to be found, or are looking for help. The fact that they are still in the streets means they are elusive. And for good reasons, they don't trust nobody. We can't just show up and offer them a Fellowship. Most of them are like "F you and your F-ing program. Get the F**K out of my face. I don't need that shit." Most of the folks we are engaging have survived on the street by not trusting anyone. We cultivate trust by being consistent. Just showing up. One day we might just see them but not talk. Then they might ask their big homie, "What's up with dude?" And they start hearing stuff about us. Then they hearing your story and they checking you out. And then slowly, they might start talking a little when you come around. You can start to see the comfortability starting to happen. Some days just listening and maybe offering them a ride. Other times it's serious conversation or a meal. It's a "slow dance."

The NCAs often face more rejection than acceptance, and that can be demoralizing. In the beginning of the street outreach process, most of the NCAs are accused of being "snitches" or working for the police. All of this makes the NCA's job even harder and more stressful. James noted,

It's hard to build trust with a person who doesn't know how to trust. You need to be there not just for them but also their other homies and family. Really showing you care and are for real. Even when, and especially when, they reject us, we need to go right back and show up and seek them out. It's essential they know, and we don't ever, affiliate with the police. Our word is how we build trust, and they, for good reason, do not trust anything or anyone working with police.

A FOCUS ON HEALING FROM TOXIC STRESS

Once recruited, the Fellows are asked to commit to the eighteen- to twenty-four-month Peacemaker Fellowship, where NCA, Fellows, and the entire Advance Peace community of supports and staff commit to an everyday assistive, corroborative, and healthy surrogate-like relationship. The Fellowship is intentionally informed by public health, restorative justice, and healing-centered strategies that have demonstrated effectiveness in developing people. It isn't oriented around or focused on stopping gun use. Its purpose is to communicate to a population of mostly young men of

2.1 James Houston performing street outreach with Fellows.

color that has been forgotten, left to kill, die, or be incarcerated, that "we see you, respect your power, you are important and valuable, are deserving just because you are here, are our family, and we want to offer you an opportunity to experience love firsthand, to be loved, then to love and live." A key aspect of the Peacemaker Fellowship theory of change is that by delivering these messages along with the accompanying practical supports and services to those currently shooting, they will stop, they will start healing, and there will be peace within themselves and their entire communities.

The Peacemaker Fellowship helps create peace by leading with love and healing, not threats. Leading with healing does not mean describing those trapped at the center of gun violence as "diseased," and thus needing to be fixed or cured. We also do not start by approaching gun violence as a contagious disease, which often implies that those involved need to be inoculated or "treated" by outside experts. While we embrace some public health strategies, like prevention and working to get at "root causes," we fear that an overemphasis on health might lead us to imagine that gun violence could be ultimately eliminated through precision medicine, neurotechnology, or a pharmaceutical product rather than intensive people-to-people relationships.[2]

We do recognize that almost all of our Fellows have been hurt—both emotionally and physically—and this unaddressed trauma and pain is frequently at the root of their decisions to use guns.[3] Our Fellows suffer from the effects of repeated insults and stressors in their lives—most of which they had no control over creating nor chose to be exposed to. What we are talking about is the structural violence of racism, segregation, and dehumanization that African Americans have confronted for centuries. Structural racism and violence—from lack of affordable housing, living with pollution, intergenerational poverty, underresourced schools, systemic disinvestment, and more—create chronic or toxic stress in the lives of our Fellows, and contribute to gun violence.[4] This stress can contribute to Fellows being abused and neglected by adults, and exposed to interpersonal violence, shootings, and gun homicides.[5] Not everyone responds the same way to these traumas and stressors, but many experience post-traumatic stress disorder anger, lack of impulse control, and hypersensitivity to threats, which can validate a preemptive assault.[6] Other frequent responses to this chronic stress can be unhealthy behaviors, including substance abuse. As the saying goes, "Hurt people, hurt people."[7] This cycle, if left unaddressed, impedes cognitive development, and impairs our brains' ability to interpret whether situations are safe or violent so as to regulate our emotions as well as trust and love.[8] We can't create peace until we help those who are hurt to heal and ultimately change the conditions that are contributing to the trauma in the first place.

The antidote to toxic stress that helps create peace is a combination of positive experiences and healthy, consistent relationships—sometimes called social connections—along with participating in ongoing efforts toward dismantling structural inequities.[9] Feeling valued, connected, purposeful and part of something larger than oneself is what underwrites the Advance Peace approach. Providing healthy adult relationships and supports are a known pathway toward reversing the adverse influences of trauma on our bodies and brains and contributing to post-traumatic growth.[10] By focusing on post-traumatic growth, Advance Peace doesn't romanticize toxic stress but rather works to create the social conditions for and provide resources to those harmed to help them have greater appreciation of as well as see new possibilities in life itself.[11] This type of healing aims to change a disconnected, angry, and hurting shooter into a peacemaker interested in living and promoting life. Healing is also about deploying grace, restoring all of our humanity, and identifying what harmed us. Furthermore, it is an ongoing process of addressing those traumas in a way that helps to restore self-love and care for oneself as well as others.[12] We build on Shawn Ginwright's framing of a healing-centered traumainformed approach and show that the Peacemaker Fellowship approach

- combines individual supports with group or community supports
- is culturally grounded and responsive while confronting anti-Black racism
- builds on participants' (NCAs, Fellows, and communities) assets, not just traumas
- invests in a circle of healing where providers, elders, and Fellows support one another

As Ginwright notes, "In communities ravaged by violence, crime and poverty, care is perhaps one of the most revolutionary antidotes to urban violence and trauma because care ultimately facilitates healing. Care within the Black community is as much a political act as it is a personal gesture because it requires Black youth to confront racism and view their personal trauma as a result of systemic social problems."[13]

THE LIFEMAP

One unique strategy that Advance Peace uses to embody and implement the healing-centered approach is for the Fellow and their NCA mentor to cocreate a life management action plan (LifeMAP). The LifeMAP sets goals that the Fellows and NCA are committed to work on together—all of which is intended to address the hurt and trauma that may be contributing to gun violence. It also is intended to give them hope and recognition that they can change. James emphasized that a LifeMAP sets short-, medium-, and long-term goals for personal safety, secure housing, education, employment, anger management, conflict resolution, creating positive social networks, financial literacy, behavioral/medical health care, substance abuse support, parenting skills, recreation, and spirituality. Some typical short-term goals might be working on substance abuse or anger management issues; medium-term goals might be improving a relationship with a family member; longer-term goals might be obtaining a GED, Social Security card, driver's license, or job.

Each Fellow in the Peacemaker Fellowship gets their own, unique set of LifeMAP goals, and works with their NCA mentor and the entire NCA team to achieve those aspirations. Frequently, multiple Fellows will have the same LifeMAP aim, such as secure stable housing, but require different actions to get to that point. For example, one Fellow might need to save money and get proper identification to fill out rental applications, while another Fellow might need to first address anger issues, substance abuse, and keeping their job before they are able to get their own apartment. Part of the LifeMAP is for Fellows and NCAs to cocreate a "road map" for the Fellow to get engaged in something they care about that doesn't involve violence as well as to provide a space for dreams and hopes.

The LifeMAP is both a mechanism for ensuring that Fellows define their own healing needs (i.e., for them, by them) and a "social contract" with a strong, caring, consistent adult who is willing to take a risk and believe in them. "We see each one of the Fellows as the essential antidote to this urban epidemic of gun violence," James told us. According to van der Kolk, agency addresses trauma through "the feeling of being in charge of your life, knowing where you stand, knowing that you have a say in what happens to you, knowing that you have some ability to shape your circumstances."[14] This sense of control strengthens future orientation, which is central to developing hope for the future. A LifeMAP is also a living document because it is updated by the Fellow and their mentor every few months to reflect new life goals along with the changing relationship between mentor and mentee.

THE "DOSAGE": SUPPORTS, SERVICES, AND TIME

Along with the LifeMAP comes everyday check-ins between the NCA and their assigned Fellow. During these engagements NCAs deliver basic supports, like food and housing, but also work with their mentee to help them overcome negative thoughts and action that can contribute to anger and gun use. An NCA is skilled in "street cognitive behavior therapy" or how a credible messenger can help a Fellow identify trauma triggers, learn coping skills, and create a new, trauma-informed but not dependent narrative. Moreover, the NCAs are expert social service navigators as they help clients identify and get access to the myriad of often disconnected supports, organizations, and programs in their communities.

An NCA's everyday closeness to their Fellows and their inner circle helps them identify the supports and services they might need to heal and make healthier decisions. The entire NCA team in a city works together to identify these supports since each NCA is expected to get to know each Fellow. In this way, team insights offer collective support for each Fellow. An NCA described the work this way:

Sometimes you see it yourself, like a parent or teacher or coach might recognize: "this kid needs more than I can give or some other kind of professional support." But sometimes our closeness to them, our intense care for them, might blind us to something, which is where the entire team comes into play. We respect what each team member brings to the table, and collectively we seen and experienced a lot. It ain't just on you as the mentor; it's on the entire team. We are like the caring family, maybe with that crazy uncle too!

An important aspect of the Advance Peace approach is that NCAs spend time screening service providers to ensure they can support the population in the Fellowship. As Sam Vaughn, director of Richmond's ONS and long-time outreach worker, explained,

We won't just send them anywhere, since most have been let down, dismissed, and dehumanized by these same services in the past. They might even encounter a rival on the way or during their visit there. Even those nonprofits and counselors claiming to work with "at-risk" youths or people, they generally aren't ready to work with our guys who are the risk.

Even once a trusted service partnership is established, the NCA will physically take their Fellow to the service and frequently accompany them for the first few sessions. As one NCA put it,

Even the best therapists or well-intentioned programs aren't prepared to handle the issues and anger our Fellows might have. We referred a Fellow to a substance abuse counselor, and they got high before going in. The first thing the counselor asked was, "Are you high?" The Fellow says, "Yes, of course, that's why I'm here." But the counselor sends them away and says come back when you're not high. Same thing with anger management classes. So we must accompany the Fellow to the service, help them navigate the bureaucracy, [and] support the interaction to ensure they are getting quality and useful professional services.

NCAs often keep a reluctant and skeptical Fellow attending a service, and if it isn't working, help them seek other supports. There are only a few mandated services or programs assigned to the Fellow, since the goals defined in LifeMAP along with the evolving learning of each Fellow by the NCA and the Advance Peace team are what determines a Fellow's services and supports. For some it might be helping stabilize a family or substance abuse issue, for others it could be ensuring they meet with their parole officer, and others might need regular mental health supports.

COLLECTIVE HEALING

The Peacemaker Fellowship recognizes that addressing trauma and focusing on healing requires both individual and collective, often community-involved experiences too. Some of the collective and community involvement in the Peacemaker Fellowship includes group life skills classes, healing circles with elders or community OGs, and participating in community building (and healing) projects, such as park rebuilding and beautification, tree planting, and city council policy discussions. Collective healing can also be facilitated through out-of-town travel experiences carefully curated by the Advance Peace team. The life skills classes are more like dialogues where groups of Fellows focus on a particular topic over a series of weeks or months, facilitated by an NCA or skilled professional. The topics are often dictated by the needs of the Fellows, but typically include discussions about what it means to be "a man," group cognitive behavioral therapy, understanding the forces of structural racism, or how to be a good parent. These classes usually meet multiple times per week.

For Joe, the classes are important to model how to respond when someone is "acting crazy" or disrespectful. He noted,

> In the streets and in their everyday lives, that type of thing happens all the time and the conditioned response is to hit back. Meet force with force; wisecrack with wisecrack. But we have to model there is another way. Not laugh even when it might be funny. They are always testing us, and the classes are as much about them learning what it means and how to be healthy in a group. They need this before they can walk into a job or something else we might be trying to set them up with.

TRANSFORMATIVE TRAVEL

A unique component of the Peacemaker Fellowship that few, if any, other CVI strategies use to heal their participants and prevent violence is travel to new horizon-building locations. Advance Peace calls this "transformative travel," and the privilege to experience this is earned. Fellows must be enrolled in the Peacemaker Fellowship, committed to working every day on their LifeMAP, attending life skills classes, and in daily contact with their assigned NCA. The transformative aspects of these experiences are many since it is generally the first time Fellows have voluntarily left their communities (most involuntarily left going to prison), stayed in hotels overnight, experienced expensive restaurants, or traveled by airplane. Transformative travel provides an opportunity for our Fellows to simply breathe, slow down, and feel safe outside their home turf "war zones." Creating this opportunity for rest is especially important for those caught up in "the grind." It can help restore and rejuvenate, and is part of a lifesaving revolution for Black people, as Tricia Hersey reminds us.[15] Black Americans tend to get less sleep than other groups, and this is associated with deadly conditions such as high blood pressure, heart disease, and strokes.[16] When Fellows travel out of state or out of the country as part of their Fellowship experience, they must be willing to travel with their crosstown rivals. This ambitious and critical element is well curated to be transformational.

As we discuss in much more depth in later chapters, travel offers all of us the opportunity to stimulate and help rewire our brains in healthy ways through new challenges, experiences, and eventually a sense of accomplishment. Yet these mind-blowing and positively altering experiences have long been denied to Black Americans—from slavery, through segregated buses and death threats during Jim Crow, to racial profiling today.[17] So the very act of formerly incarcerated (mostly) Black men taking a group of young Black people that most of society has deemed expendable and "thugs," on a trip to a museum, college visit, Broadway show, or other cultural settings is at once radical, restorative, and transformative.

MILESTONE ALLOWANCES

Another component of the Peacemaker Fellowship is that all Fellows are eligible for direct financial supports should they invest in themselves as well as peace building in their communities. Once a Fellow is working on their LifeMAP for at least six months and achieves 65% progress toward their goals, is regularly attending life skills group classes, and has committed to nonviolent conflict resolution, that Fellow is eligible for a LifeMAP milestone allowance. This is not guaranteed, formulaic, or predefined; it is based on effort by the Fellow, and in turn their NCA, investing in themselves and moving toward peaceful change. The LifeMAP milestone allowance can reward a Fellow up to $1,000 per month. The allowance is just one way to recognize the value of each Fellow and signals to them that they are a community asset worth investing in. The reality is that while one might think money is a motivator, the Peacemaker Fellowship has never spent more than $40,000 per eighteen-month cohort that had at least twenty-five Fellows. Even if Advance Peace did so, that amounts to spending about $90 per month on each Fellow. As we show in later chapters, one shooting or firearm homicide can cost a city from $500,000 to over $2 million in emergency response, policing, health care, and criminal justice expenses. When Advance Peace Fellows decide not to shoot, they are saving taxpayer money. The milestone allowance is a "peace dividend" that also sends a message to each Fellow that we value their hard work to improve themselves and the community.

The milestone allowance has elicited national headlines such as "Paying Criminals Not to Shoot," "Should Cities Pay Criminals Not to Commit Crimes?," and "Crime Pays."[18] As we look at in later chapters, the Fellows and NCAs both state that the money isn't what motivates them, keeps them engaged, or changes their mindsets. It is a nice reward that might help a Fellow pay some bills, get diapers for their baby, and stay away from potentially illicit activities.

Other collective healing components of the Peacemaker Fellowship are subsidized internships and attending an elder circle. Advance Peace will match Fellows who are ready with a local employer and subsidize their salary for a period of six to twelve months. After that time, Advance Peace requests that the employer pay the salary costs if the experience is a positive one for both. Most Fellows have never held a formal job, so the internships offer them a new experience of what it means to get to work every day, be part of a team, and have deferred gratification. Job readiness skills and preparations are done for months before these experiences are offered.

Community elders are folks who have wisdom to share from their lived experiences. The Peacemaker Fellowship includes younger people who have rarely meet a successful OG, allowing them to discuss life and overcoming challenges together. The NCAs also benefit from these dialogues since it helps them understand the different pathways toward success. The elder circles act as spaces where elders can speak to the impact of trauma on their own lives and how they managed to turn that into positive growth.

All the components of the Peacemaker Fellowship are relational, meaning they must work in combination and are intended to improve interpersonal relations (figure 2.2). The daily check-ins by an NCA with their Fellow supports the creation of LifeMAP goals and identifies needed services. Group life skills are facilitated by NCAs and others, and promote restorative justice. The NCA helps the Fellow navigate those services, and rewards them for achieving goals through the allowance, travel and internship opportunities, and meetings with elders.

LIFEMAP GOALS

SOCIAL MEDIA MEDIATIONS

DAILY CHECK-INS

MILESTONE ALLOWANCE

ELDERS CIRCLE

PEACEMAKER FELLOWSHIP

TRANSFORMATIVE TRAVEL

INTERNSHIP OPPORTUNITIES

SOCIAL SERVICE NAVIGATION

SERVICE REFERRALS

LIFE SKILLS CLASS

2.2 Components of the Peacemaker Fellowship.

COMMUNITY PEACEMAKING AND PEACEKEEPING

Advance Peace demands more than the Peacemaker Fellowship. In addition, NCAs are required to interrupt conflicts and ensure they do not lead to gun use. This is because there are few, if any, organizations in the streets every day with the credibility to interrupt conflicts, de-escalate beefs, respond to shootings, prevent immediate retaliation, or scan social media to flag an insult that might lead to face-to-face gun violence. The NCA street mediations are ongoing, and happen before and frequently in the absence of any police response. Perhaps the most critical violence interruptions that NCAs perform on a regular basis is what we call cyclical and retaliatory gun violence interruptions (CRGVIs). These are disputes between rivals where guns are present and the NCAs get in the middle of it, literally putting their lives on the line to mediate. The NCAs also respond to shootings in their cities, since we know that retaliation is most likely to occur right after a shooting when emotions are high. Our NCAs seek to understand the dynamic behind the shooting, and possibly engage with and diffuse any potential for retaliation.

A 2018 article in the journal *Pediatrics* noted how social media posts are contributing to gun violence, and that posts on Twitter, Instagram, Facebook, and others have created a "'digital street' where youth experiences in violent neighborhoods are depicted with aggressive and threatening text, video, and images."[19] James described how some young people are posting live accounts of their gun use on social media—what is known as "internet banging"—often in the hope of making a name for themselves, but this can spread the retaliation to a wider circle of those who like the post.[20] All the NCAs spend a few hours every day scanning social media to review posts that might be interpreted as insults or lead to potential conflicts. As James described it,

Like everything else, social media can just speed up the conflict and be interpreted as a personal threat. Our guys will be friends and follow the Fellows' social media accounts, and we try to diffuse a situation online too. We tell him to take down a video or delete a picture of a gun or a post that might be seen as a threat. It's a part of this work I never thought about when I was getting certified in nonviolent communication in San Quentin.

All of these actions help build trust in the community, and revitalize a greater sense of safety and peace. The reduction in shootings and perceptions of safety can also contribute to other community-based organizations and services reinvesting in our neighborhoods and families, restoring supports that may have been vacated due to fears of violence and injury. The full model of change for Advance Peace appears as figure 2.3. Here we show how community interventions and the Peacemaker Fellowship combine to build healthier communities and young people and adults. On the bottom row are the stages of the Peacemaker Fellowship, where NCAs build trust with active firearm offenders and recruit them into the Fellowship. The Fellowship delivers the full suite of supports and services—healing centered—based on the needs of each participant. These supports aim to turn a shooter into a peacemaker by helping them

2.3 The Advance Peace model for ending urban gun violence.

heal from their traumas while experiencing new life opportunities. The NCAs perform community violence interruption too—the top "steps" in figure 2.3. This demands forging community trust and credibility, and then mediating conflicts. Together, the Peacemaker Fellowships' influence on active shooters along with the NCA's community peacemaking and peacekeeping contribute to healthier, safer people and communities.

WHAT HAPPENS IF THEY SHOOT OR ARE INCARCERATED?

Since Advance Peace is focused on engaging those who are actively or likely to be shooters, we expect some to "remain in the game." The pull and pressure from their peers and crew, combined with the fact that they are probably somebody's target, means they are not going to just put down their guns when an NCA shows up in their lives. As one Fellow described it,

Even now, I got my bobblehead on a swivel. I still be spooked. When these 'hoods are at war, it can go sideways quick. I'm still a trophy to some of these dudes. If you can kill me, your name go tenfold.

We also don't quit them if they are arrested and even in jail since we know most of them will get out in a short period of time. Even those locked up for longer periods often still want and need our support, such as regular visits or supporting family on the outside. When a Fellow is incarcerated, we do not automatically remove them from the Peacemaker Fellowship. Instead, the NCA team in that city will discuss the circumstances of the arrest, how the Fellow was doing in the program, the likelihood of them getting adversely influenced inside prison, and the needs of loved ones at home. Since Advance Peace is a gun violence elimination program that achieves its objective through trusting relationships, supportive services, and healing-centered unconditional love, we can never just abandon a Fellow in a time of crisis.

WORKING FOR PEACE

The work of James, Joe, and the Advance Peace NCAs is ongoing. The public health approach to gun violence—namely, the healing-centered strategies—can sometimes seem like small, incremental change that isn't getting at the "big picture." Yet as communities like Richmond have success with the Peacemaker Fellowship, momentum for policy and institutional changes has followed. Sam Vaughn of Richmond's ONS explains that after over a decade of healing-centered, gun violence prevention work, the city saw its lowest number of gun homicides in over forty years in 2023: eight compared to forty-seven the year the ONS started. Sam reflected that ending gun violence is a marathon, not a sprint:

We are part of changing the narrative: away from victim blaming; away from more policing and prisons; away from communities don't know or can't do; away from us as being thugs or dangerous. Not only has society, but our Fellows have internalized these false narratives. We're changing that story day by day, little by little. We are doing things differently. We look different then city public safety employees. We are saving lives, and show our community and others like it that we need more policy support for this to have an even greater impact.

INFUSING LOVE INTO PUBLIC POLICY

Civil rights lawyer Bryan Stevenson says there are four things necessary to confront injustice in the United States: getting close to the issue, changing the narrative, fighting hopelessness, and getting uncomfortable.[21] The Peacemaker Fellowship is oriented toward accomplishing all four, which we will explore in more depth in the following chapters. We will show that our NCAs and Fellows are as close to the issue of urban gun violence as you can get. The NCAs and Fellows are knowledgeable about the causes of and potential solutions to urban gun violence. The city of Richmond has been at this work, using this strategy for more than sixteen years. Most of the

Richmond team members have been together during this entire period. This commitment of service has allowed the team to develop a high level of trust within the impacted communities. The city's long-term investment and subsequent stability has aided the team in becoming immersed in and one with the heartbeat of potential violence so they can get in front of it often before it manifests. The Richmond team also highlights that formerly incarcerated community members are experts, as are the young people at the center of gun hostilities, in generating solutions for ending firearm violence. This dynamic seems to hold the potential to change the narrative about who is "expert enough" to address the United States' urban gun violence epidemic. As one former NCA asserted,

You want to talk about the significant drop in crime? Talk to these young people. They control the flow of gun violence. So if they're the ones controlling the flow, let's make sure they know that we care about them. As a city, a community, we care about you. And the way we show you that we care about you is our willingness to invest in you.[22]

The Peacemaker Fellowship along with all of its built-in supports and opportunities aims to address much of the hopelessness experienced by far too many Black and Brown young people in cities today. What we will examine in the following chapters is that Advance Peace is making people and institutions uncomfortable, changing the narrative around "who keeps us safe" and public safety more generally. As James described it, "For the first time in these young men's lives, they have city government seeking them—not with a badge, not with a gun—but seeking them, saying, 'We need your help, we need your partnership, and we want to help you.'"

During a 2019 presentation, Clinton Lacey, former director of the District of Columbia's Department of Youth Rehabilitation Services, captured the spirit and practice of what Advance Peace is striving to do:

We need to shift the conversation to what heals people, what restores people, what empowers people to have options, to make other choices, to be positive parts of the community. . . . Ultimately, we need to reimagine what justice is and what a justice system can be. We need to suspend reality and imagine something different, something healthy, something caring, something—I'll use an unscientific term: "loving." We need to imagine what love can look like in policy and how that can translate into practices and policies.[23]

This is exactly what DeVone set out to do when he created the first ONS in the country with a Peacemaker Fellowship.

3

CREATING AN OFFICE OF PEACEMAKING IN CITY GOVERNMENT

Peace is a daily, a weekly, a monthly process, gradually changing opinions, slowly eroding old barriers, quietly building new structures. And however undramatic the pursuit of peace, that pursuit must go on.
—John F. Kennedy

In June 2005, the Richmond City Council was about to declare a fifteen-month state of emergency that would have included installing cameras in all high-crime neighborhoods, occupying these same areas 24/7 with a coordinated federal, state, and local law enforcement presence, and deploying police canine units throughout these communities. The council requested that the city make a special budget allocation of $2 million to support the effort. The ultimate goals of the emergency declaration were to reduce gun violence in what the council called neighborhood "war zones." Councillor Maria Viramontes said the city's gun violence epidemic required "extreme measures" that would limit residents' civil liberties, stating, "This is not normal. So, we have to treat it not normal. We give up certain rights in a war zone, don't we? All of us do."[1]

Yet Richmond mayor Irma Anderson, who had organized protests with Martin Luther King Jr., expressed reservations about the council proposal. She responded by noting, "There's no doubt we have crisis here, a severe crisis. I don't know if it's right to call it a state of emergency. We don't need the National Guard, but we do need a focused strategic plan to reduce violence."

Gun violence was at epidemic levels in Richmond, reaching forty-seven firearm homicides per hundred thousand people in 2007, ranking Richmond as the third most dangerous city in the United States behind New Orleans and Detroit. Mayor Anderson managed to put a pause on the 2005 proposed heavy-handed policing strategy in part because the $2 million to pay for it was supposed to come from a half-cent sales tax along with still pending federal and state grants, all while the city was experiencing a $35 million budget deficit. The pause was also justified because the city was in the process of identifying and hiring a new police chief, who would start in 2006. Furthermore, Richmond had just hired a new city manager, Bill Lindsay, from the neighboring suburb of Orinda. Lindsay, a middle-aged white guy with a Wharton MBA, was learning how to juggle the demands of a complex city with a population five times the size of his previous job, and one that housed the largest oil refinery west of the Mississippi River, dilapidated public housing, the highest crime rates in the Bay Area, an organized and active set of community organizations, and whose population was mostly working-class people, African Americans, Latinos, and Asian immigrants. With new leaders learning the ropes, a concern was that a stern, military-style police strategy would return the city to its racist and violent past.

Instead, in 2006, Richmond authorized the nation's second Office of Violence Prevention (OVP), naming it the ONS. The first government office of its kind to solely focus on reducing gun violence through a non–law enforcement lens, the ONS became a city department staffed mostly by formerly incarcerated leaders who perform street outreach work every day to address eliminating gun violence. The ONS officially launched in 2007, but began fully deploying its outreach staff in early 2008, after a start-up period of recruitment and training. Its intensive Peacemaker Fellowship, which includes dedicated mentorship and enhanced supports for Fellows, kicked off in 2010. After sixteen years of implementation, Richmond's ONS has served over 220 Fellows, with 95% still alive today. Of those graduates, 77% haven't been injured by a firearm, 80% are not a suspect in a new gun crime, and 88% are not incarcerated. Many have gone from the streets to college, and others have become reliable parents, spouses, coaches, and security guards, or served in the military and even pursued becoming cops. Although other Fellows still struggle to make ends meet, they do so in a much more peaceful Richmond.

Gun homicides and shootings with an injury in Richmond have steadily declined since 2009, as figure 3.1 reveals. Even during the spike in urban gun violence that occurred across the United States during the 2020–2021 COVID-19 pandemic period, this urban city managed to maintain its low rates of gun homicides and shootings (perhaps a direct reflection of the long-term investment in and commitment to the ONS by the city as an institutionalized part of its public safety plan, and being woven within the fabric of the most impacted neighborhoods over a fifteen-year period).

TACKLING THE CHALLENGES OF CITY-BASED PEACEKEEPING

Rosy though this picture may seem, getting to those successes was not easy. Concerns were raised about everything from staffing a peacekeeping office with former felons, most with a gun charge in their background, to what such a government department should look like. Would it need to be embedded in the police department? How would the office avoid duplicating the work of nonprofits and community-based organizations? DeVone and early staff members also wondered what metrics of success would suffice, particularly among a skeptical, distrusting public. It quickly became clear that for the ONS to be an effective part of local government, it would need to have dedicated funds of its own in the annual budget, much like planning, parks and recreation, housing, public works, and other departments.

KEEPING CVI OUTSIDE LAW ENFORCEMENT

One of City Manager Lindsay's first major decisions was to hire Chris Magnus, a white police chief in Fargo, North Dakota, as Richmond's new police chief. His hiring initially rubbed many of the city's Black and Brown residents the wrong way, although his presence spurred the formation of the peacekeeping office.[2]

Magnus took over a force that had been grappling with a few racially based scandals for more than a decade. Richmond officers were facing criminal charges as well as resigning due to excessive force, verbal and sexual assault charges, filing false reports, and accusations of racism against the

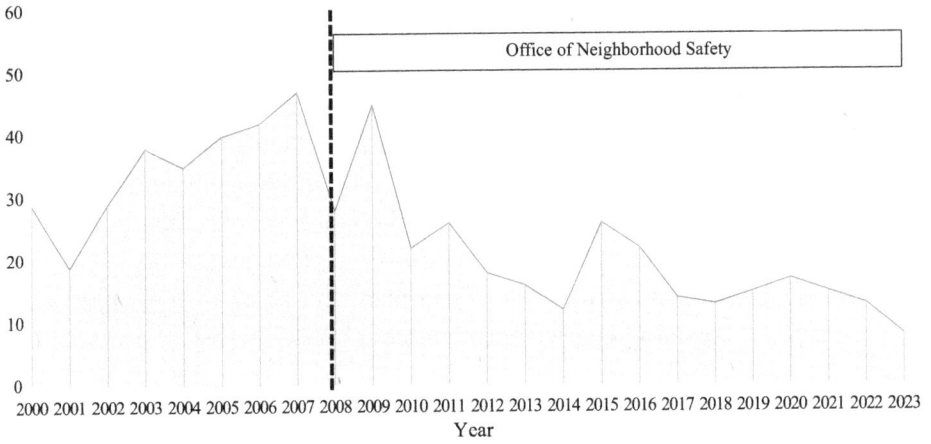

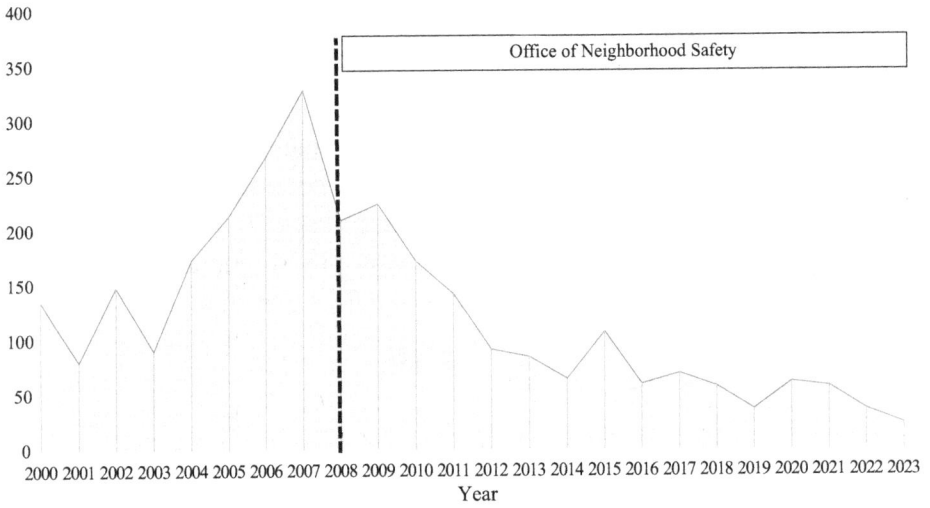

3.1 Richmond, California: Firearm homicides, 2000–2023 (above), and injury shootings, 2000–2023 (below).

Black and Latino population.[3] Trust between the Richmond police force and the public had reached a standstill in 2002, when the city's Police Review Commission issued a vote of no confidence in Chief Joseph Samuels.

The corruption and racism within Richmond's police force dates to at least the 1980s and 1990s. A group of self-described white supremacist officers, known as the Cowboys, had attracted national attention back then for their excessive brutality on Black residents.[4] The National Association for the Advancement of Colored People (NAACP) eventually filed a federal lawsuit against Richmond and the Cowboy cops, challenging their middle-of-the night, extrajudicial killings, which they had modeled after slave patrols and the Ku Klux Klan (KKK).

In 1983, the *New York Times* wrote about the racism and police violence in Richmond:

a civil suit in Federal District Court against the city has focused attention not only on the upsurge in violence and the problems of law enforcement here but also on racial tensions that have combined with hard times to trouble and divide this community, where there is a Ku Klux Klan chapter.[5]

The NAACP argued that the police Cowboys in Richmond encouraged their members to shoot unarmed Black people and this blatant racism was condoned within the force.[6] During a public trial covered by the national media, Black police officers testified that they had to create a counterterror group called the Guardians of Justice that patrolled the city at night, often in plainclothes, to prevent the white Cowboys from killing innocent Black people. An attempt by the Richmond City Council to settle the lawsuit and pay compensation to the families of Black victims of police shootings was rejected by both white and Black council members, including African American council member Nat Bates, who publicly stated, "We have a department and a reputation to defend."[7] The refusal to settle was described by a nationally viewed CBS News *60 Minutes* segment as condoning an openly racist police chief, Leo Garfield, and the city's deep institutionalized racism.[8]

Given this backdrop, it's not surprising that the *San Francisco Chronicle* would ask in December 2005, "How is a 45-year-old white guy from Fargo, which averages one homicide every two years, going to take charge in a racially diverse town that so far this year has seen 38 killings, one of the highest per-capita rates in California?"[9] In addition, seven high-ranking

Black Richmond police officers would sue the city of Richmond by 2007 for racial discrimination, alleging that they were blocked from advancement in the department, and that Magnus and former Deputy Chief Lori Ritter, both of whom are white, made racist jokes.[10] Yet City Manager Lindsay stuck with Magnus, largely because the new chief claimed he was committed to developing an innovative, community-oriented policing strategy for Richmond.[11] Lindsay later shared that the city was interested in doing all it could to reduce violence, describing an initiative he and council members pushed as a response to the crisis:

We had a process where I asked all city departments to generate ideas for how we could reduce violence in Richmond. I had heard about David Kennedy and the "Boston Miracle" program that radically reduced gun violence there. It was a public health model and a whole-of-government investment. I was convinced it was possible in Richmond. We came up with tens of proposals. Tom Butt, the pragmatist on the city council at the time, suggested we needed a "violent crime czar" in the city to coordinate all the ideas. The city decided to hire a consultant team to advise it on what type of gun violence program it might support.

BUILDING A STRATEGY FROM THE COMMUNITY OUT

Richmond hired consultants in August 2006 from the Mentoring Center in Oakland, California, and charged them with analyzing Richmond's gun violence issues and making recommendations for action. The consulting team consisted of coauthor DeVone as well as David Muhammad, Greg Hodge, Deborah Dias, and Ruth Cashmere, all known as the OVP development team. The team spent eleven months meeting with community-based organizations, city and county officials, activists, foundations, victims of violent crime, and law enforcement.

As I (DeVone) remember it, while the city was committed to launching an OVP; there wasn't any consensus over what that meant, such as where in city government it should reside and who should lead it. Greg and David would eventually leave the work, turning the principal consultant role over to me. I didn't have a background in gun violence prevention. I had never to this point worked on issues related to gun violence. As I was meeting with people, I was reading and studying everything I could about the subject. It became clear that few in the community believed that any existing effort was working or helping to change the situation in Richmond, or that anything new would either.

I started by talking to everyone in the community I could find and who would talk to me. I went to prisons and talked to those from Richmond locked up for gun crimes. I spoke to pastors along with probation, parole, and police officers. I spoke with families that had been victimized by gun violence and those whose child may have committed gun crimes. I met with leaders of almost every community-based organization and after-school program that claimed to be serving "at-risk" youths. I talked to as many social service, mental health, and other nonprofit providers as I could find or people recommended I meet. The overwhelming sentiment was that nothing had ever worked in Richmond and some outsider like me wasn't going to change that.

Our team continued to compile data to inform our feedback. We released a report titled *Violent Crime in Richmond*, which found that since the mid-1980s, violent crime was actually on the decline in Richmond, but gun crime was persistently high.[12] The report revealed that between 1988 and 2005, violent crimes in Richmond (measured by combining all the homicides, robberies, aggravated and sexual assaults, and domestic violence incidents) had decreased by 52%, but gun homicides were increasing on average 10.2% a year, with the city averaging about thirty-five gun homicides a year during this period. The report also highlighted that between 2005 and 2006, 92.5% of Richmond's gun homicide victims were male, 68% were African American, 16% were Latino, and 75% of the victims were between the ages of eighteen and forty-four years old. We found that most gun-related murders were occurring between 10 p.m. and 6 a.m., and about 50% of the murders happened within just four police beats, located in the Richmond neighborhoods of the Iron Triangle (beats 5 and 6) and Central/South Richmond (beats 2 and 3). These data confirmed community and on-the-street perspectives: the local gun violence epidemic centered on young Black men, but everyone was impacted.

LEARNING FROM BOSTON AND CHICAGO

I continued my education into community gun violence prevention by visiting the cities with the "best practices" around the country. I went to Boston and Chicago to look at the Operation Ceasefire and Cure Violence models. I spent hours and days observing their practices as well as talking with violence interrupters, law enforcement, and community members in those cities. I soon realized that some of what I saw in Boston and Chicago likely wouldn't work in Richmond. The first reason was that neither Operation Ceasefire nor Cure Violence made identifying and addressing racism/racialized trauma a central issue or practice. This was an issue I had heard repeatedly from Black leaders like my father, elders like Arnold Perkins (the former public health director for Alameda County), and my mentors Dr. Wade Nobles and Martin Jacks as something that any violence reduction strategy in a long segregated, dehumanized Black community needed to take on explicitly. The programs in Boston and Chicago also appeared way too "cozy" with law enforcement, which seemed to limit their ability to build the required protective and trusting relationships with elusive gun offenders. And I was disappointed that the programs were so purposefully apolitical and none attempted to become a regular function of city governance. Although my charge was to report back to city staffers who were eager to create something within local government, it had become clear that the Boston and Chicago gun violence strategies, while informative, didn't offer a model for the city of Richmond.

Another concern was that these alternative CVI approaches wanted to "treat" gun violence in a disconnected way, as if it was a disease rather than focusing on how gun violence offenders were victims themselves too. I had spent my entire career up to that point mentoring young people who had experienced traumas. One thing I saw often in that mentoring work was that "hurt people can hurt other people" at no fault of their own. Unaddressed trauma in young people frequently led to unhealthy behaviors. Yet neither program was talking about or confronting the racist violence along with related traumas in communities like Richmond that continue today, acting as a major contributor for some to respond to conflict violently.

I knew then that—given the legacy of racist policing in Richmond as well as the spatial racism that had created dangerous and dehumanizing living conditions—we would need an explicitly antiracist and trauma-informed approach. All of my mentoring experience told me that the best way to inspire change was through building a trusting, authentic, and loving relationship. These two principles—unconditional love and antiracism—started to become foundational to what I would share with Richmond leadership.

I also knew that the "focused deterrence" I saw applied to those involved in gun violence in the Boston and Chicago programs wasn't consistent with these values, nor my instincts about how to inspire meaningful change. The deterrence approaches involved law enforcement, backed by lawyers and even clergy, trying to "scare straight" the likely gun users in their cities. I thought to myself, "Are threats from police and others really going to convince an already angry and traumatized young person to change?" Gut instincts and a lifetime of working with youths of color told me otherwise. I could feel the distancing in folks' body language when required to do call-in meetings. I mean, these are young people who aren't afraid to die, so threats from the police without legitimate authority would mean absolutely nothing to them. Law enforcement's role was to do its job and share information with CVI strategies, but to generally stay out of the way and not undermine this challenging, community trust-building work.

I left those visits to Boston and Chicago deeply committed to not retraumatizing individuals in local neighborhoods with whatever became Richmond's gun violence prevention program. Further, I wanted to create a program founded on seeing the humanity of the actual or likely firearm offender—that they weren't just the sum of their worst acts and instead were victims worthy of healing supports of their own. A healing-centered, humanity-uplifting gun violence reduction program wasn't the norm at this time, but I returned to Richmond committed to creating this approach.

A CITY AGENCY STAFFED BY FORMER FELONS, ENGAGING SHOOTERS

After eleven months of community conversations, field research, and in-depth study, we made our recommendations to the Richmond City Council. At its core, our proposal suggested that the city adopt a violence prevention system based on a public healing model, not just a potentially disengaged public health one. That meant the city's program staffers should see their work as mentorship first, and from there, relationship building as the pathway toward ending gun violence. The focus would be the three most impacted neighborhoods in Richmond; North, Central, and South. We also recommended hiring formerly incarcerated, street credible, violence interrupters to be peacekeepers in each neighborhood. When we presented the recommendations to the council, new mayor Gayle McLaughlin suggested calling the initiative the ONS, which stuck. Our goal was, after all, to improve public safety for entire communities.

Perhaps more controversial, we proposed that the new ONS be a permanent department located in the city manager's office with the same status as any other city agency. The expectation was that proposing that this government agency revolving around public safety be largely divorced from the police and its new "community-oriented" chief would make the most waves. But I believed, and most on the city council supported, the notion that for new peacemaking staff to build trust with and offer services to those who had frequently been dehumanized, abused, and pursued by the police, the ONS needed to be independent of law enforcement. From the look on his face, I suspected Chief Magnus was skeptical. Magnus didn't publicly oppose our recommendation, perhaps because City Manager Lindsay was a vocal supporter and the new chief wanted to remain on his good side.

The ask was for a minimum of ten years and an annual budget of $2 million, half of which would go toward community grants to organizations that could deliver counseling and supports to those at the center of gun crime. The proposal emphasized that "to reduce violence, we must place concentrated energy and resources with those currently engaged in and impacted by serious criminal and violent behavior." This was our way of saying we should "focus on the shooters." I had seen and studied those gun violence prevention programs that worked with "gang-involved" and "at-risk" youths. We were proposing something different: a city agency focused primarily on likely shooters and those most likely to be the next victim of a retaliatory shooting.

What was initially controversial was our recommending that the ONS be staffed by "formerly incarcerated firearm offenders who have turned their lives around," and were committed to helping promote the end of the bitter and deadly turf rivalries between the three warring neighborhoods. A few council members expressed skepticism that former felons could be trusted to do the work. To my surprise, some community leaders were also skeptical that former felons were the right folks for the job. The details of that aspect of the proposal was tabled during the council presentation to concentrate on the authorization of the ONS. The negotiations of hiring staff would be up to the yet-to-be hired program director.

With such details still to be ironed out, and vocal support from the mayor and city manager, the Richmond City Council voted unanimously to create the ONS in July 2007. Yet the city only authorized $750,000 toward what we had recommended, and $250,000 of that was shortsightedly given to a local community-based organization. They left open the search for a director of the new office as well. It seemed like a job doomed to fail. We were recommending the new ONS director hire former felons with street credibility, train them to interrupt and end gun violence in neighborhoods they had once terrorized, and convince the city these interrupters should be permanent city employees—with a budget of only $500,000. I couldn't imagine anyone wanting such a job.

ESTABLISHING AND STAFFING THE ONS

Leading the new office had never crossed my mind until Deputy City Manager Leslie Knight and other community members asked that I consider doing so. Once the city council ratified the ONS, I had quickly packed up my office and moved onto other contractual obligations. I politely declined each time, though. Even my trusted friend and colleague David (Muhammad) weighed in with his support of the idea, and I heard that Lindsay felt it would be good if I could be involved in the ONS at a high level.

In fall 2007, I began to reconsider, from a love of challenges. Directing the ONS would likely be the most challenging thing I would have done up to that point in my career. Also, my competitive nature played a part after I heard many whispers from within and outside Richmond that it was a "pipe dream" to think of successfully helping reduce gun violence and establishing the proposed ONS.

I leaned on what I lean on when making difficult decisions—prayer. I also gained my wife's approval to really consider applying, due to the sacrifice required of Nerissa and my family (I would be absent a lot for the first couple years of building the department and a pay cut was certain). Nervous and excited, I applied and studied hard to be prepared for the interviews.

The short-listed candidates were all called into multiple, daylong interviews, with the final panel consisting of the city manager, deputy city manager, city attorney, finance director, and police chief. There was some opposition to hiring me. Rumors were circulating that I had wrote the ONS proposal with a director position only I could fill. Not only was this the furthest thing from the truth, it wasn't the sentiment of the hiring committee. After a long, drawn-out process, I became the inaugural ONS director and started in October 2007. Tom Butt, a city council member at the time and former mayor of Richmond, stated, "We have done something few, if any, cities in the United States have done by breaking new ground, establishing the ONS, and hiring its first director, DeVone, who is, in turn, staffing up as fast as he can with geographically based street outreach strategy workers. He is hard at work, meeting with many people, both outlaws and peacekeepers, and establishing collaborations with numerous public agencies, nonprofit organizations, and faith-based organizations to focus on the challenge." It was clear expectations from the city and community were as high as what I'd put on myself. In my mind, this couldn't fail. I couldn't fail. I knew instinctively that this could be a game-changing moment for helping to heal communities from the harms of firearm violence, and I had to be all in. I immediately knew I needed the best, most credible community leaders in Richmond to help me be successful in this new position.

MY FIRST HIRES: ACTIVE FIREARM OFFENDERS

I started the job much like I had done the consulting work—talking to respected community people and others in the field of gun violence prevention. I was looking for mentors who had credibility in the streets of Richmond. I made multiple trips to San Quentin prison to meet with inmates who were part of the Richmond Project—a group of felons (many serving life sentences) from the city who wanted to give back to their community. I met with Richmond Project chair James Houston, Vaughn Miles, and Jason Green (all of whom would eventually be hired by the ONS as NCAs after they were paroled). I valued and trusted their insights about people on the outside who might be viable, street-credible outreach workers.

Yet before I made any full-time hiring decisions, I decided to hear from youths similar to the ones who would receive mentoring experience. Based on insights from the community, I hired three youths from Richmond who were suspected active firearm offenders and had avoided the reach of law enforcement. In part, these young men were from North and South Richmond, and were in groups that had formed a recent peace alliance. So while they were from rival hoods, they could be in a room with each other without animosity. These youngsters were real and raw. They were willing to tell me, and they did often, "that [shit] ain't gonna work" when I introduced some of my ideas to them.

My interns were not just checking me with their "smell test." They were the very folks the ONS needed to reach to be successful; each had been shot multiple times before I hired them, and two got shot multiple times while interning for the ONS. One of them was committed to improving their craft as a shooter and eventually went to prison for life for murder. What was crucial was that these young people, living through it, were shaping every aspect of the ONS. As we built trust, they told me what they thought a "shooter" would need to get them to change their ways. Among their early insights that really shaped the future work of the ONS was sharing that even among "active" shooters, most of the young people didn't really want to be in that life. If they could find a way, an excuse, anything that protected their "name" but allowed them to get out of the game, they would likely do it. Their reaction when I told them they would be paid $1,000 a month as an intern also proved valuable. I classified them as "administrative aides" within our department. And when I gave them their first paycheck, their eyes lit up, a wide smile appeared on their face and an "Are you serious?" was heard throughout the office. I was thinking, "Hmm, you tuff guys from the neighborhood and $1,000 (minus taxes) got you excited like that?" I took that as a lesson for the program and made a mental note that a little legitimate paycheck for making a positive contribution to your community could excite the very young people we were trying to engage.

Another crucial insight from those youth interns was helping me identify what qualities were needed for an effective violence interrupter and mentor. I mean, the interns could smell BS. If a name came up in the office or an affiliation and they rolled their eyes, I knew it wouldn't work out.

They helped in finding credible people, screening new hires with relevant questions, and ensuring staff could connect with young adults like them.

The interns also helped shape what would eventually become the signature program of the ONS and Advance Peace—what I called at first the Operation Peacemaker Fellowship. They confirmed that no one they knew was receiving any social services, whether it be from a school-based program or nonprofit. Most of the community centers or programs they joined were reluctant to serve them, since they were suspected of carrying and using guns. The aha came from learning that some of the angriest, most disconnected young people in the community weren't being touched by the nonprofits, clergy, or community-based services available. It was clear we needed trusted community caregivers to ensure Fellows could get the supports they needed.

THE ORIGINAL NCAS

Community leaders, the interns, and an ex-girlfriend of a candidate helped me identify Joe McCoy, a former dealer from North Richmond who had worked with some of the city's nonprofits on violence prevention, but left disgusted that they weren't really committed to that goal. Joe had credibility in North Richmond, a community being ravaged by gun violence, yet thought I was another "poverty pimp" and was initially skeptical. But I convinced him to give it a try.

Through another contact, I was introduced to a former Latino dealer with wide influence in Central Richmond. Sal Garcia was working with a developer and running his own small construction business at the time. When I first met Sal he looked real hard, and had long fingernails and ponytail, but also had a presence about him. Importantly, Sal was a youth football coach in the community and seemed to know every kid in Central Richmond. To confirm their credibility, I reached out to Gonzalo Rucobo, a former gang member running an organization called the Bay Area Peacekeepers, and Kevin Grant, a street outreach worker I knew in Oakland. Both offered ideas about what to look for in a violence interrupter.

Perhaps defying conventional wisdom for reaching young men, I hired outreach workers Diane Gatewood and Valerie Arce. Val was already doing work inside San Quentin and on the outside with the Bay Area

Peacekeepers. The two women would work a few years as excellent NCAs. They could find and connect with anyone we needed to connect with, without trepidation.

I sought out and then hired two more female NCAs, Kim MacDonald and Arlinda Love. Kim was hired to work mostly with the parole and community team in Richmond, so that people from Richmond who were about to be released from custody were prepared to come home with a nonviolent sensibility. Arlinda was connected to several factions in the city and had lost her own son to gun violence there. Arlinda's mother, "Ms. Timmons," was known and respected by many, and a strong community advocate for our work too. Without this community elder and the women on our team, it would have been difficult to get as close to some of the individuals and/ or situations that we needed to reach to prevent future gun violence.

I also bucked my own credentials list after I heard of a youth pastor who was working to stop gun violence in Richmond and leading community events. Kevin Muccular grew up in Richmond, and on a football scholarship, went to Florida A&M, where he majored in criminal justice and psychology. He returned home, all six foot four and almost three hundred pounds, to serve his community and promote peace. "Big Kev" was a genius in speaking life into people. After five minutes with him, you would be inspired and convinced you were meant for greatness. He had organized a successful campaign with clergy called Not Today aimed at ensuring all houses of worship opened their doors and did whatever it took to prevent a shooting each day. I knew his unyielding compassion and spiritual commitment would add tremendous value to our team.

Charles Muhammad came to me through a colleague's involvement with the Nation of Islam. Charles was an elder leader in the Bay Area nation and known as a guy who sought to enforce "justice" within Richmond when injustice surfaced its ugly head. He was from a different era and street ethic, but as a barber, he "could talk to anyone and had dirt on everyone." Early on, his role on the ONS team was not public, even to the team itself. That meant he could bring high-level street intelligence about my own teams' activities as well as from a variety of potential and actual shooting incidents happening within the community. He would get me street intel that gave me credibility with my team. They would ask, "How'd this square know shit we don't?" They didn't know I had eyes out there, watching them too. This helped me to help them improve their service to the community.

Another Kevin, Yarborough, was later hired. He'd returned to Richmond after seventeen years in prison for a gun-related offense, and described being an NCA and working for peace as "living my life for a second time." He was a leader in South Richmond, particularly a housing project known as the Manors, and had been shot five times and lost five cousins to gun violence. Kevin had been shot by an ONS team member in Joe's crew back in 1989, but they were able to move beyond old rivalries. Both Kevins were tall and imposing guys, but teddy bears inside deeply committed to their communities.

I was introduced to Sam Vaughn by guys in the Richmond Project inside San Quentin prison. My first impression was that this guy was warm, thoughtful, and well-informed, and could talk to anyone about anything. He had just returned home from ten years in prison for attempted murder and was waiting to get back into the construction industry. Sam asked me to help him get a contractor job with the city's public works, but when I inquired, the department said he wasn't eligible because of his felony conviction. I had other plans for Sam anyway. Recognizing his intelligence, fearlessness, and leadership capacity, I knew he would make an immediate impact with the ONS!

WORKING ON BUILDING TRUST AND FINDING ALLIES

The first task of the NCAs was to build relationships with those at the center of gun violence in Richmond. As Sam described the process of his NCA teammates, "If they [young people] are on the corner selling drugs, we are right there next to them. We spend that time talking, getting to know them, and building trust. We take the help to them, and after they reject us, we come back the next day and the next day."[13]

One of the first tasks I gave to Joe and Sal was to attend meetings organized by the Contra Costa County Parole and Community Team, a group focused on supporting returning people and developing a reentry support program. Joe and Sal went to weekly meetings, and I asked them to get the names and phone numbers of every service provider who was present, offering support to this reentry population. I then had them call each service provider to set up in-person appointments and examine what services they were offering, and whether the services could support the youths and young adults engaged in gun violence. Few service providers, however, were picking up their phone calls. Joe and Sal went to their offices, but the doors were locked. We experienced a lot of good-sounding talk and presentations, with few groups actually providing any services. I knew if these organizations weren't really "open for business," they were clearly unprepared to provide supportive services to the hardest-to-reach populations we were engaging. Yet many of these same, so-called providers sent me proposals, seeking city funding, for how they were going to help end gun violence in Richmond. There was little shame in putting proposals in front of me that were clearly self-serving.

This confirmed what my three interns had already shared with me about widespread resistance from the very service providers and nonprofits I thought would eagerly support the "shooters" we were about to engage. What I learned was that many in the community impacted by the gun violence happening in Richmond were often too jaded to be helpful to our new efforts. It turned out that other community members weren't going to cooperate because their project wasn't getting the city's money. Many service providers saw the new ONS as a potential cash cow for their organizations. The clergy, particularly many charismatic individuals, were already in the spotlight in this space and ignored us.

With all of that in mind, I went back to the drawing board and hashed out another plan. If there weren't many legitimate service providers, I decided that we would raise the money to hire our own and have them come to the ONS, rather than having our clients go to them.

Between January 2008 and December 2012, sixteen- to seventeen-hour days were the norm for me. I would leave the city after a full day's work, have dinner at home, and maybe attend an event that involved my kids, then go back to the office and work late into the evening. I would frequently get up in the middle of the night to send an email to my team members instructing them to adjust their outreach strategy or come to the scene of a shooting. I was learning by doing, listening to contacts on the streets and my outreach workers. I accompanied my outreach team in responding to shootings and meeting the young people wherever they hung out. The focus was on building credibility and trust with the community in the streets, where I was an outsider. Family time was a casualty of this war we were trying to end. My life-work priorities were often in conflict.

Gaining word of mouth about the hardworking ONS team mattered too. The ONS team and trusted community members came up with the idea that the ONS should sponsor some weekend-long sports camps in the city's most violent neighborhoods. This would capitalize on the coaching and athletic backgrounds of myself and some of the NCA team members, and increase our visibility to hundreds of kids and their families. The camps were free to any kid who wanted to come, and all the young people who participated got ONS-labeled T-shirts. We turned it into a block party atmosphere, and people came out. The community started taking more notice of the ONS and the street outreach team after that. We created a presence, and now instead of watching us—like, "Who are these people?"—the neighborhood could put a face to a name.

SHIFTING FOCUS FROM PLACES TO PEOPLE

In 2008, Richmond had 28 homicides compared to 47 the year before, but in 2009, gun homicides were back up to 45. In early 2010, I knew we needed to adjust course. I needed more staff. Firearm offenders are intelligent and mobile, and the neighborhood-centered strategy, targeting North and Central Richmond, wasn't reaching all the potential shooters in the community. Around this same time, other public safety leaders invited me to a meeting with local, regional, state, and federal law enforcement working gun crimes in Richmond. I was just an observer in this meeting, but I heard them say that they believed there were 17 people responsible for 70% of the 45 homicides in 2009. I thought, if we could successfully engage those 17 people in a more focused, intentional, deliberate way, then positive change was possible.

I left that meeting thinking maybe I was making the strategy harder than it needed to be. I reflected on the Boston Gun Project's Operation Ceasefire report in 2001 by David Kennedy and colleague, where they had found that few gang members were gun offenders. Similar research found that entire communities weren't violent. Rather, there was a small number of offenders driving shootings in certain places in Baltimore, Los Angeles, Minneapolis, and other cities. With this similar knowledge about gun violence in Richmond, we changed course. Instead of a high-intensity concentration on the three rival and warring neighborhoods, we were going to invest our resources in identifying and engaging the 17 to 28 "hot people" most likely responsible for a majority of the gun violence. I told my new team that the answers to ending gun violence in all of Richmond was with those few people.

We went to work to engage this group every day. I asked the NCAs to bring the 25 individuals most likely to engage in firearm violence to city hall for a meeting. The NCAs got most of them there, and I explained to that group that we were going to support them with services and opportunities daily for the next eighteen months. I told them, in my suit sitting in the most exclusive city hall conference room, that *they* were the power brokers in this city. Most laughed, and some nodded their heads. They were powerful because their actions are determining whether economic development, new businesses, schools, or playgrounds get serviced or whether that money instead goes to police overtime. Now more heads were nodding. There were no threats made at that meeting—just an offer and commitment. The ONS was committed to engaging with them respectfully because they mattered, and we were going to give them opportunities they had never dreamed would come their way. Their commitment to us was to reciprocate—meet with their mentor multiple times a day, attend group life skills classes, explore social services, and most important, dream of an alternative future to the one they have today. As mentioned earlier, we would eventually offer many of them the chance to meet and engage with a group of elders from their community, opportunities to travel outside Richmond, subsidized internships that helped them move toward "legit" work, and a financial allowance, or monthly stipend, as a reward for making these commitments and participating in our program. All of these ideas for services and supports were things that my three interns suggested they needed and could get excited about. I knew that the milestone allowance, as we came to call it—a monthly stipend contingent on deep engagement with the program—would be especially controversial, but the effectiveness was made crystal clear after seeing the youths' reaction on receiving their first monthly paycheck. We packaged all of these elements into the essential components of the Operation Peacemaker Fellowship.

We managed to enroll 21 of those 25 invited to the city hall meeting into the first Peacemaker Fellowship cohort. We courted, catered to, chased, and counseled those 21 in ways they had likely never been treated before. Even if they slipped back into behaviors we were hoping they would avoid or change, we showed up and offered them more of the same. We didn't expect any immediate changes in their behaviors. It was truly unconditional love as public policy.

Compared to our neighborhood-based strategy, the first year of the Fellowship seemed to be delivering results. While during our neighborhood-focused violence interruption strategy shootings and firearm homicides went up and down, after twelve months of concentrating just on those 21 potential shooters, there were 21 gun homicides, down from 45 the year before. We doubled down and engaged them more intensely, ultimately taking some rivals on out-of-town trips. By the end of the first cohort of Fellows, Richmond had 18 gun homicides, the fewest in over fifteen years. During the first Peacemaker Fellowship, there were 314 firearm assaults, a 44% reduction from the 562 firearm assaults that had occurred prior to its launch. By the time I had my five-year review as director of the ONS, I remember City Manager Lindsay telling me, "You were a suicide mission; you aren't supposed to be here. Neither am I. We both were supposed to fail. But you are here because of who you are and the hard work of your staff."

We didn't abandon our neighborhood focus entirely. Ongoing feuds between North and Central Richmond rivals seemed to peak in the summer months. So in 2012, I mobilized all the NCAs to occupy the street corners of the five entrances and exits in and out of North Richmond from June through August. They would flag down a car they knew shouldn't be there and turn away any groups suspected of coming from Central Richmond. The intervention was called the Summertime Gun Violence Interruption Initiative. By August 31, 2012, there hadn't been a single gun homicide in North Richmond, and there were only 4 citywide between June and August 2012. By the end of 2013, Richmond had 16 gun homicides—another historic low. We even managed to get an officer from the Richmond Police Gang and Special Investigations Unit to report publicly that the bottom line is the Office of Neighborhood Safety saves lives. [The] ONS engages the most dangerous young men in our community and gives them an alternative to a violent lifestyle. For every killing they prevent, human capital is preserved, negative social costs are minimized, and millions of dollars are saved. Like them or not, [the] ONS has shown [itself] to be effective in saving human life and preventing violence in our city. Were it not for their efforts, more young men would have been shot and killed in our city.

The data in figures 3.1a–b show the trends in violence reduction that this initiative provides. The year the ONS started, not only were there 47 firearm homicides, but there were 329 shootings with an injury. By 2014, after just two cohorts of Peacemaker Fellows, there were 13 gun homicides in Richmond and 65 injury shootings; by late 2023, Richmond had 8 gun homicides and 24 injury shootings—the lowest numbers since 1971. Gun homicides have remained at all-time lows for the better part of the past decade in Richmond, even during the spike in urban gun violence that occurred across the United States at the start of the COVID-19 pandemic in 2020 to 2021.

SUSTAINING PEACEMAKING AMIDST LOCAL INTRANSIGENCE

As the first ONS director, I was building the plane while we were flying it. Listening to my team and the Fellows while adjusting accordingly was in some ways the easy part. What I found much harder was the daily negotiation of racism, skepticism, doubt, and underhandedness from within government as well as among potential allies. Confronting systems—government and nonprofit—that were so firmly resistant to change and committed to the status quo was more traumatic than I had ever anticipated. Rarely would a month go by in those first few years with the ONS where I wasn't told by my superiors, law enforcement, pastors, social justice activists, you name it, that "you can't do that" and "that isn't going to work." I was constantly being called into meetings of officials who wanted a "progress update," and then being judged and graded by policymakers and elites who didn't have a clue about the actual work we were doing, how hard it was, and the toll on my team. I took the heat for them many times and was willing to be the "troublemaker"—or in my case, the angry Negro man—in the room as I regularly justified the existence of the ONS.

Going against the city government and even nonprofit models of violence prevention—like focusing exclusively on shooters, ensuring we were engaging shooters who were from rival groups, and treating them with humanity when most others saw them as thugs—likely contributed to our success. But constantly justifying these choices and defending my team took a toll on me as well as my family. I was away from home responding with my team at late-night shootings or being called to testify late into the evening at city council meetings. To stay the course, I frequently turned to my mentors and family for support. Much like the mentorship we were offering our Fellows, I relied on experienced elders to bounce ideas around, vent frustrations, and connect to other resources that could strengthen my hand with the city.

Even with such resistance, I felt lucky to be in a community as well as working with a city manager and council that was willing to be radically imaginative, take risks, and give our strategy the time required to grow, learn, innovate, and find ways to be sustainable. One key moment for the ONS helped prove that we could likely survive through the roughest of times. We were stretched thin in the office on this particular day in October 2011. Our NCA team was spending less and less time at city hall due to summer and fall gun violence reaching significant highs that year. At the same time, our office at city hall had become a "safe space" for many of our Fellows. They would usually call to see who was in the office and ask if they could come by for a visit. This was a rule. There are no metal detectors at the door, nor are people frisked before entering the ONS office. Another rule was: people can come as they are to our office. Knowing who was coming gave our staff members time to ensure that established safety protocols were exercised to keep them safe. On this day, neither of the rival groups called to ask if it was OK to stop by.

As chance would have it, they showed up one after the other, while only our administrative staff occupied the office These were rivals from groups that had been actively trying to take out one another in the days preceding this confrontation. Insults were exchanged. No one was backing down. The groups made their way into our office kitchen, closed the door, and locked it, and a fistfight ensued. A nose or maybe two were broken. Blood ended up on the walls, and worried office workers called 911. And this is all happening at the ONS, adjacent to city hall.

Our administrative staff managed to calm the situation. The police investigated, but there were no charges, arrests, or retaliation. The media nevertheless tried to make it into a scandal, depicting it as the "brawl at city hall" and "the gang melee at the ONS." Many were demanding that the ONS to be shut down, seeing the fight as "proof" that you can't "coddle criminals." Council member Corky Booze called for a controversial "forensic audit" of the ONS, claiming that our unconventional approach was misusing public resources. Booze, like me, is Black, and tried to rally our community against the ONS and our staff.

The problem for naysayers was, we had the numbers to show success. By this time, the ONS had engaged over fifteen hundred people though our street outreach; forty-two of the forty-three Fellows we had enrolled were alive, thirty-nine of those had no gun-related hospitalizations or injuries, and thirty-six had no new gun charges.

In addition, our team recognized that a fistfight was a sign of progress. What we told the media, city leaders, and law enforcement was that the fight was between rivals who regularly used guns to resolve conflicts. As a Fellow, you are already someone with a strong propensity to use firearms. Yet this had been an old-school "fade" (fistfight). The young men decided to pick up their fists instead of a gun. Everyone walked away. No parent had to bury their child. That was a clear sign of progress and that the Peacemaker Fellowship was working.

I would leave the ONS in 2016 with the goal of bringing this work to other cities around the country by creating a new nonprofit organization called Advance Peace. When I'm asked what distinguishes Advance Peace from most other CVI work or other programs like ours, the answer is that we're not simply trying to interrupt gun violence; we're trying to develop and help heal people. It's all about seeing these individuals' potential, despite themselves and what they've done. Ultimately, we see them as human beings.

4

AN ANTIRACIST APPROACH TO ENDING GUN VIOLENCE

The problem [of equality] is so tenacious because, despite its virtues and attributes, America is deeply racist, and its democracy is flawed both economically and socially. . . . [J]ustice for Black people cannot be achieved without radical changes in the structure of our society . . . exposing evils that are rooted deeply in the whole structure of our society. It reveals systemic rather than superficial flaws and suggests that radical reconstruction of society itself is the real issue to be faced.

—Martin Luther King Jr.

Building from the Peacemaker Fellowship experiences in Richmond, Advance Peace launched in 2018 first in Sacramento, and then Stockton and Fresno. While designing the program in Fresno, we traveled the city with some future NCAs. They described their place today, but also revealed the importance of ensuring that history and context was reflected as well as addressed in the Peacemaker Fellowship.

Crossing the railroad tracks from downtown into Southwest Fresno is literary crossing the color line. The mixed ethnicities, newly constructed baseball stadium, and commercial storefronts of downtown give way to abandoned lots, barred-over windows, and liquor stores. Rod and Syrup, two future NCAs with Advance Peace in Fresno who grew up in Southwest, narrate our drive through the neighborhood.

"There wasn't nothing here except dealers and addicts. That's what you saw as a kid and that's what was expected you'd be," explains Syrup.

"If my daddy was a police officer and my momma a teacher, I probably would have been one too. There ain't nobody here that's any of those things. We a product of this environment," Rod claims.

The Southwest has been hypersegregated since at least the turn of the twentieth century. At that time, African Americans came to Fresno to find farmworker jobs, as did immigrants, and escape the Jim Crow South. Almost all the affordable housing at the time was built in the Southwest. In the 1930s, the federal Home Owners' Loan Corporation "redlined" the Southwest, meaning it was labeled a risky investment, meaning avoid Black neighborhoods and don't lend to people of color. Banks adopted the recommendations, and denied new home mortgages or other loans to the mostly African Americans living in the already segregated redlined areas. Lack of capital further depressed land prices in the Southwest while attracting new, polluting industries to serve the area's growing economy. State Highway 99 was completed by the 1960s, and created another physical barrier between east and west Fresno. "They called Shaw Ave. Fresno's Mason Dixon Line," another NCA told us.

Private property deeds further restricted any nonwhites from purchasing homes east of that line. Driving around the Southwest, we saw that every street has a tooth-gapped look with empty lots in between abandoned buildings, and the occasional occupied house or corner store. There also weren't many people walking the streets, adults or children. Rod told us, "Lots of people here live in fear. They afraid of the unknown . . . a crackhead or a stray bullet. For most of us the only protection is sports or gang life, and neither provided much. I remember when our football team went to the other side and it was like they was an NFL franchise, with nice grass fields, fences, and equipment everywhere."

The structural violence of redlining, restrictive covenants, highway construction, polluting industries, and disinvestment from schools created a "landscape of despair" in Southwest Fresno. The California Environmental Protection Agency would state that the living conditions in Southwest Fresno contributed to the area having California's highest Black poverty, infant mortality, and unemployment rates—consistently for over forty years. Structural violence in Southwest Fresno is a mirror of that in other communities. Urban neighborhoods that experience racial residential segregation, historic redlining, and other racially motivated disinvestments have thirteen times the rates of shootings compared to predominantly white and other areas.[1]

In the Southwest, it is about the everyday disasters that the city tolerates, takes for granted, or has officially forgotten. Life expectancy in Southwest Fresno is dramatically lower: 59.8 years as compared to on average 80.6 years for those living across the tracks a few miles away in the city's Northeast.[2]

Southwest Fresno has about 30,000 and some 23% of the population is Black; 40% of the residents live below the poverty line, with a median household income of just over $38,000. Perhaps it comes as no surprise that Southwest Fresno suffers from gun violence as well. In fact, since at least 2011, the Southwest has recorded the highest firearm homicide rate in the city. From 2011 to 2021, the Southwest had a firearm homicide rate of 50 out of 100,000, also making it one of the most gun violent places in the United States. In Fresno, African Americans make up about 8% of the city, but were killed by a firearm in Southwest Fresno at a rate of 84 out of 100,000 between 2010 and 2021. There was an average of 71 nonfatal shootings per year in Southwest Fresno from 2014 to 2021, or a rate of 236 per 100,000.

ANCESTORS MOVEMENTS TOWARD PEACE

The expansion meant being explicit about the insights that shaped Advance Peace, and sharing with these new communities how the Peacemaker Fellowship was different from any other CVI program they might have heard of. The Peacemaker Fellowship was designed to be about ending urban gun violence through redressing some of the traumas and harms done to Black people for hundreds of years. There were 244 years of slavery, after all, and 81 years of Jim Crow in this nation.[3]

Elements of today's Peacemaker Fellowship derive from lessons learned in studying the history of Black resistance and peacemaking movements within our communities. For example, mutual aid organizations existed, such as the African Society in 1796 Boston and the African Lodge of Masons, which offered refuge for free Black people to find support and peace. They collected dues from those who could afford it to redistribute to those in need. The African Meeting House in Boston became a site for abolitionists to organize and assist with the Underground Railroad. While true peace and justice were largely out of reach for Black people, organizing before and after the Civil War offered some protection from white terror. Inspiring leaders such as Ida B. Wells called for Black-led institutions as the only way for Black people to gain true liberation and healing.

BLACK SETTLEMENT HOUSES AS EARLY PEACEKEEPERS

One inspiration for today's peacemaking comes from the Progressive Era, a period near the end of the nineteenth century when "care" emerged as a driving social value. In particular, the Black-led settlement house movement, such as the Negro Fellowship League in Chicago, inspired generations of Black self-help movements. Most coverage of the Progressive Era and settlement houses discusses white reformers such as Jane Addams, Julia Lathrop, Florence Kelley, and John Dewey. These important urban reformers focused largely on improving living and working conditions for impoverished immigrants, protecting children, standardizing education, and advocating for women's rights.[4] For all of their supposedly progressive ideas and innovations, the settlement houses were segregated places that failed to serve and largely ignored the needs of African Americans.[5]

A Black-led settlement house movement also existed that provided an alternative to the white-dominated approach of the day. This included Wells's Negro Fellowship League, Lugenia Burns Hope's Neighborhood Union in Atlanta, and the White Rose Mission in New York.[6] These Black settlement houses were founded and led by Black women. Hope left Hull House in Chicago to found and lead the Neighborhood Union, which delivered nursing, sanitation, housing, employment, and political organizing for the Black community.[7] The creation of the union was inspired by the concerns of Black residents of Atlanta's Westside after searching for a local woman who was missing and ultimately found dying alone.[8]

The Neighborhood Union was formed with a "community consciousness," and the first task was to get to know each family in the neighborhood. The union also recruited Morehouse College students to interview residents and document who was living there, making the formerly invisible Black residents and neighborhoods more visible. It then supported the students and residents to construct solutions, such as installing water and sanitation services in homes and schools, increasing the amount of streetlighting, delivering health care, and building recreation and play spaces in vacant lots. The union used its historically Black college or university connections in 1914 to purchase a property that was formerly part of the Spelman Seminary and turned it into a community-centered space, staffed by newly trained Black social workers.

A frequently overlooked aspect of the Black settlement houses was that they focused as much on building up people as they did on improving physical infrastructure. The Atlanta Neighborhood Union was explicit about engaging with the "undesirable" members of the community—from gamblers to prostitutes—and hired "zone workers" to visit "houses of ill repute" as well as engage these folks.[9] Eventually, the union hired eleven men, led by Gary Moore (future chair of the sociology department at Morehouse who also helped create the Atlanta School of Social work), to support residents on probation and juvenile offenders.[10] These men were a Black version of the "friendly visitors" who Hope had witnessed supporting immigrants at Chicago's Hull House.[11] What emerged from all of this was a new type of Black-led social work committed to reaching out to those whom white society had deemed criminal and unworthy.[12]

In effect, Black settlement houses undertook what today we would call the work of community healing. They brought together multiple generations of Black folks, created processes for sharing lived experiences, and used these experiences to create the newly emerging civil rights movement. It should be noted that the movement was led by formerly underemployed, "everyday" Black folk, not just the Black intelligentsia of the day.[13]

As was typical of the United States when Blacks created a positive, enlightening, uplifting initiative "for us and by us," white power structures were threatened and worked to dismantle the Black settlement houses. The Black street outreach workers were critiqued by white social workers as being unobjective and too "attached" to their clients. Elite whites were also challenged by the notion being put forward by Black leaders—not just within the settlement houses of the day—which emphasized that Blackness was something sacred, not pathological, and that what was needed was a collective approach to survival and prosperity, not just individual behavioral change.[14] Ultimately, many Black settlement houses struggled to obtain funding from white philanthropy, and those that managed to survive were forced by their donors to shift attention away from criticizing such things as institutional racism and police violence, and focus more on volunteerism, self-help, and physical changes to their neighborhoods.[15]

CONFRONTING MYTHS ABOUT BLACK CRIME

An important legacy of the Black settlement house workers was that they refused to perpetuate US myths about Black crime. They were not alone in going beyond being fierce advocates of Black self-help to providing a counternarrative to the white-dominated, criminal-justice-only-focused approach to public safety. Wells and others were critics of the white domi-nant, eugenic perspective that Blacks were inherently inferior and predis-posed for criminality.[16] These critiques have ranged from W. E. B Du Bois's look at Black "crime statistics" to Michelle Alexander's *New Jim Crow* cri-tique of the "war on crime."

In 1897, Du Bois moved to Philadelphia's College Settlement House, where he would prepare the landmark study *The Philadelphia Negro* and make astute field studies of criminality in the Black community.[17] Du Bois was already perhaps the most important voice against the racist, pseudo-science of eugenics. His critiques detailed how Black arrest and impris-onment data were not "evidence" of criminality but rather a reflection of the harsh application of Jim Crow laws, discriminatory punishments, and intense racial surveillance that had been institutionalized since at least the 1890s.[18] Moreover, Du Bois highlighted the rampant racism within municipal police forces and the legal system, noting that noth-ing "is easier in the United States than to accuse a Black man of crime."[19] While native-born white and immigrant crime was on par with that of Blacks from the latter third of the nineteenth century through the 1920s, criminality of whites was frequently described as "part of the structure of urban life," while immigrant crime was dismissed as part of the processes of "social inequality" and challenges of assimilation.[20] Black crime, on the other hand, perpetuated white racism.

As Khalil Gibran Muhammad has argued, "For white Americans of every ideological stripe—from radical southern racists to northern progressives—African American criminality became one of the most widely accepted bases for justifying prejudicial thinking, discriminatory treatment, and/or acceptance of racial violence as an instrument of public safety."[21]

As whites perpetuated the dual narratives of Black inferiority and criminality, this helped justify white terror groups such as the KKK, and place blame on Blacks for rising unemployment and white poverty in the post–World War I era. In fact, summer 1919 came to be called the "red summer" due to the violence by white terror groups inflicted on Black communities that had increasingly established their own businesses and were gaining employment in urban industries (although in the most dangerous jobs). This white-inflicted violence against prospering Black communities included the destruction in 1921 of the vibrant Black economy in Tulsa, Oklahoma, known as Black Wall Street.[22]

THE TRAUMAS OF "NEGRO REMOVAL"

By the early 1940s, concerns about World War II and national defense supplanted some concerns over urban racism and crime. The postwar period, however, saw expectations about the role of government shift as a US populous that helped "win the war" looked to government institutions to now promote opportunity and social order back home.[23] What followed was President Franklin Delano Roosevelt's sweeping New Deal legislation, which underwrote opportunities for whites, but not Blacks, and acted as what Ira Katznelson called "white affirmative action."[24] The New Deal ensured that federal employment legislation discriminated against Black participation, the GI bill didn't apply to returning Black soldiers, and new housing legislation created access to cheap mortgages and new suburban opportunities reserved only for whites.

This era was also the height of racially restrictive covenants written into the deed restrictions of homes barring the owner from renting or selling to African Americans as well as other racial minority groups. This would limit where Blacks could live and concentrated them into increasingly impoverished urban neighborhoods.

As we noted about Southwest Fresno, spatial racism was perpetuated by restrictive covenants and New Deal subsidies for white, new home purchasers through the practice of redlining. The federal Home Owners'

Loan Corporation sent thousands of auditors into neighborhoods to rate the risk of offering new home loans to those living in urban areas. An area was given an A rating if it was an optimal area to lend, and a D rating was applied to areas of high risk, where no loans should be given. In what was a state-sponsored system of racial segregation, the D or risky areas were color-coded red on maps, based almost entirely on whether there was a large Black population.[25] The federal government encouraged that mortgage insurance be given instead in areas that were labeled green, which meant only whites could obtain mortgages there to buy homes, further concentrating Blacks in urban ghettos.

Federal housing policies went further in the 1940s through the 1960s, pushing through a policy and practice of urban renewal, largely under the guise of and with support from public health.[26] Urban renewal razed entire neighborhoods and justified this destruction by determining that an area was "blighted," which was a vague definition that included everything from older housing to a community with few services, poor health, and abandoned properties. Due to decades of Jim Crow racial segregation and disinvestment, restrictive covenants, and a real estate practice known as blockbusting, Black neighborhoods were already starved of resources and investment, and thus disproportionately labeled as blighted and subject to demolition.[27] James Baldwin would call the urban renewal program "Negro removal," as thousands of mostly Black neighborhoods were demolished in the name of public health and social order with the empty promise of rebuilding new, modern communities.[28]

Redlining, racist housing policies, and urban renewal devastated the economic as well as social fabric of Black urban neighborhoods. Businesses couldn't get loans, landlords couldn't get the capital needed to improve existing older housing, and declining property values decimated public schools reliant on the local tax base and further segregated them by race. According to urbanist and psychiatrist Mindy Fullilove, this complete disinvestment from Black urban communities was a form of state-sponsored violence. Fullilove has called the impacts of urban renewal "root shock," or the "traumatic stress reaction to the destruction of all or parts of one's emotional ecosystem."[29]

According to Fullilove, urban renewal contributed to trauma-related mental illnesses, stress from losing family wealth and housing, and prolonged grief, all of which increased hypertension, stroke, heart disease, and other conditions in African American communities for current as well as future generations. For Fullilove, when the people, institutions, and built environments of urban places are preserved and nurtured rather than razed, this can act as an "exoskeleton" that protects us from social and physical harm along with promoting well-being.

FOUNDATIONS OF CVI

In an attempt to reclaim this protective "exoskeleton" and protect ourselves, Civil Rights leaders advocated for peaceful resistance to violent state discrimination. MLK Jr. would articulate a powerful vision for peaceful social change, stating: *"Darkness cannot drive out darkness; only light can do that. Hate cannot drive out hate; only love can do that."* Black urban leaders were already working on how to 'infuse love into public policy' and everyday community peacemaking, as exemplified by two prominent Black-led civil rights groups.

THE BLACKSTONE RANGERS IN CHICAGO'S SOUTH SIDE

For example, Chicago's Blackstone Rangers was a group (some called it a gang) that organized to protect itself in the violent Woodlawn neighborhood beginning around 1959.[30] The group, while accused of extortion and enrolling unwilling South Side youths, decided to organize residents and seek peace with other, supposedly rival groups across Black Chicago. According to an investigation of the group published in the *Atlantic* magazine,

Ranger Nation has been credited with keeping the South Side of Chicago "cool" during the summer of 1967 and the spring of 1968, following the assassination of Dr. Martin Luther King. It has been said that they have kept drugs, alcoholics, prostitutes, and whites hunting for prostitutes out of their neighborhoods. They have also been credited with making genuine attempts to form lasting peace treaties between themselves and the Disciples to decrease the level of gang fighting on the South Side.[31]

The Rangers were the target of much Chicago police and Federal Bureau of Investigation (FBI) activity in the 1960s and early 1970s, even while the group advocated for peace at city hall, lobbied its alderperson, and campaigned for peace and employment for all Blacks on the South

Side. A Harvard University newspaper, the *Crimson*, described the Rangers as a threat to both the state and civil rights groups claiming to represent the people's will for change. The report noted,

The Rangers are a symbol, representing the way toward a better future for the members of the gang and other youth in Woodlawn. The Rangers wield more power in Woodlawn than any civil rights group or social action committee. . . . The success of future programs will hinge on the police department's ability to establish a firm—and possibly sometimes friendly—rapport with the Rangers. This can only happen if the police begin to treat the Rangers fairly and communicate with them as individual youngsters with distinct problems.[32]

The influence of the Rangers would be diminished after it partnered with Chicago civil rights organizations and the police department to obtain a federal government literacy and job training grant.[33] After many of its leaders were arrested, the Rangers faced further criticism from law enforcement by partnering with the Vice Lords (Bloods) and Latin Kings to form an alliance in Chicago known as People Nation, for which it was accused of perpetuating a violent rivalry with the Folk Nation (Crips).[34]

THE BLACK PANTHERS

The Black Panthers were another important resilience and self-help movement that successfully combined an agenda of healing, protest, and prosperity for Black communities.[35] The Panthers mobilized in the face of police killings of mostly young Black men and built an institution that filled a void left by an absence of state services. They organized Black-led armed neighborhood patrols, community "survival conferences," free school feeding programs, and health clinics as well as prevented housing demolitions, and campaigned against medical discrimination and other racist institutions.[36] Yet much of the influence (and whites' fear, which led to the FBI's counterintelligence campaign to spy on, infiltrate, discredit, and disrupt Black freedom movements) of the Black Panthers came from their politics that combined armed self-defense, a critique of legalized apartheid in the United States, and the effective delivery of life-supporting social services. While their organizing and arms patrols obstructed the brutal policing of Black communities, they also exposed the failures of the federal War on Poverty programs along with the previously mentioned housing and other policies. Importantly, the Panthers promoted a revolutionary Black nationalism that was distinct from the civil rights movement of its day, and this also was ultimately too much of a threat to incrementally minded activists and white power structures. As Douglas McAdam wrote in his book *Political Process and the Development of Black Insurgency, 1930–1970*, disagreement within civil rights groups over things such as the legitimacy of armed personal protection, if nonviolence was the only path to political reform, and whether civil disobedience that resulted in property destruction and physical harm was a legitimate form of resistance fractured the movement and weakened interracial solidarity.

URBAN STREET OUTREACH AS RESISTANCE

What the Rangers and Panthers taught us is that not only must peacemaking and peacekeeping be led by the community but it must help restore harm already done too. Peacemaking for them was at once about preserving and protecting individuals as it was doing so for entire communities. Like the Black settlement house and human rights movements before them, it was through collective work that healing can and must happen. Healing contributes to peace among ourselves and our communities.

The collective notion of healing was later enshrined into the 1960s' civil rights legislation, particularly the Economic Opportunity Act of 1964. What is important for us was that this War on Poverty program centered street outreach as a pathway toward community improvement and healing. Prior to the 1960s, street outreach was largely framed as a way to interrupt "delinquent" youth gangs, which in early twentieth century were described as mostly white and European immigrant social and sport clubs.

It wasn't until the 1950s that urban street outreach began to look like what it is today. At this time, urban street outreach initiatives such as the Boston Special Youth Program were launched in neighborhoods like Roxbury. The goals of these 1950s' street outreach workers were to reorient youth gangs away from delinquency by providing social services to them and their families while also creating local infrastructure for community self-help. In other words, street outreach was viewed as a temporary step to get delinquent youths back on a productive track and establish more lasting community-based support systems for them.

The 1960s' street outreach models, as mandated in the Economic Opportunity Act, went a step further than those of the 1950s. This new government-funded group of outreach workers needed to come directly from the local neighborhoods where poverty was endemic. What was also different was that the 1960s' street outreach workers were not instructed to be "extension agents" of the state and deliver prescripted law-and-order messages but instead were charged with serving as "agents of change." These agents of change were supposed to help communities mobilize and organize socially as well as politically to address inequitable economic, housing, and other conditions.

The broader change agenda of the 1960s' street outreach workers was not only controversial but also contributed to critique and ultimately defunding by the federal government. One major criticism was that street outreach workers didn't do enough to stop crime, although this wasn't an explicit aspect of their job descriptions. The perception of lawless city neighborhoods—particularly in Black ghettos—gave rise to the 1968 passage of the Omnibus Crime Control and Safe Streets Act, which shifted urban street work from the War on Poverty to a war on crime. This new "war" was led by newly resourced police departments, which were incentivized to increase arrests for petty crimes, use military-grade weapons, and criminalize most community organizing because it was characterized—again almost exclusive in Black neighborhoods—as gang behavior.

Then came Daniel P. Moynihan's 1970 advice to President Nixon to call for "benign neglect," or a strategy of ignoring the needs and claims of groups such as the Black Panthers as well as neglect of issues such as poverty, inequities, and violence in Black communities. The challenges this brought were exacerbated by another government practice that also took hold in the 1970s called "planned shrinkage," where cities closed fire stations and hospitals, and stopped collecting trash, in Black and Brown neighborhoods under the guise of saving money. These are just two examples of how public policies and practices shaped the presence as well as persistence of traumas in Black urban neighborhoods—many of which are still with us today.

The federal "war on drugs" followed, intentionally designed to punish Black people, as John Ehrlichman, President Nixon's domestic policy chief, would later admit.[37] From the 1970s into the 1980s, the political narrative had shifted. Crime control led by increasingly militarized police was the answer to urban poverty and despair, not improving housing, offering education, or providing social services. Government drug policies, implemented by police, public prosecutors, and judges, sensationalized by the media on nightly TV, coupled with a destruction of Black-led social movements and service providers, amplified the presumption of guilt assigned to Black people since slavery and entrenched the racialization of criminality that began in earnest with lynching.

GUN VIOLENCE AS A PUBLIC HEALTH ISSUE

Gun violence, particularly its disproportionate adverse impact on young Black men, was increasingly recognized as a public health issue. In 1980, the surgeon general's report *Promoting Health, Preventing Disease* emphasized that healthy communities were only achievable by reducing violent behavior; it called for reductions by 1990 in the rate of homicide among Black males fifteen to twenty-four years of age.[38] By 1985, the *Report of the Secretary's Task Force on Black & Minority Health* identified homicide as a major cause of the disparity in death rate and illness experienced by African Americans and other minorities relative to non-Hispanic whites.[39] In the same year, the surgeon general's Violence and Public Health workshop recognized violence as a national public health problem. By 1993, the Centers for Disease Control published *The Prevention of Youth Violence: A Framework for Community Action*, which included guidance for a public health approach to youth violence prevention. The set of strategies proposed by the Centers for Disease Control in the early 1990s included the adult mentoring of youths, teaching conflict resolution and social skills, support for parenting centers, home visitation, therapeutic and recreational activities, and work/educational experiences.[40]

CEASEFIRE AND CVI

Even as urban gun crime was increasingly being viewed as a public health crisis, President Bill Clinton signed the Violent Crime Control and Law Enforcement Act in 1994. This law, known as the Crime Bill, allotted billions to local government to increase the mass criminalization and incarceration of Blacks, including such provisions as mandating life imprisonment for anyone with a third violent felony, allowing for sentencing enhancements if someone is accused of being "gang affiliated," and empowering prosecutors to charge thirteen-year-old children as adults.

While a majority of the members of the Congressional Black Caucus did vote for the Crime Bill, most Black politicians and activists were pushing instead for full employment, quality education and drug treatment, and reining in police brutality as the key ways to reduce crime.[41] In fact, the caucus proposed an alternative to the Crime Bill, part of what it called the Racial Justice Act, which included investments in community-based prevention, alternatives to incarceration such as drug treatment and putting $3 billion into youth intervention programs, and allowing defendants the use of statistical evidence of racial bias to challenge death penalty sentences.[42]

While the Crime Bill entrenched greater police arrests, harsher punishment, and heightened surveillance in Black communities, some criminologists were advocating for a greater attention to deterrence as a way to prevent gun crime. Just a year after the Crime Bill, the Boston Police Department partnered with Harvard University's David Kennedy to launch the Boston Gun Project. What Kennedy and colleagues' research found was that there was a small number of highly active firearm offenders in Boston, and, if given a choice, even they would rather not kill to settle mostly turf disputes.[43] This strategy, which came to be called focused deterrence, was antithetical to the Crime Bill's massive investment in punishment and incarceration.

Kennedy managed to mobilize the probation department, juvenile corrections, district attorney's office, and faith-based leaders to work together to collectively "deter" these active gun offenders. They would use "every lever possible" in a program called Operation Ceasefire. The strategy would be described as the "Boston Miracle" because it seemed to successfully reduce gun homicides. Chicago and tens of other cities would later adopt Operation Ceasefire.

At the heart of Operation Ceasefire is the "call-in" meeting. Those thought to be involved in or influencing firearm violence, those who have firearm charges in their backgrounds, and those on parole or probation are required to attend a meeting with all the partners—law enforcement, prosecutors, social workers, clergy, and so on. In those meetings, they are told, in no uncertain terms, that if they don't stop using guns, they and their group (or gang) will feel the full force of the law and prosecutors.[44] As Kennedy described it, the call-in message goes something like this:

Violence stops now, the adults are taking over, and the new penalty structure says that if anybody in your gang puts a body on the ground, the whole crew pays, and fast. Every unserved trespassing warrant will get served; every petty parole or probation violation will get enforced; smoke a joint in public housing and you'll get evicted; open a single beer on the street or piss on the sidewalk and you'll go to jail.[45]

Operation Ceasefire aims to combine an intensive law enforcement effort with peer pressure and some degree of social services, all with the aim of stopping gun violence. While evaluations of Operation Ceasefire suggest it has had some success in reducing gun crime, there is little evidence we could find that the program helped (or even attempted to) heal historically traumatized Black youths or those living in these communities.

THE PUBLIC HEALTH ORIENTATION OF CURE VIOLENCE
Somewhat dissatisfied with the close relationship Operation Ceasefire had with law enforcement and seeking to inject a more public health (meaning preventing and treating gun violence as a disease) approach, physician Gary Slutkin created a spin-off of Operation Ceasefire called Cure Violence in 2000.[46] Cure Violence explicitly aimed to approach gun violence like a doctor or public health practitioner would an infectious disease. Slutkin explained the strategy this way:

For violence, we're trying to interrupt the next event, the next transmission, the next violent activity. And the violent activity predicts the next violent activity like H.I.V. predicts the next H.I.V. and TB predicts the next TB.[47]

According to an evaluation of Cure Violence, the street outreach workers, called violence interrupters, are the agents who stop the transmission of violence, such as

when one person is injured or shot, the victim's friends and known associates are likely to seek revenge. The Violence Interrupters from Cure Violence sites seek out those associates and try to "talk them down," or persuade them that there are other ways to negotiate the conflict without engaging in more vio-lence that could risk their liberty and even their own lives.[48]

Unlike Operation Ceasefire, Cure Violence does not work closely with police, uses street outreach workers who work to interrupt gun violence, and employs separate adult mentors to offer gang members social services and jobs. The interrupters focus on conflict mediations while the men-tors practice case management revolving around changing the partici-pants' attitudes and behavior related to violence. To participate in Cure Violence, an individual must meet at least four of seven criteria:

(1) carries or has ready access to a weapon; (2) has a key role in a gang; (3) has a poor criminal history; (4) is involved in high-risk street activity such as dealing in illegal drugs; (5) is a recent victim of a shooting (in the past 90 days); (6) being between 16 and 25 years of age; and finally, (7) being recently released from prison or a juvenile facility for a criminal offense against a person.[49]

COMMUNITY VIOLENCE INTERVENTION (CVI)

Both Operation Ceasefire and Cure Violence place a heavy emphasis on community-level interventions, much like a public health disease preven-tion strategy might. These educational, social marketing, and programing strategies are mostly aimed at changing what is perceived as unhealthy community norms that do not condone gun violence. For example, Cure Violence staff will train community residents to help them spread mes-sages of nonviolence and enroll them to canvas neighborhoods to hold vigils in response to shootings.[50] This aspect of community-based violence intervention works to "denormalize" gun crime, and again referencing public health campaigns like those to stop smoking or change one's diet, aims to mobilize a critical mass of individuals who no longer make certain behavior acceptable in a community as well as encourage this message and practice to spread throughout the community like a "positive epidemic."[51]

Both Operation Ceasefire and Cure Violence have also shaped what is today defined as CVI. At the core of CVI is the use of "trusted messengers who work directly with individuals most likely to commit gun violence, intervene in conflicts, and connect people to social, health and wellness, and economic services to reduce the likelihood of violence as an answer to conflict."[52] The US Department of Justice further defines CVI as a set of multidisciplinary strategies that "engage individuals and groups to prevent and disrupt cycles of violence and retaliation, and establish relationships between individuals and community assets to deliver services that save lives, address trauma, provide opportunity, and improve the physical, social, and economic conditions that drive violence."[53] Advance Peace is one CVI initiative and differs from some of the others in important ways—namely, that it is explicitly antiracist, invested in the healing of staff, participants, and communities, works solely with those closest to firearm hostilities within impacted communities, and does not work with the police.

HOW ADVANCE PEACE IS A UNIQUE APPROACH TO CVI

Perhaps the foremost difference between Advance Peace and other CVI approaches is that it was created as well as informed by the history of Black resistance and liberation briefly summarized in this chapter. What this means practically is that our leaders are African American, most (though surely not all) of our participants or Fellows are Black, and the neighborhoods where we work are primarily (although not exclusively) suffering the toxic legacy of decades of racial residential segregation.

Another implication of being on the shoulders of Black movements for liberation and justice is that we lift up, trust, and promote the excellence, assets, and potential within the Black community. Our outreach staff members are formerly incarcerated folks from the communities where we work. We value their intelligence and experience, which is viewed as essential for shaping the content of the Peacemaker Fellowship. Our clients or Fellows are viewed as valuable assets too, not problems, thugs, terrorists, or any other often racist connotation society places on them. We see them as both victims and healers as well as capable, with the right supports, to be leaders and positive influences on their communities. Too frequently our "indigenous" approaches are co-opted and undermined by well-meaning white allies. The fact remains that the urban gun violence epidemic in the United States disproportionately impacts the Black community, so peacemaking and peacekeeping ought to be viewed as paid work toward reparative justice.

A second aspect of Advance Peace that distinguishes it from other CVI strategies is that we are primarily focused on healing and building healthy people through intensive healthy relationships. It is through these relations and human development that we achieve gun violence reductions. Compare the Advance Peace goal of healing with those of Oakland's Ceasefire strategy, which includes reducing gang/group-related shootings and homicides, decreasing the recidivism and incarceration rates of individuals participating in the intervention, and strengthening police-community relations.[54] Advance Peace reduces firearm crime in a community through healing those already traumatized as well as providing them with healthy adult mentors and supports, and through these activities, delivers peace, safety, health, and equity to the entire community.

Third, and building on the previous two characteristics, Advance Peace integrates a discourse of everyday and institutional racism into the work, as both a driver of participant's trauma and source of collective strength. For example, Advance Peace has learned from and builds on the insights of the Black-led settlement houses, Black Panthers, and others, that we must first identify the "structural violence" imposed on African Americans, name it, and then dismantle its bodily and place-based impacts. These historical movements also taught us that we must first change the people who shape and drive the institutions that make public policy as well as occupy our public institutions, from criminal justice and education, to housing, employment, social services, and more. In other words, we must start with changing people along with healing ourselves and our communities, so that the institutional, policy, and place-based changes that must follow are sustainable, and have people in power who are deeply committed to peace.

We put our Fellows and NCAs in positions to confront existing "institutional violence" (i.e., segregated housing practices, dehumanizing policing, underfunded public schools, planning that allows more liquor stores than libraries in predominantly Black and Brown neighborhoods, etc.), often through telling their personal stories in meetings with government officials, teachers, private sector leaders, activists, and others. Our Fellows learn from their Black and Brown elders (i.e., our elder circles), and get opportunities to travel to historically significant Black cultural sites, universities, and museums around the country. This is about empowering them, arming them with knowledge of self and culture, and using this renewed awareness to love themselves and our community. This love translates into a desire to live, hope, dream, and act for peace.

Fourth, unlike Operation Ceasefire's call-in approach, Advance Peace never uses threats to encourage participation. What type of relationship begins with a threat? Certainly not one that has sincere and genuinely caring roots. Advance Peace explicitly aims to avoid retraumatizing its Fellows through threats or other potentially triggering experiences. As we see the humanity of all of our Fellows, this demands compassion and forgiveness from the outset. We practice radical Black self-love. As in other healing-centered strategies, we first ask our Fellows, "What happened to you?" versus telling them they better change or else.

Fifth, Advance Peace does not focus on group or gang norm change. Advance Peace acknowledges and respects that most people in gangs are not violent, and most who live in some of the most violent spaces within neighborhoods are also not and have never been violent, and have no intentions of ever becoming violent. We believe that a way to transform groups and community safety is to offer attention, intensive mentorship, and alternative life opportunities to the those most likely to use guns. Again, we see these folks as victims. This might be thought of as "precision" public safety, and is consistent with other CVI strategies that concentrate on the most influential and chronic offenders, not entire communities or neighborhoods.

A sixth difference is that Advance Peace is tailored to those who we recruit into the program. We invite them to join voluntarily. There is no threat or sanction if they refuse, at least not from Advance Peace. We do not have a manual or "off-the-shelf" set of engagement strategies. While it is true that we deliver trauma-informed supports to all of our Fellows, such as cognitive behavioral therapy, culturally competent counseling, and life coaching, these are tailored to the participants' needs and experiences. This is done through our unique Peacemaker Fellowship, where each participant cocreates a LifeMAP with their NCA mentor. As described earlier, LifeMAP is a tool for identifying the strengths of each participant, charting out the partnership between Advance Peace mentors and Fellows, and setting short-, medium-, and long-term goals as well as actions for transforming one's decision-making in healthier, more peaceful directions.

While some Fellows might need safe housing or mental health supports, others might require anger management and family conflict mediation. Still others might need literacy and chronic disease supports. All Fellows get one-on-one and group healing supports, such as restorative justice and elder circles. Critically, the Fellow is not given their LifeMAP but instead cocreates it with their assigned NCA. Advance Peace believes that those at the center of gun violence are intelligent and capable of identifying the solutions for reducing gun violence, and do not need to be threatened or told what to do by those disconnected from and unfamiliar with their lived reality.

A seventh aspect that sets Advance Peace apart from other CVI strategies is that all Fellows are engaged every day, multiple times a day, by their assigned NCA (mentor) and other members of the NCA team in that city (and sometimes from other Advance Peace cities). What this means is that Advance Peace does not have some outreach workers performing street violence interruption, others doing community conflict mediations, and still others doing mentorship, life coaching, or social service navigation. The Advance Peace NCAs are trained and supported to do all of these things—and more. The NCAs go out daily to chase, court, counsel, and cater to our Fellows, no matter where they are. Advance Peace has learned that intermittent contact and engagement with active firearm offenders is insufficient in the process of helping to deliver optimal healthy outcomes for our Fellows.

Eighth, the Peacemaker Fellowship was the first and only CVI effort for a long period of time to invest in its strategy participants, the Peacemaker Fellows, through such things as travel and financial allowances. This was controversial, even by so-called progressive CVI organizational leaders. We were criticized, as noted earlier, for "paying people to stop shooting" and "taking criminals on vacations." On the contrary, these activities are intentional and part of our healing-centered strategies; traveling with other people can act as a form of group therapy, and money is used as one type of reward for our Fellows' commitment to investing in peace. We describe both dynamics in more depth in later chapters. In short, we view travel and financial stipends as elements of ensuring our Fellows have unique opportunities to participate in community healing and are seen as valuable; both are intended to give them something to live and strive for.

Ninth, Advance Peace explicitly invests in building and supporting the personal as well as professional development of a national and global "family" of formerly incarcerated outreach workers. Advance Peace is unique in its extensive investment in and focus on staff training and development. We pride ourselves on being intentional in delivering learner-centered, performance-based training and development support to our teams. Advance Peace aims to deliver an elite standard of care to the communities where it works by constantly investing in the skills, knowledge, and professionalization of NCAs. It recognizes that outreach and violence interruption work is intensive. It's often underappreciated that our credible messengers are dealing with their own traumas, families, and personal needs, but most have little, if any, experience in formal workplaces. We build up and empower these local leaders to not just serve the Advance Peace clients or Fellows but also be change agents in their own lives, families, and communities.

Finally, Advance Peace believes that the conditions that contribute to gun violence in urban (largely Black) communities were created in part by city and county government practices (or a lack thereof), and therefore cities and counties must commit to redressing these harms by showing support for CVI practices such as Advance Peace. For Advance Peace, this means not being part of or too close to the institution of policing. Similarly, Advance Peace does not include an emphasis on reducing the number of guns in a community, which again is something that many working closely with law enforcement frequently center on. While not explicitly partnering with law enforcement, Advance Peace is committed to working with and being embedded in local governments. We acknowledge this requires strong leadership in order for our population to be seen and welcomed as part of local governance. Our history suggests that ending the epidemic of gun violence cannot be the responsibility of charities, churches, nonprofits, or police alone. There should be an intentional peacemaking and peacekeeping municipal workforce made up of formerly incarcerated community residents who are deployed in our most impacted neighborhoods. City councils, mayors, and support staff in every department can—and should—play a role in urban gun violence reduction.

5

NEIGHBORHOOD CHANGE AGENTS

To every man there comes in his lifetime that special moment when he is figuratively tapped on the shoulder and offered a chance to do a very special thing, unique to him and fitted for his talents. What a tragedy if that moment finds him unprepared or unqualified for that which would be his finest hour.
—unknown

PREVENTING A STREET WAR

A gang war seemed like it was about to erupt in Sacramento. A prominent rapper affiliated with Lavish D was killed in the Meadowview neighborhood. Another well-known rapper, Mozzy, who is from a rival neighborhood called Oak Park, was calling for revenge. The city was on edge. The two rappers had already had another dispute that led to a brutal fight at the Arden Fair Mall. Only a year or so earlier, the Sacramento police had shot an unarmed Black man, twenty-two-year-old Stephan Clark. That incident had set off local and national protests. The National Basketball Association's Sacramento Kings and Boston Celtics wore warm-up T-shirts a week after the killing with Clark's name on them. The Oak Park Bloods were ready to "slide" through Meadowview, territory of the Starz gang.

It was at this moment that something unexpected occurred in Sacramento that had never happened before: there was peace in the streets. It wasn't as if there wasn't tension, beefing, and threats. There were, and plenty of them in the streets and on social media. Even the local and underground media in Sacramento was counting the hours until the deadly violence arrived.

According to a Sacramento probation officer, "There was no doubt in my mind, knowing who was likely involved in all of that, the insults spreading across social media, the anger and trauma those young folks were dealing with, that the city was about to be on fire. The morgue was about to be full."

What was different this time was that there was a team of NCAs from Advance Peace focused exclusively on those most likely to shoot in Sacramento's neighborhoods. Two of these NCAs, Marcus (called MAK) and Freddie, were known on the south side and in the neighborhoods likely to kick off the war. They were former gangbangers themselves, having returned from prison with a new outlook, set of values, and skills centered on ending the gun violence they had helped perpetuate in Sacramento.

MAK and Freddie tapped into all of their networks. They showed up at every spot, street corner, and trap house where something might be plotted. They scoured social media to flag any potential conflicts. They barely slept and spent night after night in the streets. They called and got in the face of every potential shooter they knew in South Sacramento, and got everyone else they trusted to spread the word: "keep the peace, there is no retaliation this time."

"We were in their ear everyday, multiple times. Talking them down from the hurt, anger, and reaction they were being encouraged to do. Just trying to get them to stop and take a breath for a second," recalls MAK. "Everybody was amped up. Streets was hot and heads on a swivel," as Freddie remembers it.

A week passed and no shootings. Not even an attempted drive-by. Two weeks later, nothing. A month later and still no retaliation.

Advance Peace Sacramento launched the Peacemaker Fellowship in July 2018. From July 2018 through December 2019, in the first cohort of the Fellowship, there was a 21% reduction in gun homicides and shootings in the city. In one year, July 2018 to June 2019, homicides went down by 50% in Oak Park and South Sacramento, two of the city's historically most violent neighborhoods. There were no youth homicides in Sacramento in 2018 or 2019–the first time that had happened in the city in over thirty years.

The daily street presence of Advance Peace NCAs not only prevented this likely street war in Sacramento but also was—and still is—largely responsible for reducing gun violence in this city and providing opportunities for those at the center of gun violence along with giving them reason to come out of the shadows and turn their lives toward peace.

WHO ARE THE NCAs?

When it comes to how this CVI approach differs from others, the most important ingredient in the Peacemaker Fellowship strategy and ending the epidemic of gun violence is people. Specifically, it is the street outreach workers / violence interrupters / mentors called NCAs, and the participants or Fellows. You'll learn here about several NCAs working in different cities because it's so important to see that the qualities, experiences, skills, and dispositions of the NCAs make the Peacemaker Fellowship what it is. This Fellowship model of change is a concept or blueprint, but the NCAs and Fellows collectively make it a reality.

The Advance Peace NCAs can be considered "community clinicians" much like the community health worker (CHW). Their skills extend beyond the "street social worker," as they interrupt gun violence, mediate conflicts, mentor traumatized Fellows, and deliver healing counseling as well as other supports and opportunities. They put themselves in the middle of potential shootings on a regular basis. They bring a wealth of street knowledge and professional training to the job, and are often described as credible messengers.[1] NCAs are also effective because they are wounded healers in the sense that they too are working on their own traumas, which likely contributed to their involvement with gun crime at another phase of their lives. Like the addiction counselor who was once an addict, they have lived the experience of being at the center of gun violence and are still healing from those traumas. A healer can share that experience, and offer it as an opportunity for others, faced with similar circumstances, to engage in healing and turn adversity into positive growth.

Regarding the logistics, NCAs are full-time and well-compensated employees. They are persistently trained formerly incarcerated members of the community where they work. Putting yourself in harm's way, mentoring frequently reluctant and violent young people, and navigating social service bureaucracies and programs that aren't intended to support marginalized Black men, can be and is taxing on one's body and mind. You might wonder who these people are, and what it takes to do this kind of work.

WHAT MAKES A CHANGE AGENT EFFECTIVE

An NCA is a life coach and violence interruption clinician who works in a tailored fashion with their assigned Fellow, helping to diffuse the cyclic and retaliatory gun violence that surrounds our Fellows. Each NCA is thoroughly screened and observed through a robust interview process. Those selected have demonstrated sound character traits, personal integrity, above-average emotional intelligence, game-changing potential and talent, healthy work ethics, and an ability to identify, engage, and positively influence active firearm offenders who have avoided law enforcements' reach within impacted neighborhoods in their city. Talent alone is not enough; the NCA must fit into the existing "chorus line" of skilled outreach workers in their city too. This assessment is made by considering the leadership potential in each, with the support of the national network of Advance Peace staff.

As the "neighborhood" in their title suggests, NCAs are expected to not just change individuals but have a broader vision of community change as well. This community orientation is part of the inspiration for the public health and healing-centered approach Advance Peace uses as its way to prevent gun violence. Our NCAs are more than just an outreach worker, violence interrupter, or credible messenger as they are frequently called in the field of CVI. They work to support young people at the center of gun violence to recognize their inherent and authentic humanity, genius, and beauty. NCAs also work to ensure that those around that Fellow—their peers, families, and other influencers in the neighborhood—are prepared to eventually receive and support the rebirth of the Fellow's authentic self.

As community clinicians, our NCAs are what psychologist Carl Gustav Jung described as wounded healers:[2]

The intelligent psychotherapist has known for years that any complicated treatment is an individual, dialectical process, in which the doctor, as a person, participates just as much as the patient. . . . We could say, without too much exaggeration, that a good half of every treatment that probes at all deeply consists in the doctor's examining himself, for only what he can put right in himself can he hope to put right in the patient. It is no loss, either, if he feels that the patient is hitting him, or even scoring off him: it is his own hurt that gives the measure of his power to heal. This, and nothing else, is the meaning of the Greek myth of the wounded physician.[3]

The key factor is the healers' disposition toward sharing their own journey with others along with the willingness and ability to do so. Yet as the name implies, the wounded healer is still processing, so their own healing is part and parcel of that of their "clients." The NCA is a *wounded* healer because they must simultaneously empathize with similarly hurt clients while transforming their own past into a source of wisdom to be drawn from even as they are acting as a trusted mentor.[4] In these ways, the wounded healer aims to move with their Fellow from trauma-informed care to post-traumatic growth.[5]

Post-traumatic growth is an approach that does not romanticize trauma but rather identifies the positive changes that can come from adversity when one has healthy supports to process those experiences. It can include greater self-awareness and identification of personal strengths, a strengthening of interpersonal relationships and compassion for others, enhanced spiritual development, a greater appreciation for life, and an openness to discovering new possibilities or purpose in life.[6]

A key difference in the Advance Peace approach compared to other gun violence prevention initiatives is the way we see and prepare our NCAs. While other approaches place a primary emphasis on detecting and interrupting conflicts that could lead to gun violence, our NCAs are primarily charged with building trusting, meaningful, and nurturing relationships with those at the center of gun violence.[7] Fundamentally, the NCAs choose to love their Fellows in the way M. Scott Peck defines love as "the will to extend one's self for the purpose of nurturing one's own or another's spiritual growth."[8] Love, then, demands intention and effort.

The NCA is central to acknowledging each Fellows' authentic self, and where they are encouraged to understand and embrace their autonomy as they move in a healthier life direction. Our model of the NCA builds on the work and writings of the Burkina Faso–born Maladoma Patrice Somè, who wrote in his book *The Healing Wisdom of Africa: Finding Life Purpose Through Nature, Ritual, and Community* that there are certain things without which young people cannot survive and flourish, and mentoring is one of them. Westerners see adolescents as fundamentally naïve about life. By contrast the tribal mentor sees a youth as someone who already contains all the knowledge that he or she needs, but who must work with an older more experienced person to "remember" what they know. A mentor therefore is not a teacher in the strict sense of the term, but a guide who shows the way, working from a position of respect and affinity, addressing the knowledge within the young person. The pupil is not an ignorant person in the eye of his or her mentor. The pupil is seen as a storehouse, a repository, of something the mentor is quite familiar with and very interested in, something the mentor himself has and knows very well. The mentor perceives a presence knocking at a door within the pupil, and accepts the task of finding, or becoming, the key that opens the door. There develops a relationship of trust between mentor and pupil motivated by love and without which success would be unlikely.[9]

As a point of reference, Advance Peace NCAs combine skills typical of CHWs, social workers, and street violence interrupters. CHWs provide community members with culturally relevant health education and supports, conduct street outreach, and advocate for individuals and communities that might be voiceless—too intimidated or not yet ready to advocate for themselves.[10] In these ways, CHWs are regularly seen as critical "bridge builders" and "culture brokers" between community residents, health care delivery systems, and other institutions of support. Meanwhile, community social workers, particularly in the Black community, aim to strengthen already existing community network ties as well as enhance social supports in a place by linking those able to provide advice, emotional support, and tangible aid to those who need it.[11] Black social workers have traditionally integrated insights of how racist systems of oppression work to perpetuate trauma, but also deliver supports that identify and lift up unique strengths in the Black community.[12] Since its origins with the Freedmen's Bureau, Black social work has aimed to support Black self-determination in the pursuit of social change, emphasize collective identity and healing over individual culpability, rupture racist and white supremacist thought that characterizes Black culture as "pathology," and centers racism as an essential factor for understanding and addressing trauma.[13]

The definition of skills for this relatively new field are being developed, which is worth considering. In 2016, the National Uniforms Claims Committee created a new provider code, eligible for Medicaid reimbursement, called Violence Prevention Professional, which they defined as follows:

Prevention Professionals work in programs aimed to address specific patient needs, such as suicide prevention, violence prevention, alcohol avoidance, drug avoidance, and tobacco prevention. The goal of the program is to reduce the risk of relapse, injury, or re-injury of the patient. Prevention Professionals work in a variety of settings and provide appropriate case management, mediation, referral, and mentorship services. Individuals complete prevention professionals training for the population of patients with whom they work.[14]

This definition led to efforts to define the "prevention professionals training," and some in the field of CVI issued a set of minimum core competencies for these workers that included trauma-informed care, managing traumatic stress, de-escalation, conflict mediation case management, and understanding violence as a public health issue.[15]

In 2022, the American Public Health Association recognized the violence reduction roles for CHWs and passed a new policy that calls for training them in violence prevention.[16] The association interestingly describes the work and tasks of CHWs in a similar way as we (and the field of CVI) do, claiming that CHWs provide cultural mediation among individuals, communities, and health and social service systems; offer culturally appropriate health education and information; supply care coordination, case management, and system navigation; provide life coaching and social support; advocate for individuals and communities; build individual and community capacity; offer direct services; implement individual and community assessments; conduct outreach; and participate in evaluation and research.

Yet the above reveals there is no one definition of a gun violence interrupter, mentor, and wounded healer. To better understand who these professionals are and how they do what they do, here are profiles of a few NCAs regarding why and how they do what they do, the struggles they face, and how they manage those challenges. Because they come from the same neighborhoods as Fellows, their formative experiences also provide a window into what it is like to be in their clients' shoes.

JAMES

James Houston is a lead NCA and program manager in Richmond's ONS. James's story, as he tells it, is about putting in the self-work to understand the sources of one's own anger and trauma. Becoming an NCA for James was a natural progression from this self-exploration and healing since he is able to share his ongoing journey with others who may have been similarly harmed.

James arrived in prison in 1996, having just turned twenty-one. He bounced around to numerous state prisons, most of which made him want to do nothing but, as he described it, "be the same guy I was on the streets, doin' the same things." Yet that began to slowly change once he was transferred to San Quentin prison. James spoke of his early days there:

> I was working on death row, sweeping. I wanted to go, you know, to school, go to college, but the hours conflicted with this job. I talked to someone there who became a friend and he talked to some people and got me shifted from that job to another job. I was able to take a college course. I never had a man really give me something and not want nothing in return. . . . [F]or someone who just genuinely wants to see the best in you, it sparked something in me. So I started following these men and seeing, Are you real? Is this really you? And it turned out they were.

This same group of OGs were, like James, "lifers," meaning none were likely to ever get out of prison. They nonetheless encouraged James to continue with his classes and address his anger issues because, as he stated, "it was going to get me killed in there."

The OGs encouraged James to join a prison program called the Victim Offender Education Group (VOEG), run by the Insight Prison Project that helped set him up for his current outreach position. VOEG uses skilled facilitators and other prisoners to facilitate a self-awareness, healing, and emotional skill-building curriculum designed to help prisoners decrease violent and negative behavior, better understand and experience the mind-body connection, and improve and increase their impulse control, conflict resolution, and communication skills. An end goal is to develop healthier relationships with others, including family and friends, and empathize with the victims of their crimes. The VOEG process starts with a year of intense weekly meetings, where groups of prisoners learn to open up, trust each other, and begin to tell their stories. The process has been described as focusing on supporting prisoners to identify and address unresolved trauma, connect to their feelings and emotions, and be witnessed in their truth and bear witness to others.[17] The program also supports the development of new life skills, like mindfulness, emotional regulation, and anger management.

VOEG is explicitly informed by research highlighting that ACEs frequently contribute to adolescents having problems with emotional processing, and when unrecognized and unaddressed by caring adults, contribute greatly to substance abuse and criminal behavior.[18] The second year of the VOEG program enhances skill building and prepares participants for a "restorative justice" circle, where offenders and those impacted by the crime meet and dialogue to humanize each other.[19] Those who remain with the program in the second year are also trained with a new cohort of participants to be VOEG facilitators.

James reflected on his journey and what he learned in the VOEG program:

You grow up with that mentality, where I have to be hypermasculine. At six years old, I seen my mother being abused by my father and I remember my brother who was five years old, he was the one who went up to my father and bit him on the leg. My father picked him up and threw him over a table onto a couch. And for me, in that moment, it was fight, flight, or freeze . . . and I froze. And from that moment on, I kind of felt like a coward. Shortly after that, my mother picked us up and moved us to California, and I felt that I had something to prove. Like I was the oldest. I had to make a name for our family out there.

He continued:

I was in the streets selling drugs. I had been shot at before. I was carrying a gun. I had no conflict resolution skills. I was an angry young man. I was frustrated because I had a son who was ten months. I didn't know how to be a father. All I knew, at the time, was money. Get more money. I didn't know the power of being there in his life and the impact of that. How more important that was. So I'm coming home from the store. I started drinking a lot more. I seen my neighbor, who was a friend of my mother, in a conflict with her boyfriend, who I also knew and I had actually sold drugs to. I went over there. I confronted the guy arguing. I said, "Give her money back." He said, "No." I pulled out my gun to kind of intimidate him with the gun. He reached for it. I pulled back and shot him.

James explained how the VOEG process helped him see his actions and himself in new ways, particularly what it meant to be brave:

Even though I did a lot of negative things in the community, in my way, I felt like I was the type of person who would look out for you if you needed me in a violent situation. Even talking to my family, most of the things that I was there for them was for violent situations. I had never let go of that feeling of being a coward. I was always constantly trying to make up for that moment. And so when that situation came with my neighbor, I had to realize, you know, because when I first committed the crime, I never thought that I would get that much time or an eighteen-to-life sentence. I felt like I should be rewarded, like I did something good. Over time as I looked at it and got to know myself and know my own story, because I ran from it so much, so long, I realized that it wasn't about conflict going on. It was about that little boy who is six years old, trying to prove that he wasn't a coward.

With his in-prison experiences and self-work, James was recruited to join the ONS as an outreach worker in Richmond once he was granted parole. But to this day, he continues to work on his own self-awareness to be an effective mentor to others.

JULIAN

Julian was raised on the streets of Stockton and is a former leader of the Norteño gang there. He has a warm smile and welcoming demeanor behind his barrel chest and the extra-large Raiders football gear that he frequently wears. Julian has become one of the most valuable NCAs in the entire Advance Peace organization, but by his own admission, he didn't ever imagine life would wind up this way.

Even after word got out that Advance Peace had hired him soon after his release from prison, a police officer in the city's gang unit told the Advance Peace program manager, "That's one of the most violent guys in this city and he ain't never gonna change." They were wrong, and Julian's life experiences growing up in the rough-and-tough Latino community in Central California still drive his work today.

My uncle was a crack and heroin addict, but he was also the guy I looked up to. I had no other consistent adult males in my life. My older brother went to prison before I was a teenager. My uncle, he paid attention to me. Of course, that was because he used me to rob for him. I was a little kid, and he would tell me how to rob and help him get money for drugs. I might get a little, but it was the attention that I liked the most, so I kept doing it. Then he started coming to my house and stealing from me—our food. There would be nothing left to eat after my mom went shopping. No money or food, so I went out and stole so we could eat.

My uncle was the only adult male family influence in my life. What I took from that, you know, was that you needed to be stronger than everyone else. I remember that movie, *Karate Kid*, it had an influence on me about how to be an adult, a mentor. I took that lesson from that movie, where they are in the dojo, learning to fight. The leader says, "Strike first, strike hard, no mercy. Mercy is for the weak. In the streets, a man confronts you, he is the enemy. An enemy deserves no mercy." That made total sense in my life at the time. When I was raising my young son, two to three years old, that was all I taught him. I'm dropping him off at preschool, I signed him in, and then told him, "Strike first, no mercy," type shit. Now at twenty years old, he is serving 125 years to life for murder. I carry that with me every day. Every day, that motivates me to give these young Fellows another story. Another way to be. I look at this as an opportunity to right a wrong.

Julian's contagious charisma and wit helps him connect to future Fellows and bring them into the Advance Peace program. He shares his own stories of abuse and neglect as a child, how he had little choice but to join a gang to survive as an adolescent, and how he transformed from a gang leader to a peacekeeper.

The work for many NCAs, including Julian, is personal and frequently involves family members. He couldn't get to his son in time to avoid violence and a life prison sentence. He reflected on how personal the work has become for him, including trying to get his nephew to take advantage of the Peacemaker Fellowship. Julian slowed his voice, took a deep breath, and explained the shadow of his drug-dependent uncle in his life:

He would steal food from my house and even rob me. He put my mom through hell. But he was the only man of family. He used me, and I grew up hating him. Fast-forward, and my younger sister started using meth. I was like, "Well, she better get it from me, 'cause I had good stuff and not laced shit." That was my mindset. I was doing my sister a solid by selling her drugs.

5.1 Julian, NCA, Stockton, California.

For my nephews, I was the only family man around, and in their eyes, I was my uncle. I was to them that same evil guy I hated in my uncle. They blamed me for turning their mother out; she became transient, living in the streets, addicted.

One of my nephews now has this real deep anger toward me. He takes that anger into the streets. He shoots and is also selling meth. He goes to jail. Still won't talk to me.

He gets out; I give him a place to stay. I'm still trying to repair this relationship with my nephew. He moves into my place with his girl and two babies. I got four new people living in my small house. I'm paying for their food. I'm buying his babies clothes. I'm driving DoorDash to make extra cash to help pay for all of this. I even set him up with a job.

I tell him, "OK, I'm here for you. I help you. You just got to not shoot, not smoke weed for thirty days, not get drunk in my house. Show up at that job I got you.".

He shows up one day. Next day, he's too high and hung over, blows off the job.

I tell him, "Bruh, you just using me for somewhere to stay. You not even trying."

He is just so angry with me, he don't want to do nothing. I think, what we dealing with, ain't easy. Sometimes, it's the people we love the most, people we get closest to, that take the most advantage of us. When we treat people with love and genuine intentions, it's not that they gonna just say "thanks, I appreciate you." They still gonna hate. Still gonna be angry. Still gonna sabotage themselves and their families. It's like that is what they know and expect, so giving him love and stuff, unconditionally. I mean I asked him to change, but I didn't make it a condition of him staying, eating my food, you feel me?

I mean, I was ready to slap him and tellin' him to get the fuck out. I'm committed to sticking with it. With him. Not giving up on him like my uncle did on me. Seeing that I let my own son down. My nephew is gonna shoot again or get caught up in that if he doesn't have anyone in his ear offering something else. So I'm not lettin' another one slip. I'm not quittin'.

In addition to the challenge of close family relationships, Julian has the constant one of being seen as that "other guy," the person he became known for in the streets. He described visiting a grave site a few days earlier and leaving some flowers for a deceased friend. When he was at the cemetery, he saw an older woman who he knew from his neighborhood. He remembers buying her groceries as well as helping her and her family numerous times. He knew she had lost a son to gun violence. Julian approached her, offering his hand and the flowers he had brought for his friend's grave. She looked at him and said, "I know who you are and what you did. Stay away from me."

"It's a constant struggle," Julian reflected. "You carry yourself as a peacekeeper, not a killer no more, but people remember and don't forget easily. It's just about being consistent, swallowing your pride, trying to understand where they comin' from, the hurt that lingers in them, and how it may be my calling, my challenge to show and prove every day, every moment I'm challenged, every time the temptation is there, to not be that other guy." He continued regarding the trust difficulties of outreach:

People always talk. They talk often and negatively about things that they don't know about. People are afraid of what they don't know, and uh, you know when I took this job, I got a lot of pushback from some of the members in my community, you know the "fellas," if you will.

You know, everybody automatically assumed that we were somehow connected to some sort of law enforcement agency or you know all of these other types of things. I even got a call from prison from the Nortenos higher-ups demanding that I go and meet a representative and explain myself. It just got really crazy like that. I stood my ground. I just continued to dispel the negative narrative that some certain people had about the program. And everybody who was a naysayer before is now all over me about how they can be a part of it. And it was just a matter of standing your ground and being consistent. I always tell everybody there's a formula. The first thing, they watch you, then they judge you, then they follow. So that's pretty much how that's been.

FREDDIE

Freddie is a leader and former NCA who now coaches other NCAs for Advance Peace. He was born in Salinas, and raised in Seaside and Sacramento. He describes growing up "with all the traumas and abuses" you can imagine. His first memories were his dad beating on his mom. He was three or four. By this time his mother was on drugs and his dad in prison, so he few options but the streets. He can't count how many times he was told his dad was coming for him and he was waiting by the window with his football in hand. His dad never came. By the time he was nine years old, he was in the California Youth Authority (CYA) for stealing and several other offenses. Yet the abuse and trauma only increased while in juvenile detention. For Freddie, a gang was his only family, and just surviving at ten or eleven years old was a way of life. Freddie, who is part Mexican and part Black, recalls having to be his violent self just to survive.

I remember having these split personalities growing up. I loved school. It was my escape. I knew I'd get to eat. I was protected. After school I had to go back to the block. I'd hide my gun in the bushes, and after school, I'd go get it and head down, back to the street life. Put a different mask on. I was book smart and street smart.

I experienced so much abuse coming from every adult. It happened while I was in foster care, when I was in CYA, all of them therapists they throw at you, they were part of the sexual and physical abuse. I created an alter person, called Loco ["crazy" in Spanish]. This was me as a superhero, not Freddie, but Loco. So you couldn't fuck with Loco. If you brought him out, I would go literally crazy on you. Whatever it took. I hurt a lot of people along the way as that guy.

I just got used to being abandoned by adults. It wasn't until I was in my late thirties, serving another prison sentence—my last chance before a life sentence—that I was able to take a class called Abused Boys, Wounded Men. That was the first time, approaching forty years old, that I finally understood what all the abuse, all that happened to me and why I am this way. I spent a lifetime pushing away people who love me. Why? Being regularly abandoned and not wanting to feel that pain again. I went back to being a kid getting dropped off at school and knowing they wasn't coming back for me. I'd grab their leg. I just kept behaving like that as an adult. I would hurt anyone who got too close to me in any relationship before they could hurt me. It also made me loyal and very protective—of course, a good gang member. I refused to lose what I love, or thought I loved, and protected it, literally, to death.

I'm a coach. I got into coaching my kids and then every team sport I could. It was a way for me to be a different adult than I had experienced. I also got to know all the little homies in the community. I was well-known. In my church, youth groups. All of that. Parents trust me. I was showing up at the hospital after a shooting. I was stepping in for them at parent-teacher conferences. I'm taking kids to their doctors' appointments. I was filling that father or parent, big unc, void for the kids on my team. In all of my kids, I could recognize the abuse and hurt in them. I could see it in their eyes. I could "smell it." I was also seeing myself. It motivated me. It was my calling to help these kids. To help them not become me. Go through what I went through.

I couldn't always control Loco, and I get sent away again. Now I've got two strikes on me. One more and I was going away for life. One of my players. I'm watching TV, and they reporting on him getting shot and killed right before the game. It hit me hard. I landed on that yard and told myself I'm gonna take advantage of all the programs in here. I'm gonna get out and do something to help these kids and be a different dude.

I took classes and got an AA degree. I took all of these self-help classes. I got certificates. I became a facilitator. I took the parenting class six times before I felt like I really got it! Then they said, "OK, now you need to teach this class." Soledad to Solano [prisons], I stopped hanging on the yard. I was in the books all day. I took classes that really only lifers have to take because I wanted to learn.

I also met and realized there was a lot of other people who went through shit as bad or worse than me. A lot of them right here in prison next to me.

I came out with all of my notes, papers. I was doing construction, but coaching and with youths was really where my passion was. I was called. I wanted to help. I started a youth program called Ready for Change. It's like, when someone came to talk to me, therapists, with a suit and tie or whatever, I didn't hear nothin'. When someone came to talk who looked and sounded like me, I heard them. I know its like that with these kids. I look like them. They hear me, they feel me.

Freddie is a student of life, which makes him a good fit for being a mentor. He developed a habit of keeping notes about what he was learning in school and prison, and continued that as he became an outreach worker. He is committed to continually learning and "refining his game," as he put it.

Perhaps no other outreach worker we met has spent as much time in hospitals after shootings as Freddie. On or off the clock, Freddie is the night owl who will leave the club at 3 a.m., hear about a shooting, go to the scene and emergency room to check in on the victim, counsel the family, and try to prevent retaliation. It is his calling, he claims, to not let it happen again. It is also personal for him. He reflects,

About two years in, I've got all of these Fellows. They are like my kids. My kids are all grown. I had one particular Fellow who is really doing well. This is a guy who was really 'bout it. Instigating and behind lots of gun violence. We had him focused on a job, and he is dating my daughter. This Fellow is literally like my son. I treat him like that, and we are very close.

I get the call from my daughter. Little homies been shot. I rush to the scene. Daughter is covered in blood. People all around amped up. Tensions are high. I'm holding my young life in my arms. Trying to stop the bleedin'.

We follow the ambulance to the hospital. My daughter is loosing it. We are all crying. It doesn't look good for him. He was shot a number of times. He dies. You know, I pretty much knew who shot him. It was another one of my Fellows. It was like that. It was deep for me because I went away after a shoot-out after one of my supposed "brothers" snitched on me. All of that gangsta shit came back to me and almost got me life in prison.

So my first reaction was my young life, "Loco," and to go get this m*fucker. Seeing my daughter hurting. Hurting myself. But I watched that come and go. I had let go of all that shit in prison. I was a different person, even in this most hurtful, angry, stressful situation.

One of the hardest moments was going back to them streets, going back to the group that likely killed my "son," and seeing them as humans, hurt humans. Talking them down from more violence. Talking to my daughter's friends. All

5.2 Freddie, former NCA, Sacramento, California.

ready to ride. Spending time with them. Crying through the anger and pain, but not letting them react violently to that pain.

I really had to use my emotional intelligence skills to not let my emotions override my intelligence. I had seen like three kids dead that last week. At the end of the day, what mattered was that everyone alive would make it home safe and sound. I was about not lettin' nobody else die. That was the goal every day.

For me, doing this job, keeping the peace, and mentoring young people to be and do better, its like double Dutch. You got to know where to jump in and where to stay out. Timing is important, but you also can't be in it if [you] don't show up. You got to know the rhythms of those holding the rope; feel what they doing and their pace. You need determination and careful calculation. When it looks easy, it's like you dancing over that rope, but that takes practice and mastery. Don't crisscross. Sometimes you don't get a second chance and you get tripped up. Be focused and put in the work. Double Dutch ain't something you can do by yourself. It only works if everyone gets involved, everyone gets into the rhythm, everyone gets a turn. That's what gun violence work looks like to me.

MARC

Marc, or MAK, is the program manager of an Advance Peace city and a former NCA in Sacramento. He was a well-known drug dealer, gang leader, and "known entity" in South Sacramento. One side of his family migrated to California from Louisiana, bought some land, and built wealth. He describes his childhood as somewhat different than most of his NCA colleagues:

I had a great dad around. He was always trying to get me to stay in school to keep off the streets. He was in school, working a job. All I saw was he was working all the time. Why would I want to do that? My biological mom, she literally dropped me off at my dad's front door when I was like eighteen months old next to a paper bag. I didn't see her again for more than two years. We all have our struggles, in my teens we got close. My Dads family was no nonsense church bearing folks, my moms on the other hand kept it poppin! It was a struggle with my stepmom. She was always telling me what to do. No matter how good my Dad, Stepmom and all the family from that side loved on me I always wanted my mom and I just seemed to always gravitate toward her side of the family. It felt right with my uncles, whom some weren't much older than me. Watching them I started to learn the game.

I was also a good student and athlete. I was popular in different circles, which also made it easier to be a successful hustler. One day in like third grade, my mom's boyfriend gave me like $100. It was more money than I'd ever seen. They was testing me to see how I'd handle it. Could I hold the money in my pocket?

I went to school the next day, and bought all of my homies, all the kids on free school lunch, like tacos and pizza. You know, what the kids with money could buy. Not the ghetto lunch. The place went bonkers. Kids was going crazy. They was loving me. The school thought I stole the money, so I got suspended from school for that!

I was always seen as a leader even if it was hustling. Hustling was also addictive. I thrived off the adrenaline. The thrill. If I wanted something right now, I could just have it if I do this. Instant reward, but the stress level was high. I didn't realize that until much later. What it was doing to me and my body.

I didn't listen to no one back then. I was so successful at eighteen in the streets, I acted like Lucky Luciano and created the commission; I was overseeing all the dealing in my area and beyond, and keeping the peace to ensure business was good. I had the plug. I wasn't down with any violence. I didn't just jump a dude for no reason. It is also bad for business. If there was beef, it was just a fade, no guns.

Music was big from both sides of my family and that has shaped me. I often remind myself and my Fellows to take advantage of a good thing that's right in front of them. When we was making music, we got an record deal offer. A big label. We were gonna be the first on BMG and walk away with like a hunnid and fifty thousand each. Not so much compared to what we was doin' in the streets, but it was sitting on the table. I wanted it, I'm not gonna front, but I didn't push as hard as I shoulda because in our minds, we was doing so much in the streets and we thought we had so much momentum that we thought we could make a million on our own. So we didn't take the damn deal.

I drop my first record in 2000; it does OK. We come out with another like compilation that had all high-powered names on it. I'm like alright, I'mma get these dudes from my neighborhood and we gonna be like a dog pound from out here. We had another label say, "We give you fity up-front," and then for each time it sells. At that time we making five dollars a CD, so we really can win if this thing crack. I got the damn graphics done for the song; they done the commercial that was gonna run on BET, plus the flyers. Got sent the masters. The same day I came back from the Bay with all the stuff, promotionals paid for and masters ready to go. They was like, "Come pick up the check." I'm celebratin' bruh. I'm done with the game. I ain't hustlin' no more. We was gonna flip this legal money 'cause to me if I got fifty grand legal plus my album sale, I can kick back. I ain't got to sell dope no more. That was where I was at in life. That same day, my door got kicked in. Feds kick in the doo'. I wasn't doing no hustlin' at the time, but it didn't matter. And I've never seen the streets again.

They didn't have shit on me but I knew the truth and what it could turn into. I took a deal that sent me away for ten years in federal prison. I didn't snitch on nobody, even though they knew as large an operation as I was running couldn't be just myself. So I get to prison and people know me. They heard about me and what went down.

When I first hit the yard, first day, dudes was like, "So how much time you got?" I'm like, "Man I got ten years." They like, "Oh you short timin'?" I'm like, "Short timin'?" He's like, hell yeah, I've been walkin' down a thirty. Or I've been down for forty-five. You get perspective and start asking yourself, "Am I gonna use this as an opportunity or what?" Y'all not just going to take ten years of my life, and I'm going to get out and just be the same dumb ni**. I'm going to do something with this shit job you keep me in, with all of these criminals and shit, and I'm gonna learn some shit. I'mma make sure I understand the game, and I'm gonna be the motherfuckin' big homie. The real big homie.

I started listening to the older dudes. I went to church. I listened in on the white dudes talking about investing. In the feds, these were high-level criminals. These are like the masterminds of crime in one place. They was there for all sorts of crimes and being leaders. It was the first time I listened and learned how other people were leaders in their shit. It was my college-like experience. I'm not saying it was easy like that, but for me it was where I learned from other elders and mostly how to not be a criminal mind. How to be better in my life, and with ten years, get out and live differently. Take my creativity and channel it to something uplifting. I was like, How they gonna take ten years of my life and not figure out how to turn this into a positive? Do something with this?

I came out, and after a stint in transitional housing in San Francisco (which was a trip, more drugs than in prison), I had to move back in with my dad. He helped me try to go legit. I got rid of the fancy, expensive car and apartment. I got a job offer to counsel former dealers and gang members. It was easy-peasy, talking to people like me and no one else had the experiences I had. But I had to take a class to get certified in counseling former dealers and gang members. For real, I coulda taught that class better then them . . . but it was the humbleness of riding the bus to the class, not being paid for months, no money, no flashy lifestyle anymore. That was challenging my whole persona, who I was in the streets, MAK. Kizzle! That was a big ego and identity challenge. I sat in the uncomfortableness, focusing on what I really wanted at that point in my life.

I got the job as a mentor and running the classes I was recently certified in. They never had nobody like me working for this nonprofit. I was still really a street dude, never had a job before. So I brought that hustle to this nonprofit

5.3 Marc, program manager, Yolo County, California.

job. For real tho', it fuckin' blew them away. I could code switch. . . . Maybe it was my dad as an educator . . . and one minute be the street dude, and the next giving a PowerPoint presentation to the board, and . . . whoop de whoop . . . feel me? We had all of these new kids joining up. People I could connect with that no one else in the organization could. I was rewarded with more and more responsibility. Then Advance Peace came calling.

MAK spent four years on the streets of Sacramento as an NCA and field coordinator, which is a position like the captain of all the NCAs in a city. His success in Sacramento contributed to him being selected to lead a new Advance Peace program in a neighboring city called Woodland. He now leads the Advance Peace work for all of Yolo County, California.

ROD

Sitting in a Fresno café, you would never know from Rod's calm demeanor and peaceful delivery that he was once a feared gang leader. Now the program manager for Advance Peace Fresno, Rod has been in the nonprofit space and giving back to his community of Southwest Fresno ever since he returned from his last prison sentence. He sees a homeless person outside and steps away to give them some cash. He exudes warm energy, inviting you into his story, and you can feel his genuine desire to help people. He admits, however, that he wasn't always this way.

I mean it's no story hasn't been told before. I didn't get no love at home so the street would take anyone in. There was lots of drugs in my house, and people coming in and out the house. There was a fight between my mom and stepdaddy. I wind up stabbing my stepdaddy. I was nine. Punctured his lung. I was protecting my mom. But a month later, stepdad is home from the hospital. He was a big guy. He confronts me. . . . "You got heart kid," he said. He had a knife in his hand and puts his other hand out to shake mine. I knew it was a setup.

I was out the house. It was self-preservation. I had three siblings. At ten years old, I was forced to steal food. Got caught and sent to foster homes. I was always running away. It was like I was never allowed to be scared and always be in self-preservation mode.

An Advance Peace colleague of Rod's tells us that a few weeks earlier, Rod ran up on a guy he didn't even know who was carrying a pistol. Rod took it from him and talked him down from whatever was possibly leading this guy to want to kill another human. As his colleagues watched with trepidation as the encounter between the two guys seemed to be winding to a close, the two men embraced in a bear hug. Rod and the stranger held one another like they had known one another for life. Shaking his head and smiling, Rod's colleague reflected, "That's just Wade" (Rod's last name).

I was the small dude who always did shit. I didn't care. I did it if it needed to get done. It probably came from not trusting nobody as a kid. Always having to do things myself. If you in a snake pit, you got to be a king cobra to survive. I embraced it entirely. I didn't care if there was a gang, or someone claiming a certain area or control the dope trade. I left the local gangs and started my own because I wanted to do it myself. I was the leader.

I was the salutatorian of my middle school class, a star athlete, and a dope dealer. I was in high school [and] my pager would go off. I'd just get up and leave school, go take care of business. I'd ace the test on Fridays, played football, center field on the baseball team. I played with many future pro athletes. I wound up getting kicked out of school and told myself I didn't care. I did tho' and know I threw away many sports opportunities my friends wound up gettin'.

In prison, like in school, he rejected authority and it cost him. He got sent to the hole (solitary confinement). "I just didn't care at that point," he recalls. While doing time in the feds, some older guys from Fresno got in his ear, telling Rod that he needed to change his ways, and join a group working to uplift the community and decrease the violence. Soon after coming home, with many of his homies dead or in prison, Wade's cousin was killed. He remembers his guys giving him the AK-47, and he just looked at it and in that moment decided not to retaliate. That urge, however, was again put to the ultimate test when his nineteen-year-old son was killed.

He was killed trying to shoot at someone else. I was mad. Thoughts of revenge consumed me. I had to leave town, 'cause I knew I was gonna catch up with the killer sooner rather than later and have to make a decision. My family pulled me out of it. They said, "Bro, don't ruin it for your daughter and your other son. They need you." Some of my guys like Aaron (Foster) also sayin' the same thing, and he had lost a child to gun violence too. It was also when I realized people out there thinking about me, caring about me. I don't remember feeling that until that point in my life.

One of my boys connected me to a group of ex-gangbangers called Fresno Street Saints. They was doing stuff in the Southwest to stop violence, address poverty, housing, that type of stuff. It was a way to channel my energy. We did real talk, life skills, and job training for young people from the neighborhood.

Soon thereafter, Advance Peace was launched in Fresno and hosted by the same organization that was hosting Fresno United, the Fresno Economic

Opportunities Commission (EOC). Rod has been the mainstay and anchor of the Advance Peace Fresno work since it started in 2020. He wasn't originally selected to lead the initiative, but was hired as one of the lead NCAs. After the attrition of two program managers and a few of the originally hired NCAs, Rod stepped into a leadership role, right where we might have expected him to land given his history. After some of the original funding from the city for the Advance Peace Fresno program was cut, the CEO of the EOC asked Rod to attend the new mayor's state of the city address and council hearing. He recalls not wanting to go. He was a street dude. "I'm most effective in the streets. What is the point of going to that?" he recalls asking the CEO. She turned to Rod, and much like the revelations of his former teammates, gang members, and prison partners, told him, "You need to be there because they are all going to listen to you. You are credible."

SAM

Sam was one of the first NCAs hired in Richmond as part of the ONS. Like some of the other NCAs profiled here, he is a natural leader, charismatic,

5.4 Rod (second from left) and Advance Peace Fresno NCAs.

astutely intelligent, and intuitive as well as committed to his word. He is now the leader of the ONS—a position DeVone once held—and has demonstrated how to build on his outreach worker skill set to become a program leader and valued, high-ranking city employee. To go from street dude to civil servant isn't easy and likely not for everyone, but Sam proves that "there is life" beyond a street outreach worker. His trajectory reveals not just that it's possible but also that this work, this movement of urban gun violence elimination, needs more people like Sam in leadership positions (inside government) for this epidemic to really be squashed.

I was invited to a block party in Richmond, where I was asked to talk to the young people about staying away from violence and not going to prison, like me. DeVone was there and was introduced to me afterward. I listen to the brotha and had heard of this shit from the Richmond Project in San Quentin and others. I was like, "Oh, you part of the city? Can you put a word in for me to get a construction job?" I had a heavy equipment operator background, but after ten years in prison, couldn't find anyone who would hire me. He seemed a little surprised I wasn't that interested in working with him, but he said he'd look into it.

DeVone did eventually get back to Sam. It wasn't what Sam wanted to hear. We couldn't get him a job with the city doing construction, but we could offer him employment. We offered him a job as a peacekeeper, going to juvenile hall and talking to young people as part of the newly created ONS.

5.5 Sam (left) and DeVone (right).

I did the peacekeeper job for like fourteen or sixteen months. I was really just waiting and hoping for some construction work to pick up. I came home from prison in December 2007. By 2009, ONS was offering me something more full time. I took it. I was doing outreach in every neighborhood. I had connections from prison in north, central, and south Richmond. I'd work whatever network I had and with other NCAs to reach the guys who were shooting.

Sam was instrumental in helping DeVone shape the ONS program from the beginning. When there was an opportunity for the ONS to recruit young people into summer jobs offered by the Richmond Police Athletic League (RPAL), he went out and found young people to enroll. He also quickly realized they weren't job ready and needed to be "coached" every step of the way, almost every day, to get to a point where they were. This daily coaching and job readiness became permanent features of the ONS.

Sam also used his history as a drug dealer and his networks in prison to connect with every neighborhood in Richmond. Even when the gun violence was most intense in the North, and DeVone had selected NCAs with connections and credibility in certain neighborhoods, Sam's mentality was that a street outreach worker needed to be credible everywhere.

We couldn't be limited just to some old affiliations or neighborhoods. Richmond was too small for that, and we just weren't a big enough team. I wanted to know every Fellow and be able to go to they hood and talk to their people. Being effective in this work means you need to be able to talk to anyone and everyone, from those in the streets to those runnin' systems.

COMMUNITY PEACEMAKING AND VIOLENCE INTERRUPTION

The work of an NCA is not easy. They are available 24/7, mentoring folks facing several challenges, responding to shootings, and mediating conflicts in the streets, often where guns are present. NCAs and street outreach workers who interrupt conflicts and put their lives in the middle of harm's way to help others are also managing their own life traumas, as you heard from some of the Advance Peace NCAs. There is a growing need in the field of CVI to recognize the on-the-job stressors outreach workers deal with, and ensure they get the ongoing supports, counseling, group love, and opportunities for self-care that can make or break whether this job is sustainable.[20]

Here is just one encounter described by an NCA:

Was meeting a Fellow NCA at the park yesterday, when one of my patnas walked past me with a revolver in his hand. Not knowing what was goin' on, I ran up from behind and grabbed him and the gun. I took him in a different direction. Got him back to his car and gave his wife the gun. Told them to leave. I'm walkin' back to the scene to see who he was into it with, and it's one of my Fellows! As I'm getting his side of the story, the dude returns with the gun again. I confront him and wrestle the gun from him a second time. Put it in my trunk this time. I then got them two to try and understand the magnitude of these decisions. They was once friends, and I know 'em both. Nobody wants either one dead. Spent another few hours with 'em and another NCA, talkin' it out. We ended it cool, with a group hug. Each NCA followed one of them home, stayed on them all night making sure nothing else went sideways.

The NCAs are regularly responding to and interrupting conflicts in neighborhoods as well as responding to shootings, at all hours of the day and night. Despite putting themselves in the middle of harm's way, here's what one NCA told us:

My biggest fear, though, ain't getting shot. My biggest fear is somebody shootin' at me, hurting me, and I can't control the reaction. The repercussions of what happened. If I can't say, "Leave that shit alone," there will be an all-out war up in here.

Between July 2021 and June 2023 (a twenty-four-month Peacemaker Fellowship cohort), across ten Advance Peace cities (Antioch, Fresno, Pomona, Stockton, Richmond, and Vallejo in California, and further afield, Fort Worth, Lansing, Orlando, and Rochester), we found that our NCAs delivered 1,364 community conflict mediations for 3,976.5 hours. This means that hundreds of conflicts were de-escalated in two years that could have contributed to more violence in each city, increasing public safety for everyone. These conflict mediations included the following:

- *572 general conflict mediations for 1,537 hours.* This is when an NCA mediates a community dispute, physical altercation, or argument, such as domestic violence. These rarely involve Fellows, but are likely to impact their safety and that of the entire community, and lead to more violent or even deadly conflicts if not addressed.
- *225 after-hours conflict mediations for 660.5 hours.* This is when an NCA performs a "general conflict mediation" outside normal business hours, generally from 8 p.m.–8 a.m. This is a 24/7 job, and many community conflicts with and without guns arise in the middle of the

night, after a day of drinking on the corner or at the club. Advance Peace NCAs are on call and respond.

- *205 shooting responses for 540 hours.* This is when an NCA goes to the scene of a shooting to understand who was involved and reduce the likelihood of any retaliation.
- *251 CRGVI for 957 hours.* As a reminder, a CRGVI [cyclical and retaliatory gun violence interruption] is when an NCA interrupts a situation where guns are present and likely to be used. These conflicts do not always involve Fellows but instead are likely to influence gun activity among rival groups, including our Fellows. These are the disputes that tend to perpetuate the most lethal firearm activity in a community and act like a contagion, spreading with unknown origin or rationale.
- *104 social media conflict mediations for 265 hours.* This is when an NCA addresses a dispute on social media that is likely to spill over into a face-to-face dispute and possibly gun violence. Social media has become "weaponized," especially in our communities.[21] Posting a live video of a shooting or a music video claiming you want a rival crew killed is seen by some of the youngsters that Advance Peace engages as a way to make a name for themselves in the streets and beyond.

Some of the social media disputes are linked to "drill rap" music videos and lyrics.[22] More of it is related to young people posting live videos of themselves brandishing a firearm, boasting about a killing, or taunting, threatening, or insulting a group of people or gang they've never met because of something they posted on Instagram or Facebook. This has become known as "internet banging" or "cyberbanging."[23] These online disputes are known to spill out into the streets as physical violence.[24] At the same time, an increasing body of research suggests that mediating online disputes can reduce the incidence of urban gun violence.[25]

WHEN HELPING HURTS OUTREACH WORKERS

Recent research has found that violence interrupters are ten times as likely as the police to be shot or shot at; 12% had been shot at while working, more than 60% witnessed a shooting attempt while on the job, and over 30% witnessed a successful shooting.[26] Community violence interrupters are 80% more likely than law enforcement or EMTs to be the first responders to the scene of a shooting.

One of our NCAs shared how being the first responder impacted him:

I pulled up on a shooting with another NCA. The victim wasn't hit too bad, but was visibly upset. He wasn't a Fellow. He got on the phone to request his weapon be brought to him. Seemed like a minute, and his friends pulled up with a pistol and an extra magazine. They were very upset with us and threatening us since we were telling them to stand down and physically blocking them from moving. They brought the guy with the wound to the hospital, and the other NCA I was with followed. We knew that could be a site of retaliation.

No more than fifteen minutes later, I get a call that one of my Fellows had been shot. I got in the car and rushed toward the scene. As I'm rounding the block, I just had a feeling it was someone from that first victim's crew. I jumped out of the car, seeing my Fellow on the street. He had been shot in the head. I'm trying to stop him from bleeding out.

The police arrived about the same time as me. I'm screaming at the officers to call for an ambulance. I was telling them, "Hey, call it in. He's still breathing." The officers just ignored me. They had their backs to me and were focused on controlling the scene. I yell at them again, "Call a fucking ambulance! This is my client and he needs to be saved!"

My Fellow stopped breathing, right there in my arms. I lost it. All I remember after that was getting up and kicking the police car. Next thing two officers wrestled me to the ground. I was crying uncontrollably. Man, if we had just held all of them dudes at the first scene. If I had just gotten there a few minutes earlier. I know we can't be there all the time, but time is everything. Just wish I had gotten these guys to slow down.

The on-the-job traumas many of our NCAs experience also can retraumatize them by bringing up their past experiences with violence and death.[27] Complicating the well-being of the NCA is that after one of their Fellows experiences a traumatic event, the NCA tends to get even closer to them, their family, and their social networks. This can expose the NCA to even greater secondary traumatic stress—which is the stress resulting from helping or wanting to help a traumatized or suffering person.[28] This type of stress can be toxic for outreach workers, contributing to sleep issues, anger, poor decision-making, and PTSD. Thus self-care, stress, and trauma support along with regular outlets for healing are essential to the well-being of NCAs as well as the efficacy of the Advance Peace strategy.

MEETING MENTORS' MENTAL HEALTH AND OTHER NEEDS

In some Advance Peace cities, the NCA teams have an in-house psychologist who attends daily team briefings. It is important for this professional

to really understand the experiences of the NCAs and Fellows, be culturally competent, and build trust with the team and Fellows through their
regular presence. It is also critical that the psychologist looks and sounds
like, and can relate on a deep, often unspoken level, to the staff and Fellows. For example, the psychologist who works with the Advance Peace
Fresno team, Dr. Tucker, was born in Detroit, but never knew his biological mother. His father was a drug dealer and killer who eventually went
to prison. As a Black teen, Tucker bounced around the foster care system
until landing with a loving family that helped him gain a college scholarship. He went into law enforcement to help kids like him, but soon
realized the criminal justice system wasn't interested in making positive
change for African Americans. Tucker went back to school, did his clinical residency in Valley State Prison, and then went into private practice.

Tucker's daily presence not only helps NCAs deal with traumatic on-
the-job experiences but allows him to know the staff and Fellows more
fully too. By doing this, he can identify things that the NCAs might not,
and from there, recommend strategies and tools for addressing trauma
that can be used in both group and individual settings.

Having a Black in-house psychologist, especially with Tucker's upbring-
ing, also helps break down the stigma for staff and Fellows that talking to a
counselor is a negative thing or not needed. As one NCA described Tucker's
monumental influence on them: "Him being with us every day, we don't
need to explain everything each time, with us or Fellows. He raising our
game. He asks us every day, 'What do you live for? What is your greatest
desire for life?' He helps us speak life into ourselves and the work."

Moreover, having a culturally competent psychologist sit with the NCA
team every day in its regular debriefings has helped give NCAs the confidence to share their wisdom with colleagues in a productive way about
how best to support themselves or a Fellow. As we heard from one NCA,

Before he [Tucker] started sitting with us, our debriefs weren't that productive.
We'd just share what we did, who we talked to, which neighborhoods. He asked
us questions and created a space for us to really understand how we engaged in
each situation. Turned it back to us and the team to identify ways we could
do and be better for our Fellows. We also had more structure to the meetings.
No interruptions, agendas, someone taking notes, decision-making rules, all of
that. Now when I go to county meetings, I see how disorganized they are and
that's just wasting everyone's time.

Trauma-informed strategies, healing supports along with professional skills, have been some of the overlapping benefits of in-house psychologists for Advance Peace staff.

PROFESSIONAL DEVELOPMENT OPPORTUNITIES

Advance Peace recognizes the challenges outreach workers face, from adequate pay, familial stress, and on-the-job stressors. The interpersonal, one-on-one counseling and skill building from a Tucker is essential for our NCAs. So too is investing in staff training and building a community of support—a family of practitioners as we call it. As one of the few national CVI organizations working in multiple cities, we are better able to develop a community of practice that supports staff members' personal health and professional growth, and communicates that these mentors are valuable assets, worthy of investment.

Advance Peace explicitly supports the personal and professional development of its family of formerly incarcerated outreach workers, and is unique in its extensive investment in and focus on staff training and development. Most NCAs have little, if any, experience in formal workplaces. We have developed professional development trainings for NCAs that are intentionally learner centered and performance based. The aim is to deliver an elite standard of care to communities by constantly investing in the skills, knowledge, and professionalization of Advance Peace NCAs. We build up and empower these local leaders to not just serve the AP Fellows but be change agents in their own lives, families, and communities as well.

Leadership also means allowing NCAs to design their own professional development gatherings, which Advance Peace supports two times a year. In these meetings, NCAs often share specific challenges from their cities with colleagues from other cities and collectively problem solve. They plan group excursions, share meals, and exercise and have fun together. All of this is intentional, as Advance Peace is committed to and invests in building Fellowship among outreach workers. This is something we know is essential for self-care, collective healing, and forging a new network of like-minded professionals.

The community of practice is about building leadership too. The program managers in each city along with their field coordinator counterparts have separate biweekly calls to share challenges and strategies. They get mentorship from peers and those who may have grappled with a similar experience in their city. The national Advance Peace program staff members participate as well to offer reflections, insights, and strategies from across all the sites. On a larger scale, Advance Peace brings together all staff and many Fellows for an annual forum or "family reunion." The event developed with NCAs' input creates space to collectively reflect, honor our accomplishments, discuss challenges ahead, and partake in group self-care.

The NCAs should be considered street clinicians, credible messengers, gun violence whisperers, and perhaps other titles as they chase, court, counsel, and cater to Fellows every day, while risking their lives. Who and what our NCAs are is best captured by Marc, the NCA turned program manager we heard from before:

You have to understand that your job, one of them, is to change the mentality that leads to destructive behavior and community harm and trauma. You have to challenge the toxic street code. You have to promote positive social activity and encourage those social norms. You can be a beast in those streets, but if you aren't doing these things at a high level for yourself, you'll never be as effective as you possibly can be.

Most Fellows we dealing with aren't psychopaths. They ain't running around killing everyone for no reason at all. We are all traumatized out here, but not totally out there. You feel me? We tryin' to get to him before anything go down. We keep gettin' at him. Call him every day. He still ain't ready, but I'm not giving up. They know we coming for him. The mentality and message is: if I can change from being that person, I'm living proof, so you, little homie, can do it too. Then we got action. I believe in you.

I've got to keep on being the best man that I can possibly be, positive, so that dudes will see what you do and who you are and say, "I want to do what you do. How do I become that?"

6

THE FELLOWS IN THE PEACEMAKER FELLOWSHIP

In these bloody days and frightful nights when an urban warrior can find no face more despicable than his own, no ammunition more deadly than self-hate and no target more deserving of his true aim than his brother, we must wonder how we came so late and lonely to this place.

—Maya Angelou

Sitting in a life skills class, a facilitator, Rasheed, is smiling at the participating Peacemaker Fellows like he is looking in the mirror. He listens attentively to each Fellows' "highs" and "lows" during the class opening. One Fellow, Twan (not his real name), describes a low he recently experienced.

"Man, I was at anger management class and I disagree with dude. It got to me. I was a little fired up about it. Counselor then tells me to leave. Why I ask? ''Cause you angry,' he say! Mutha fucker kicked me out for bein' angry during a fuckin' anger management session!"

Rasheed calmly, with his baritone voice, asks, "So how did you deal with that?" The Fellow looks up at Rasheed, seemingly surprised that a grown man would ask him how he was dealing with a low, rather than telling him to "deal" or "suck it up."

The Fellow struggles for words. He stutters a bit. His voice lowers.

"I mean, I left and all I could think about was people telling me, 'You just like your daddy.' He locked up for beatin' a man. I don't want to be that guy."

Rasheed listened attentively. After the Fellow was done and then a brief pause, he didn't offer any advice or judgment but instead described his own similar experience of how he felt after his parent's separation. How he sought out his father's recognition after he had moved on and largely forgotten about his kids. Rasheed explained how he felt like the divorce was his fault, and that maybe if he was more like his now locked-up father, he would pay more attention to him. Rasheed then noted his connection with the ONS in Richmond, specifically mentors like Kevin and Sam, and how they listened and never gave up on him, even when he was actively trying to be like his dad. He spoke smoothly about what it was like for him:

I didn't want to allow nobody to get over on me. I felt like avoiding an "L," a fumble [in] your life, meant not letting someone get a pass on something. I couldn't take an L. Didn't matter if it meant being dead or in jail as a result. What I really needed was to be allowed to unbutton my top. Get a chance to release.

Twan was listening to Rasheed's every word. This life skills class seemed like the type of group healing session he could relate to and be accepted in. Rasheed continued to engage Twan and the other Fellows.

"We here and we just freestyle. I'm not about judging you or no conditions. Get open on any topic. Relationships. Fatherhood. Finances. Credit and everything. That is why asking you to share a 'highs' and 'low.' We all here to let you know you ain't alone."

Rasheed was once a self-described street terrorist. His crew protected neighborhood turf with anger and no mercy. He was also part of the first cohort of Peacemaker Fellows through Richmond's ONS back in 2010. Thirteen years later, he is in a healthy marriage, raising his children, steadily employed, and facilitating life skills classes with a new generation of Peacemaker Fellows. He is an adviser to outreach workers and an inspiration to Advance Peace Fellows in every city. Rasheed regularly attends Advance Peace events and shares his story along with the "how did he get here" journey. That journey included working with NCAs to identify the sources of his anger, learning how destructive it was to him and the people he loved, and finding allies in his own healing journey through the Peacemaker Fellowship.

Rasheed told us that even after he completed the Peacemaker Fellowship, he knew his journey wasn't done. The pull of the streets and calls for revenge by his crew were still there. He maintained a relationship with his NCA mentors. Every time that call or temptation came, Rasheed remembers asking himself, "What would Sam think? How could I talk to Kev? I don't want to miss a minute of my kids' lives."

At the heart of the Fellowship mission is Rasheed's transformation from angry and thinking "I don't give a f*ck" to "I do care, I want to live, and I want to be the man I know I can be." Most Fellows arrive at Advance Peace with similar experiences as Twan and Rasheed, having been let down by family, friends, and almost every adult and service provider who was supposed to help them. They frequently lack trust in anyone while also grappling with anger, shame, rejection, and a host of other unrecognized emotions. They don't want or trust the Advance Peace mentors or NCAs when they come around. They expect to be let down and rejected again, often because they are confident they are going to "slip up" in the eyes of those committed to helping them. Even those from Advance Peace.

There have been hundreds of other Peacemaker Fellows. Most, thankfully like Rasheed, are alive, not involved in using guns or incarcerated, and are raising children, working, and supporting their communities. Since Richmond launched its first cohort of Peacemaker Fellows in 2010, it has mentored 222 Fellows. Advance Peace has mentored 824 Peacemaker Fellows in eleven other cities since 2018. That's 1,046 Fellows—all of whom were active firearm offenders.

As of June 2024, 95% of the Fellows (thankfully) are still alive, 91% have no new gunshot-related injuries, and 82% have not been incarcerated on a new firearm-related charge. These numbers reflect the power of the Fellows themselves as well as the potential of the Peacemaker Fellowship.

WHO ARE THE ADVANCE PEACE FELLOWS?

To be an Advance Peace Fellow means you are actively using firearms to solve street conflict. You are not an at-risk person, gang affiliated, or even chronically breaking the law. We focus on shooters, those likely to be the next firearm victim, and the rivals of each likely shooter. This makes the work of identifying and transforming Fellows into peacekeepers that much more challenging.

"We shoot because then we matter," remarked a Fellow named KT. He went on to say, "Funniest thing in world to be praised. Doing this sober.

Sad about me. I hadn't lost my virginity, but I had already pulled a trigger. I loved the game. The game was put out there for us. That's all there was. At least it seemed. Be a shooter. Get a name. Get the choochie. You ain't gettin' that pushing the positive shit."

For community youths seeking attention through the violence that they have seen be rewarded around them, the justice system serves as little deterrent. The sad reality is that in Black and Brown urban communities where gun violence is common, perpetrators have a seven in ten chance of escaping prosecution for these crimes. For example, Live Free Chicago reported that clearance rates in that city in 2021 for gun homicides in majority Black communities was 21.7% while it was more than double, 45.6%, for gun homicides in predominantly white neighborhoods.[1] So most shooters get away with it and remain in the communities where they committed their crimes, perhaps even becoming more emboldened to handle conflicts with a firearm.

What we have also learned over decades of working with Fellows is that most do not want to continue with their violent, street lifestyle. They are frequently looking for a way out, but the "code of the street," peer pressures, and no legitimate alternatives are coming their way. When we looked across eleven Advance Peace cities (Antioch, Fresno, Pomona, Stockton, Richmond, Vallejo, and Woodland in California, along with Lansing, Fort Worth, Orlando, and Rochester in other states) and 596 active Fellows in 2024—71% of those Fellows said they wanted to change their lifestyle on the day they enrolled. This might be a self-selected sample since those who do agree to enroll in the Peacemaker Fellowship are likely to be more open-minded than shooters who flat out reject the program. Yet that seven out of ten want a different life runs counter to the dominant narrative that says, "These thugs want to be killers." Meanwhile, the same survey revealed that only about 16% of Fellows at enrollment are receiving any social or supportive services. Most want out; most aren't getting any support to leave the game.

So while Fellows have been rewarded, at least in their eyes, for shooting and using guns, a lack of connection means they live largely in the shadows, avoiding almost every potential service, institution, or supporter that comes their way. They aren't coming to a "midnight basketball game" or showing up at a community center. They know that today they are a "hunter" and tomorrow the hunted. For various reasons, they have avoided the reach of more than law enforcement and remain on the streets.

This includes not engaging with Advance Peace NCAs. James, an NCA from Richmond, reminded us,

These youngsters are acting out with guns; it's really just a cry for help. . . . Most have been abused, neglected, let down, and abandoned in some ways their whole lives. But as a young man in our neighborhood, you can't go to someone and say, "I'm hurting." It's shamed or seen as weak. We have to be genuine. They can see if it's fake. And invest in them when nobody has done that before. Let them know their worth, just for who they are, not anything they do or don't do.

BUILDING ON FELLOWS' ASSETS

Traumas that young people have experienced adversely impact their cognitive development, impulse response, and executive function, and contribute to related behavioral and physical health impairments. Yet too often CVI programs either do not describe or do not know the past experiences of participants. They might, for instance, treat everyone as if they are unemployed or need job training, or think that they all need similar mental health counseling. A look at the published evaluations of CVI and similar deterrence programs such as Baltimore's Safe Streets, Chicago's Create Real Economic Destiny as well as Communities Partnering 4 Peace, Los Angeles's Gang Reduction and Youth Development (GRYD), Boston's Roca, Inc., Rapid Employment and Development Initiative in Chicago, Pittsburgh's One Life, Washington, DC's Cure the Streets, Philadelphia CeaseFire, and Oakland's Unite revealed that most described participant's prior criminal justice system experiences, and if they were gang affiliated, had been shot, or had witnessed gun violence. A few captured their educational status, prior trauma, substance use, and if they were a parent. Almost all collected information on participants' age, gender, and race/ethnicity.

What was concerning is that little data from these programs revealed participant's strengths or assets. For Advance Peace this is critical, not because we want to romanticize our Fellows. It is critical because our model of change says that each Fellow

a. is not the sum of their worst acts
b. is a victim in potentially unique ways

c. has often untapped/ignored strengths and potential

d. is a potential leader of broader change

These are data-driven and evidence-based statements, not assumptions. At intake, our NCAs have a conversation with each Fellow about themselves, where they have been, what has happened to them, and where they might want to go in their life. This forms the foundation of our unique LifeMAP—the road map for supports and services that the NCA along with the program will offer the Fellow while in the Peacemaker Fellowship. These data include a survey and qualitative, interview-style responses.

That intensive approach was how the program learned that over 70% of our Fellows are open to change. It is also the source of the following revelations about our Fellows:

59% are critical thinkers

65% are charismatic leaders

63% have a strong work ethic

25% have artistic (i.e., music, arts, etc.) talents

32% have marketable job skills

These data help us see the humanity of those at the center of gun violence too. As this Fellow reflects on his new life, "The hustle I bring to the streets is the same focus I need to get an education and a steady job. I just never had nobody show me how to go in that direction. The discipline I got writing my rhyme's and getting to the studio. It's what motivates me."

THE NUANCES OF FELLOWS' ADVERSE EXPERIENCES

To change their lives, Fellows must tap into their assets while confronting the traumas and challenges they face. Fellowship intake responses suggest a suite of traumas in the home and their communities; 51% of the Fellows enter the Fellowship having been shot at, and over 43% have had a family member killed by a gun. More than 80% reported living in a community where hearing gunshots was a frequent occurrence, and almost 75% come from homes where drug or alcohol abuse was common. More than half had a prior arrest and incarceration. Fewer than 20% were employed, a fifth were still in school, and over 40% experienced homelessness and food insecurity. We also learned that only about 18% had a caring and trusted adult in their lives.

WHAT FUTURE HEALTH MARKERS REVEAL

When Jason and his University of California at Berkeley team matched ten program intake questions to the ten ACEs questionnaire, the findings revealed why many clients had much to overcome.[2] The ACEs questions were developed by researchers at Kaiser Permanente health care system to study whether abuse and household dysfunction during childhood influenced the likelihood of adult disease, quality of life, and mortality.[3] Numerous studies have now documented that while many people have experienced one or two ACEs, the more ACEs a child is exposed to, the greater likelihood of physical and mental health issues, learning disabilities, and substance abuse later in life.[4]

Four or more ACEs have been documented as a key threshold for significant adverse impacts on future physical and mental health. One study found that those reporting four or more ACEs had increased later-in-life traumas and incidents of violent behavior.[5] Others have found strong associations between ACEs and criminal behaviors, including physical violence and homicide.[6] Some researchers have documented how "hurt people hurt people," demonstrating that urban youths with a greater number of ACEs were more likely to both engage in violence and be victims of it as teens as well as young adults.[7] Developmental studies have underscored that trauma caused by ACEs can create stress-induced neurological changes (e.g., emotional and behavioral dysregulation) that increase the chance of further victimization or aggressive responses to perceived threats.[8]

What we learned is that 57% of our Fellows have four or more ACEs, the threshold of concern for ongoing trauma and future violence. Across all cities, about 30% of the Fellows had seven or more ACEs. Yet the number of ACEs varies by city. In Rochester, the Advance Peace Fellows had a mean of seven, but in Richmond, Vallejo, and Fort Worth, the Fellows had an average of four ACEs.

These data also suggest that not every city or cohort of Fellows should be approached in the same way. We found that in each Advance Peace city, the most prevalent ACE was rarely the same. While physical assault was the most frequent ACE in seven of eleven Advance Peace cities, the Fellows in some cities were more frequently grappling with the trauma of witnessing a homicide, experiencing food insecurity, or dealing with a depressed household member. Advance Peace uses these data to design targeted and specific supports within the LifeMAP, and throughout the Peacemaker Fellowship, address these different experiences with trauma. There is no one-size-fits-all approach for the Peacemaker Fellowship.

The story of a Fellow from Advance Peace in Fresno describes how he coped with ongoing trauma and what led him to agree to enroll in the Peacemaker Fellowship:

Me. I gangbanged. That's what I did. I woke up every morning and I banged. I didn't go home unless I had a body or a couple shootings on my belt. I was out here thugin'. I started when I was fifteen. My homie was killed. He was fourteen, and I was fifteen. That turned me up. Then I couldn't be seen. I could be walking through the mall or something. They be like, hey n*ga, whoop de whoop. Then it's on. I ain't no punk. So you got to move smart. That's how it is out here. I thought I was just trying to look out for my people.

At fifteen, I was sleeping on the slide at the park I used to play at. My sister committed suicide. Other family members killed. No food, no place to sleep. I felt like it was my fault, that I was supposed to do something about it. I was willing to do anything to change that. I mean anything. Always had a gun. I was out here wildin'.

I went to jail when I just turned eighteen. I was angry. I went to the hole. I needed someone to talk to. I talked to the psychologist. Someone who didn't know me. I never had a childhood. I made the best of it. My brother raised me until he was killed. Nobody talked to me, but that psychologist talked to me.

When I got out, I needed someone to talk to. My NCA became that therapist I needed. We discussed that every situation don't need a reaction. He told me, "You don't have to go big on every situation." You feel me? There was no other program that ever did that. Then they come at you, "Hey, you need this . . . do that," type shit. You feel me? It's the first time in my life that I feel like I'm around people like me. Game knows game.

GUN VIOLENCE EXPOSURES

Importantly, the ACEs do not include any specific questions about gun violence exposures.[9] In Advance Peace, we define gun violence exposure as one of the following: a gunshot injury, being shot at, a prior gun charge arrest, or having a family member killed by a gun. Exposure to gun violence has been associated with serious mental illness in young people including anxiety, post-traumatic stress, and depression.[10] Young people exposed to gun violence are likely to experience PTSD and carry unaddressed trauma, and when they do not receive any support for this trauma, are more likely to engage in gun violence themselves.[11] Young people who are exposed to gun violence or hear secondhand reports about violence are more likely to obtain guns for self-defense.[12] Hearing and witnessing community gun violence has been shown to contribute to youth and adolescent declines in cognitive functioning along with lower levels of attention and impulse control, and can have long-term impacts on aggression, anxiety, depression, and antisocial behavior.[13]

Among the Advance Peace Fellows, 60% had experienced two or more gun violence exposures, and almost half of the Fellows had both four or more ACEs and two or more gun violence exposures.

We also discovered a relationship between the number of ACEs and the number of gun violence exposures. Fellows with seven or more ACEs were eight times more likely to have three or four gun violence exposures than Fellows with one to three ACEs. Almost all (90%) Fellows with nine ACEs had three or four gun violence exposures. These data aren't just statistics, nor do they define our Fellows; they do, though, help inform the types of supports each Fellow receives in the Peacemaker Fellowship.

THE PEACEMAKER FELLOWSHIP

Each Fellow is offered the Peacemaker Fellowship for eighteen to twenty-four months. The Fellowship is the start of a journey toward individual and collective healing. The programming is rooted in the notion that steady, consistent, healthy, loving adult relationships can help an individual and groups heal from unaddressed traumas along with all of their adverse consequences on behavioral, mental, and physical health.[14] The work is also grounded in knowing that positive experiences as well as supportive relationships have been shown to help overcome the influences of ACEs and traumatic experiences, like witnessing and engaging in gun violence.[15] We recognize just focusing on individuals isn't going to be enough, and that we don't want to just help heal a Fellow to then send them back into the neighborhoods that are contributing to their anxiety, stress, and fear in the first place. That is why chapter 9 delves into how healing relationships with some of the most influential people (active firearm offenders in this case) helps heal entire communities.

The timing of each Fellows' journey is frequently driven by funding constraints and the amount of time the outreach team has had in recruiting Fellows. If the Advance Peace NCAs in a city have had fewer than six months of street outreach to identify potential Fellows and build trusting relationships, they generally need twenty-four months for the Peacemaker Fellowship. Moreover, the timing of the Fellowship can be driven by the intensity of the traumas experienced by our Fellows. The greater the ACEs and gun violence exposures, the longer the time we need to support the healing of our Fellows. This includes engaging with a Fellow who has completed a cohort, if the NCA team determines they still need support and healing. Once a Fellow, always a Fellow.

One Fellow, AW, described his experience in the Peacemaker Fellowship, including the LifeMAP:

I didn't have any vision of what I wanted to do in five years or where I wanted to be. But I set some goals and was making progress on my LifeMAP. My NCA says, "I got some financial support for you" and explains that I needed to give him my Social Security number to get it. I didn't have that, so we went and applied to get the card. Then he says I should open a bank account, but I had no idea how to do that. Didn't know nobody who did that. He helped me set that up and get that paperwork. He explained it could help me build some credit, and I was like, Why the f* do I need credit? I only dealt with cash. Then he helped me see that everything I was paying for was in my mom's or girl's name, not in my name. He explained that building credit ain't just about getting money, but it's like building trust. Are they going to trust me? I mean, it was like months of financial literacy before I even got that first check. This was the first time I've been recognized for anything since like the third grade. Nobody seen anything that I've done as positive.

Another Fellow spoke of the Peacemaker Fellowship like having a positive father figure, stating,

If there was a shooting, I would go from zero to a hundred in a second. I just reacted. Didn't even think about what to do. Just did it. Now I got this mentor in my ear every day. He showing me things. Speaking life into me. Next shooting, I start thinkin', "What he [my NCA] gonna think if I go do this?" Nobody really cared before but now I'm indecisive. But my buddies are like, bruh, you leaving us out here. I got this fear now of making the right decision. Nobody but my NCA really understands that stress of trying to change my ways and do what's right. It's not like you just walk away cold turkey from all of this one day. They get that. They walked that line. They the ones who can help take us there.

THE "DOSAGE" OF SUPPORTS

Each Fellow gets engaged three times a day by their NCA mentor while in the Peacemaker Fellowship. That means in the morning, afternoon, and evening, their mentor is checking in with them, meeting with them, and/ or taking them somewhere. In this way, Advance Peace keeps a close eye on their Fellows, keeping them busy, off the streets, and working toward achieving LifeMAP actions and goals.

Fellows describe being courted, catered to, counseled, and chased. This is purposeful. We want to wrap our arms around folks who are experiencing unaddressed trauma since we know trusting, supportive, and loving relationship are a key antidote to the adverse impacts of these traumas. We also deliver specific services to each Fellow based on their identified traumas. Frequently, we can't deliver the needed supports, so our NCAs will take the Fellow to a service provider to help them "navigate" the bureaucracy, counselor, or an unfamiliar encounter.

The diagram below shows the total touchpoints that our Fellows received over a typical eighteen-month Fellowship from 2021 to 2022. In this city, there were 31 Fellows and 52,307 engagements, or 3.1 engagements per day per Fellow. The Fellows received more than a dozen type of services and referrals over the eighteen months, as defined in the following list, and figure 6.1:

- *Life coaching* is when an NCA delivers culturally responsive and competent support for a Fellow to help them identify their strengths, weaknesses, and traumas, and aid them in overcoming obstacles holding them back

- *Cognitive behavioral therapy* is when an NCA helps their Fellow to identify and change the destructive or disturbing thought patterns as well as traumas that have a negative influence on their behavior and emotions. It helps Fellows reflect on their own thinking, slow down in key moments of conflict, practice less harmful responses in dangerous situations, and begin to adapt their behavior to a new, nonviolent identity.

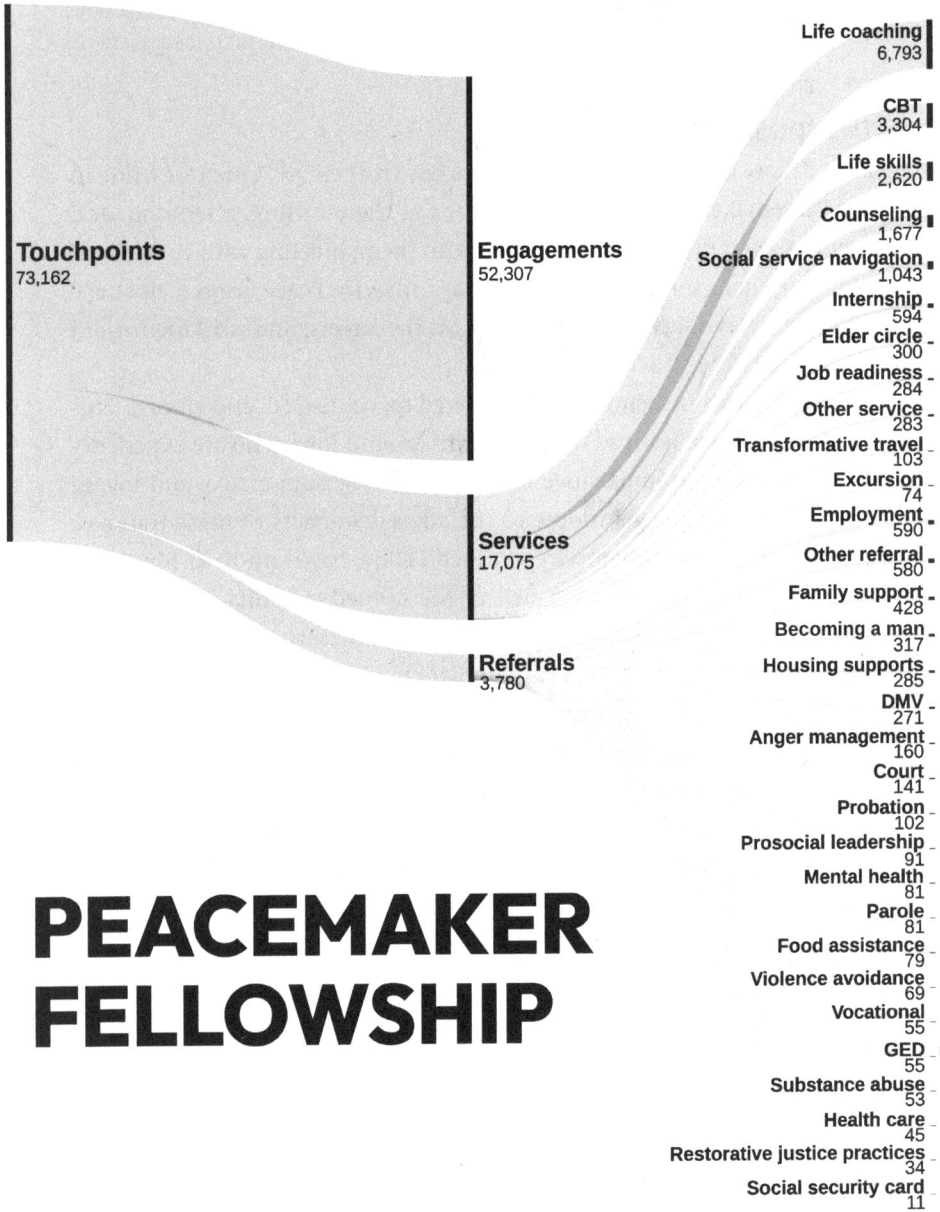

Touchpoints
73,162

Engagements
52,307

Services
17,075

Referrals
3,780

Life coaching
6,793

CBT
3,304

Life skills
2,620

Counseling
1,677

Social service navigation
1,043

Internship
594

Elder circle
300

Job readiness
284

Other service
283

Transformative travel
103

Excursion
74

Employment
590

Other referral
580

Family support
428

Becoming a man
317

Housing supports
285

DMV
271

Anger management
160

Court
141

Probation
102

Prosocial leadership
91

Mental health
81

Parole
81

Food assistance
79

Violence avoidance
69

Vocational
55

GED
55

Substance abuse
53

Health care
45

Restorative justice practices
34

Social security card
11

PEACEMAKER FELLOWSHIP

6.1   The types and numbers of services and referrals in the Peacemaker Fellowship.

- *Life skills classes* are groups of Fellows learning about important life-affirming skills, frequently facilitated by an NCA or third-party professional. Example discussions cover what it means to be "a man," group cognitive behavioral therapy, understanding the forces of structural racism, or how to be a good parent.
- *Culturally responsive counseling* is when an NCA who understands and is from a similar cultural, racial, and ethnic background of their "client" offers supports to address trauma, promote healing, and change unhealthy behaviors. This is done in a way that does not assume or essentialize a "culture," ensures NCAs approach clients with humility, and helps clients understand the ways institutions and social systems create as well as perpetuate trauma.
- *Social service navigation* is when an NCA supports their Fellow in navigating any social services, such as the Department of Motor Vehicles, housing assistance, the legal system, welfare benefits, and so on.
- *Internships* are opportunities for Fellows who are actively participating in the Fellowship for at least six months. These typically are part-time paid opportunities that prepare a Fellow for full-time work.
- *Elder circle* is a group of elder/senior community members that meet with Fellows to share wise counsel, their life experiences and ways they've avoided unhealthy traps so as to become successful in raising a family, running a business, and other endeavors. Elders can speak to the impact of trauma on their lives and how they turned that into positive growth, and model success for staff as well.
- *Job readiness* is when an NCA supports a Fellow in preparing them for employment (i.e., creating a résumé, applying for certification classes, getting an ID, etc.).
- *Excursions* are when an NCA takes a Fellow out of their neighborhood and daily routines. Usually these involve camping, hiking, amusement parks, museums, plays, musicals, movies, sporting events, and so on.
- *Transformative travel* is when groups of Fellows travel out of their city of origin, stay overnight, and take in cultural, educational, civic, and other horizon-building activities that exposes them to life-affirming opportunities. A well-orchestrated and curated activity of the transformative travel element involves rival groups of Fellows traveling out of state and/or into the country together. Transformative travel occurs after a

Fellow has been enrolled and actively participating in the Peacemaker Fellowship.

The Advance Peace Fellows range of supports, services, and opportunities is wide and deep. Their use is tailored for each Fellow's needs based on their past and their dreams for the future. Offerings are initially focused on healing from the often unaddressed traumas staff learn about, but the supports and services are as much about building toward a peaceful, rewarding, and joyful future. The story of one Peacemaker Fellow alumni, Eric, helps illustrate how the combination contributes to life-alternating transformations.

ONCE A FELLOW, ALWAYS A FELLOW

Eric was the first Peacemaker Fellow to be accepted into the prestigious White House internship program, but his gun-using past almost landed him in prison before he could get to Washington, DC. On a transformative travel experience with the ONS, Eric and the other Fellows visited their congressperson at the time, George Miller. In a chat with the Fellows, Miller suggested that if any of them applied for a summer internship, he would help them get to the White House. Eric remembers how excited he was. He recalled, "I went back to the hotel and started making a plan. I was dead set on going to college. I knew then that I wanted to study government, the law, and understanding how to make real change. I saw that internship was my ticket."

On returning to Richmond, Eric worked with his NCA mentors to apply for the White House internship. He organized the paperwork, got the recommendation letters, and filled out the applications for housing. With the daily help of his NCA mentors, he got the application out to meet the deadline. A few months later he received word that he was accepted. He was going to DC to be a legislative intern working on policies focused on preventing minors from getting sentenced as adults.

Sam [Vaughn] and the ONS program made it happen for me. It was perfect. It was like something I didn't even ever dream could happen, happened. I didn't even know the next steps, but the ONS helped me get the plane ticket and they agreed to fly out with me. They took me shopping for clothes and everything.

Just days before the flight and the start of his internship, Eric got arrested for a warrant on an old gun possession charge. His past wasn't far behind, even with the future looking bright. He remembered,

Here I am sitting in county jail, thinking like, "I ain't gonna f*ck up this opportunity." I kinda felt like I had thrown all that hard work, by me and everyone, out the window. It was like they knew I had something good coming and wanted to make sure I didn't succeed. That was kinda what we expect. Nothing good ain't really going to come our way. How crazy was it that I'm sitting in jail a few days before I'm supposed to go to DC to work on policy about preventing kids like me from going to jail!

It was the ONS and Eric's NCA mentors who stepped in to prevent him from falling through the cracks and missing his opportunity. Eric said the ONS always "saw my future, before I could, and they never let go. They had me. Got me a good lawyer who was able to convince a judge to hold a hearing on my case right away. Apparently, the lawyer told the judge about my internship, that our senator was expecting me in DC, and that I had all of these positive things going on."

Eric recalls being in that courtroom, looking around, and thinking these things just don't happen for young Black kids from the hood. There usually isn't a dedicated lawyer advocating on your behalf, getting the criminal justice system to see your humanity rather than just your priors.

That judge looked at me and said, "What the hell are you doing here? I'm going to let you out today, and I don't want to see you again or you'll serve the rest of your time." All I was feeling was just real love for my ONS brothers. I love those dudes for how they had me. Yeah, I was really feeling the weight of wanting to be successful. Almost getting there and almost having it snatched from me before I got a chance to get started. But I knew I got that opportunity because some real men chose to love me and not let go.

Eric made it to DC, and after the first few days of the internship he realized how different he was from the other interns. Of course, none of the others had ever been to jail or been shot—things Eric wasn't proud of, but he had experienced both of those things. He had first been shot at fourteen, spent time in juvenile detention, and was in and out of county lockup. His biggest revelation was watching how they moved even without any experience in the subject matter. He remembers, "Here I was trying to explain what life was like for a kid from the hood trying to avoid crime and violence and jail. Most of the other interns were focused instead on schmoozing, meeting other interns and other powerful people. They joked about shit I had never heard of."

He remembers one social hour where the group was talking about books they had read and places they had been—things that had never been offered or accessible to him. Eric took a breath and explained,

I was in a world I didn't know anything about. Yeah, none of the other interns were from the hood. They hadn't been through the shit I had. They didn't have to struggle out the ghetto to get there. But all of that didn't seem to matter in this space. What was getting rewarded wasn't what you knew but who you knew. I tried. I would go back to my room and read stuff every night. Trying to catch up with them. Sam was always calling me like almost every day, checking in. He would encourage me, and always reminded me why I was there and that I was *supposed* to be there. He told me, "They need people like you in those halls of power." Sam always looked out for me. Always treated me like an equal, not a kid or a Fellow.

Eric is now living in Florida, working and raising his four-year-old son as a single father. He finished the internship and returned to Richmond. He used his experience and the help from another NCA, Kevin, to apply to a Florida community college. He got in and soon transferred to Florida A&M University. Eric went to Florida to study with another friend from Richmond, also a Fellow, who wanted to get away and start a new life. It was hard being away from home, learning to be a student for the first time, and just "feeding yourself."

Once again, the NCAs from the ONS were calling him almost every day, sending him money to stay afloat and buying him a plane ticket when he got homesick. Eric's friend didn't make it through the academic year and returned to Richmond. Eric managed, but he told us that "it was as hard as any challenge he had faced in his life." With his NCA adult mentors at his side and having his back, Eric navigated a system that wasn't designed to give him the opportunities to be a successful, college-educated Black man.

He wrote a letter to the ONS and Richmond City Council, thanking them for the opportunity and what it meant to him, part of which appears below:

Dear City of Richmond,

When I first started with the ONS, I had no clue as of what it was they wanted me to do. I was done with high school and just wanted to make money. I was in the streets after I dropped out of the union because I wasn't going to pass the drug screening. On my way home one day, I was on the phone with a friend and he was talking to another friend of ours mother. She knew a guy who was starting up some type of program. I remember being recruited by the ONS from these meetings over lunch with DeVone and two of my other friends. We would have discussions about the city of Richmond and the violence. We never spoke about anyone's business or anything that was too personal; only about how the murder rate was too high.

Anyway, I joined the ONS as an intern and got serious about college from the conversations with DeVone, Diane, and Joe. They would just elaborate about their school experiences and how they made it, or didn't make it through. That inspired me to want to do more with my life and get a career started. Before I joined the ONS I had no vision to complete college, but then the ONS introduced me to the Omega family (Street Soldiers); it was then that I really started to take school more serious.

During this process I still had issues I needed to work out, like putting myself in dangerous environments, and the bad decisions I was still making. I got in trouble, and the ONS was there in my corner to say good words on my behalf to the judge, and has been here for me since I've been home. That let me know that they truly cared about my future and well-being. The neighborhood change agents have played a big role in my journey by giving me pep talks about their history, of the struggles they had to overcome as men and women. . . . Additionally, I've been on a few trips with the ONS and met some important people. I went to Los Angeles, San Diego, Texas, Sacramento, and Florida. On those trips I had such great times because I'm in a new environment exploring around new towns. We get to eat at some different restaurants I never heard of nor been to that serve great food. I always get to meet some interesting people who play important roles in that city like mayors, city managers, executive directors, company presidents, and more, which has been so inspirational.

The ONS means a whole lot to me because without the ONS, I probably would still be running the streets. They invested a lot into me by linking me to resources, helping get my life on track, and surrounding me with positive role models. They've shown me there's more to explore in the world than just the Bay Area. Everyone in the office has been supportive of me since day one, and I'm very appreciative to be a part of this program.

My dad hasn't been in my life since I was a kid, and my mother raised me until it was time for me to get out on my own. I had to live and learn a lot of things about being a man on my own, and pick up what I can from other men on my own. The ONS showed up as a healthy guide in my life and I now realize it. I'm grateful to have a good team behind me such as the Office of Neighborhood Safety. I just hope I am doing my part with my role in the department. That's why any meeting or any type of event that's going on, if I'm invited, I will show up.

Thanks and Happy Holidays!
Eric

Eric reflected on his journey and how instrumental the healing-centered work of the Peacemaker Fellowship has been for his transformation, stating,

I was angry. I had been shot. I lost friends. I was stuck in the hood, worrying about some damn killing, being self-destructive. ONS stepped in and opened me up to other opportunities. I'd likely be in jail or dead by now. It's 2023 and I'm alive. There is more to do. Still taking steps. Getting there. You need someone to walk with you and kick-start that journey. That's what it [the Peacemaker Fellowship] does. They walked with me, they held me, they caught me before I could fall too far, and you know, they still with me. As a father, I'm taking all of that love they showered on me and giving it to my kid now. I ain't gonna let them fall too far, and if they do, I'm right there to pick 'em up, hug him, and get 'em going again. That's family. That's what Advance Peace showed me.

7

TRAVEL AS HEALING THERAPY

You have brains in your head. You have feet in your shoes. You can steer yourself any direction you choose. You're on your own. And you know what you know. And YOU are the one who'll decide where to go.

—Dr. Seuss, *Oh, the Places You'll Go!*

BEING ALLOWED TO DREAM

Eric and Rasheed from Richmond were two of the first Peacemaker Fellows to be asked to join with their crosstown rivals to travel out of state. They first went to Dallas, Texas, to attend a conference and then to Washington, DC, and New York City. They shared afterward that traveling opened their minds, allowed them to see the humanity of their crosstown rival sitting next to them on the plane, and to dream. In part, traveling allows for new possibilities to surface by providing Fellows a break from being caught up in the daily routines, worries, and modes of survival that took place at home.

"I'm listening to a senator talk about an internship at the White House," Eric recalled, reflecting on his trip to the nation's capital. "I was absorbing every detail as he talked about making policy and legislation. Some light in me went off. I remember that night. I was hella tired and crashed hard. I had a dream where I had gone to college and was in DC working as a lawyer. I saw myself that way for the first time. Then I woke up, and I was still wearing the suit I had on the day before!"

Eric's dreams would be further awakened during a follow-up trip to Florida, where a group of Fellows visited Florida A&M University. He recalls seeing "so many beautiful, smart Black people, getting along."

I was all about going to college, and I wanted to attend Grambling. For sure, a HBCU [historically Black college or university]. That came to me as NCA Kev talked to me about HBCUs. Traveling there, to FAMU, was like seeing the most beautiful women; made my heart skip a beat, I felt something inside. It was love at first sight. We walked the campus, and I was in a dream state. My body was like floating. I looked at things, and they were in a new focus, like I had superpowers. I could see all the detail. I didn't hear anything but nature. All the yappin' of the fellas was just background to this music in my ears. Like for real. It felt like I could belong here, not just be there. It was like I was destined to be there.

Eric did arrive at Florida A&M University a little over a year and half later. His NCA mentors helped him get into a Tallahassee community college and then he eventually received a BA from the university. His dream came true, and it all started from an opportunity to travel from California to DC and Florida with the Peacemaker Fellowship.

Rasheed's dreams were also radically changed by traveling. Neither Eric nor Rasheed (who eventually became a staff mentor) had ever left California or been on a plane before they were recruited into the Peacemaker Fellowship. By the time Rasheed was offered the chance to travel to South Africa with the ONS, on the condition that he go with a crosstown rival, his first question was, "How many different planes we going to take?"

Rasheed remembers one day in Soweto township, outside Johannesburg, where the Peacemaker Fellows were planning to visit a youth group near Nelson Mandela's childhood home. The Fellows were already feeling "some kinda way" after visiting the Apartheid Museum. The van they were riding in was a little lost, but eventually pulled over to where there was a group of young people dancing and hanging out on the streets. It was a scene, Rasheed recalls, that might have looked similar in his hometown of Richmond. But this place was different. Rasheed explained,

I mean, I thought we was poor, until I saw the shantytowns. No running water. Shacks like that. We seen kids in those streets strapped up with serious firearms. No handguns. It was like a battlefield in their backyard.

I started feeling much safer in that van, sitting next to a dude I was supposed to want to kill back in Richmond. We started joking, but not really, that we weren't getting out of the van. We told our the NCAs, "Hell no, this place ain't safe. We stayin' in the van."

So Rasheed and the hometown rivals refused to get out of the van. They felt safer together than stepping out into the unknown. Sitting in the van, they started playing familiar music, joking about the clothing they saw people outside wearing, and talking about "having each others' backs" in a place so unfamiliar. For Rasheed, and likely other Fellows, his view of the deadly rivalries they were perpetuating back home seem to lose significance sitting together in that van. He recalled in some detail how that experience shaped him:

I'm thinking to myself, I'm fine with this dude being by my side out here in South Africa. We were all gonna protect one another 'cause we was from Richmond. But if I was back home, we'd be huntin' one another? Nah. I'm actually starting to like this guy. Why do I want to take him out?

That night, I remember this like it was yesterday, I had a dream. I hadn't ever dreamed in my life until that night. At least not that I could remember. Only thing I remember about my sleep was nightmares. Always the same nightmares; I was falling off a building and about to land. Boom! I'd wake up in a panic. Or I'd be in a shoot-out and the clip on the gun jammed. No bullets. I'm shot. Boom! I'd wake up in a panic. I only had nightmares. I didn't like sleeping for that reason. This night in Africa, I had a real dream. What I remember was that there was nature all around and it was calm. I wasn't about to die. In my dream I was a little kid again. Playing outside. I wasn't worried about nothin'. I didn't hear gunshots. I don't remember all the details, but I seemed happy. I slept so hard that I didn't wake up on time the next day. Africa, yeah, going to Africa helped me dream again.

TRANSFORMATIVE TRAVEL AS RESTORATIVE THERAPY

Travel can be transformative for anyone, but especially those trapped physically and socially in a world of cyclical violence and chaos. That is, Eric's and Rasheed's recollection of dreams may partly reflect that getting away from trauma-heavy spaces has been tied to sleeping better and other health benefits. Travel opportunities are an essential component of the plan for participants in the Peacemaker Fellowship for this and other health benefits, and beyond. Getting outside one's neighborhood offers an opportunity for Fellows to simply breathe without having to be hyperalert about who and what is coming at them. They can slow down, reflect, and yes, even sleep deeply. Travel has been found to improve sleep since being in a new bed can help people dissociate from negative sleep patterns at home.[1]

DeVone found out how transformative travel can be after inviting a mentee to join him at a conference on positive youth development being held at Bowie State, a historically Black university. Devonte, or "D," agreed to join him. A detailed itinerary was sketched out to attend the conference in Maryland and see sights around Philadelphia.

The flight to Philadelphia from the Bay Area was a red-eye flight. On the morning of the day of travel, D was excited and ready to go. Yet when the van arrived at D's apartment later that day to pick him up for the airport, he wasn't home. There was loud music coming from the apartment complex, and the corridor had used needles, baggies with the dust of crack cocaine, and the robust scent of Mary Jane. In his small apartment, which he shared with his aunt and at least a few others, there were about a dozen people including toddlers, the TV was turned up loud, and there was smoke everywhere. After nearly thirty minutes (and a $20 bill to the van driver), D finally arrived.

After the flight and arriving at the hotel, D got his own room. The conference was early the next morning. But at the scheduled meeting time the next morning in the lobby, D wasn't there. DeVone knocked on his door and found D still in his boxer shorts, shirtless and wearing a wave cap on his head. His clothes were spread across the bed in neat piles, separated into shirts, underwear, pants, and so on. Frustrated that D was running late again, he emphatically told D that there was a schedule and the need to not be late to the conference.

"I'd like to just stay in the room today," D told DeVone, who responded with, "But we got stuff to do. I've made several plans for us. The people at the university are expecting you and me!"

D explained that he lived in a crowded environment, with drug addicts and lots of street drama right outside his door. Noise all through the night. People trying to get into his room to take his things. He explained that he would have to lock his stuff, clothes, and everything in a locker that he had purchased for himself, and sometimes that wasn't enough to keep folks (even family) from stealing his things in his own apartment.

He also said that he rarely got a good night's sleep because he was always on guard. D asked if he could just stay in the hotel room all day because it was the first time in his life that he had a room to himself, where he could have peace and quiet for long periods of time, without worry of someone breaking in, interrupting, or trying to steal his stuff.

"I just need to relax and take this in—breathe, man, I don't want to go nowhere, and I don't want to do nothin', I just wanna chill. Would that be OK?" D asked.

It turned out D didn't need too much of a travel itinerary. He just needed the space to create a healthy plan for himself. The itinerary of conference speeches, cultural sites, and social engagements could wait. For D, the trip gave him the chance to be alone and find himself again (and charge hundreds of dollars in room service to DeVone's credit card). How much this all mattered became clear when D was being driven back to his apartment on returning to California; he put his head down and said, "Damn, back to this shit."

TRAVEL AS HEALING

Traveling—or leaving one's place—is a key contributor to brain health and transforming your life outlook. The approach might seem counterintuitive to one of our core arguments for how to end urban gun violence—namely, the importance of daily engagement, mentorship, and supportive services for those in the streets at the center of gun violence. Advancing urban peace requires community-based solutions that involves credible messengers working with gun offenders in their neighborhoods. Yet our approach to travel aims to create transformative experiences, while offering comfort and connection as well when Fellows leave their place called home.

Our approach to travel as healing focuses on getting our Fellows to experience a new culture or challenge in a safe way, and often rediscover their authentic, sometimes silly selves. These experiences are essential for healthy life transformation, but for too long have been denied to those trapped in segregated, violent, urban neighborhoods. Advance Peace intentionally curates what we call transformative travel opportunities for our Fellows to create the conditions for healthy neuroplasticity.[2] Remember that neuroplasticity is the brain's ability to rewire itself and even reverse the impacts of trauma through new, positive, and supportive

experiences. Brain research has demonstrated that an enriching environment, meaning sensory and intellectual stimulation, positively enhances
the number of neuron branches in our brains, and an impoverished environment stymies brain development and our capacity to learn.[3] In part,
research suggests that our brains can reset while also being stimulated in
new ways when we are away from familiar routines and places.[4]

The Advance Peace transformative travel touchpoint purposefully
curates the kinds of external stimulation, new experiences, and daily challenges that stimulate positive brain development.[5] The types of venues
visited in new locations include museums/cultural sites, the offices of local
politicians/decision-makers, and universities. Fellows and NCAs may also
visit entertainment venues, restaurants, and when available, professional
sporting events. For Advance Peace staff, this helps because it's hard to
help someone else dream about something that you don't even know
exists. So our NCAs travel too—to see, learn, experience, and work as
teams in new places, and later curate these exploratory experiences for
our Fellows. Staff work every day to "blow our Fellows minds" on life,
but sometimes it's the unacknowledged aspects of travel that provide the
greatest impacts. For example, on a trip to Disneyland, grown men were
walking around wearing Mickey Mouse ears and being "allowed" to be kids
for the first time in their lives.

Although such experiences are essential for healthy life transformation, for far too long, they have been denied to Black Americans. Black
travel restrictions were written into the US landscape through the law and
social codes. From Jim Crow segregation to lynchings, to segregated trains,
buses, and hotels, restrictions on Black Americans from traveling freely
have robbed them of a multitude of benefits, including being denied the
healing potential of leisure and rest, economic gains from work-related
travel, and social, educational, and other benefits of tourism.[6]

Travel restrictions were about white institutions and people viewing
the Black body as captive and regulated, much like gun violence today
restricts freedom of movement and self-realization for those caught up in
its cycle. Thus Advance Peace's explicit inclusion of transformative travel
as essential for ending urban gun violence should be viewed as part of
the continual struggle for redefining Blackness as well as civil and human
rights, and confronting structural racism through "mobility justice."[7]

TRAVELING (OR NOT) WHILE BLACK

Traveling as part of the Peacemaker Fellowship is about restoring human dignity, freedom of movement, and the right to explore and discover in public places. Unfortunately, denying these freedoms and human rights has been, and in some ways remains, a way to dehumanize and "other" Black folks in US society.[8] Advance Peace is committed to the ongoing Black struggle for the freedom to travel safely and of one's own volition.[9] Yet as Mia Bey reminds us in *Traveling Black*, "Once one of the most resented forms of segregation, travel segregation is now one of the most forgotten."[10]

Black human rights struggles—which we see ending urban gun violence as part of—have been and remain rooted in freedoms to move and travel. They include Frederick Douglass refusing to leave a whites' only train car in Lynn, Massachusetts, in 1841; in 1863, Charlotte Brown, an African American woman, who contributed to desegregating whites' only streetcars in San Francisco; Ida B. Wells refusing to move to a smoking car from a "white ladies" car while in Memphis on the Chesapeake and Ohio Railroad in 1884 (she was forcibly removed and later won a discrimination lawsuit in the lower courts, although it was overturned on appeal to the Tennessee Supreme Court); and in 1882, Homer Plessy sitting in a whites' only coach on the East Louisiana Railway, getting arrested, and having his lawsuit reach the US Supreme Court, resulting in the *Plessy v. Ferguson* ruling legalizing "separate but equal" Jim Crow discrimination.

The Great Migration of Black Southerners that began in the early 1900s saw millions move to emerging industrial cities to escape the fear of death from racist whites, and as expressions of hope, possibility, and future prosperity.[11] Jim Crow America, however, made Black movement highly controlled and sanctioned. Along the nation's highways, Black travelers were routinely denied access to essential services like gas, food, restrooms, and lodging. Stopping in an unfamiliar place carried the risk of humiliation, threats, or worse. Sundown towns were all-white communities and counties where Blacks could work, but not reside after sunset."[12] In 1936, the violent enforcement of sundown town rules inspired Victor Hugo Green to write *The Negro Motorist Green Book*, which offered Black Americans a list of safe places to rest, shop, and eat along the road.[13]

It was also mobility and travel boycotts that gave visibility to the 1960s' civil rights movement. The 1961 Freedom Ride was the news story of its day and is credited with ushering in the end of segregated transportation. While the legal victories of the civil rights movement helped end official Jim Crow humiliations forced on Black travelers, informal travel discrimination persists to this day.[14] The uncertainty, insecurity, and potential humiliation that come with Black travel also contributes to self-restrictions, even when folks have the means.[15] For example, in the post–civil rights South, rental car companies would lease to Blacks, but many gas stations, rest areas, and bathrooms were hostile to, or refused to service, African Americans.

Today, profiling by police makes it a risk for a Black man or family to be driving, not to mention the risk of targeting while driving in a new-looking rental car. The danger of "driving while Black" remains a barrier and disincentive to travel, as over two decades of research shows a consistent pattern of disproportionate police stops of Black drivers.[16] African American motorists are 63% more likely than whites to be stopped (even though they drive 16% less) and 115% more likely to be searched in a traffic stop.[17] In addition, the NAACP issued a travel advisory in 2017 urging Black motorists to exercise "extreme caution" when driving in the state of Missouri. Yet few scholars have explored the psychological scars and intergenerational impacts that travel restrictions have had on social relations as well as worldviews within diverse African American communities. What impacts has the internalized desires to avoid insult and potential embarrassment had on Black families? These are important questions because travel can and does benefit our brains and bodies.

NATURE DENIED STYMIES HEALTH AND HEALING

Since travel was prohibited, or made dangerous and difficult, for Blacks of all classes, the benefits of travel have not reached many African Americans. There is still a stigma to and lack of tradition about leaving one's place.[18] These violent restrictions were purposeful since many whites viewed travel throughout the nineteenth and twentieth centuries as a way to reach enlightenment.[19] Travel and "escaping the city" to experience nature was viewed by 1800s' environmentalists as a pathway toward enlightenment too. John Muir, a naturalist, described his ventures into Yosemite and the Hetch Hetchy Valley like visiting a temple where nature could heal "and give strength to body and soul alike."[20] In 1845, Henry

David Thoreau's book *Walden* suggested that nature was essential for a "serene and healthy life," and helped define the US transcendentalist movement, which believed that nature could help men "rise to a higher and more ethereal life."[21] The city, on the other hand, was seen at this time as 'dark and dirty,' and increasingly full of "unwashed" immigrants and African Americans surviving in urban squalor.[22]

The denied health benefits of travel, especially spending time in nature, contributes to the unaddressed traumas experienced by many Black folks. Exposure to nature and spending quality time in green spaces can have multiple healing benefits. For example, one hypothesis is that nature changes our need to constantly problem solve—a process called attention restoration theory. This theory suggests that being in nature allows our brains to slow down and stop focusing on external challenges, and thus restores our depleted brains.[23] This is basically the "chill-out" theory of how nature helps us heal, which can also be applied to traveling to a new place where you can let your mind wander, imagine new possibilities, and leave behind the constant daily worries.[24]

Yet these natural and potentially healing spaces remain mostly unavailable to the urban poor, especially African Americans.[25] This so-called nature gap has resulted in Blacks being three times less likely than whites to have access to safe natural spaces.[26] Exposure to nature has been shown to have a profound positive effect on children and the developing brain, which can be critically important to mitigate the traumatic influences of ACEs.[27]

In addition, a longitudinal study of the risks of heart disease found that "men who did not take an annual vacation were shown to have a 20% higher risk of death and about a 30% greater risk of death from heart disease," and concluded that "vacationing is a restorative behavior with an independent positive effect on health."[28] Another study found that traveling for a vacation had greater benefits than a regular meditation practice; it also increased well-being, reduced stress, and increased positive affect.[29] Taking frequent vacations has been linked to reduced metabolic syndrome, or the confluence of abdominal obesity, high blood pressure and blood glucose, and low HDL (the "good") cholesterol, all of which can increase the risk of diabetes, heart disease, and stroke.[30] Thus traveling outside one's local area can provide psychological, social, physical, and even material benefits.[31]

IT'S DIFFICULT TO DREAM ABOUT SOMETHING THAT YOU DON'T EVEN KNOW EXISTS

The dreams of Eric and Rasheed along with D's newly discovered peace reflect how travel can allow Advance Peace Fellows to see themselves as full participants in the opportunities and freedoms life has to offer, and rediscover themselves and their purpose. Yet we have found that transformative travel has its greatest positive influence on Fellows' behavior when they experience it with their adult mentor or NCA. As we noted, few, if any, of our NCAs have ever traveled, and none had been out of the country before participating in Advance Peace. Part of the transformation of the Advance Peace approach to travel is that the mentor and mentee build an even deeper bond and greater trust. It has been said that you really don't know a person until you've traveled with them, and that is exactly what happened between one NCA, Julian, and his Fellows.

Julian, a former gang member and now credible messenger with Advance Peace, reflected that traveling helped him understand himself and his Fellows in a new way. In his mid-forties, Julian had never been on an airplane, just like the Fellows he and other NCAs were taking on an out-of-state trip. He recalled that as they drove to the airport together, he watched as his Fellows' smiles "turned up" and he "had the same cheese, ear to ear." He remembered that they looked over at them and nodded. None of them knew what to expect, and they were equally excited and scared.

"They saw me, big homie, be vulnerable, not afraid to admit I don't know shit about what to do in this situation," Julian remarked. "I was just following and acting like a kid again. It was important they see me like that 'cause I am, or was, just like them. They seen me be a little scared and show it, and I'm still the same person."

Another NCA, Marcus, recalled that he had to make sure his team had the experience first, so when those unknown and vulnerable times arise, the NCAs could ensure the Fellows stepped through that door. He explained,

I took my guys there first. Just the staff. We really bonded over that trip. Before we went, some of our guys were unsure. They were panicking and trippin' on all the plans: "What if this doesn't work?" "How we gonna do that?" They had no confidence in it or in theyselves because they never done it. Never traveled. I was like, "How are these guys, my team, gonna convince Fellows to go if they ain't never done it themselves?" It's difficult to dream about something you don't even know exists. We got there and you know what, all them plans I made went to sh*t. Things didn't go as planned . . . the rental car wasn't ready, the hotel didn't have our reservation, the restaurant was all full. I mean just about damn near everything went sideways! But it didn't matter. We experienced it together, got through it, and had a ball. We got back on the plane home and we was all like, "Yeah, that wasn't so hard. I can do that again. I can be a tour guide now." It was hilarious. That trip brought us together in ways a year of meetings couldn't, and gave us the confidence and language to let our Fellows know this travel sh*t is dope.

Facing difficulties during travel in an unfamiliar environment, meeting new people, and adapting to routines out of one's normal comfort zone can all contribute to mental and physical well-being.[32] Psychologist Jeffrey Kottler touches on the same reality while describing how travel experiences can be as or more important than successful therapy sessions. Kottler states,

Travel offers you more opportunities to change your life than almost any other human endeavor. People who structure their journeys in particular ways consistently report dramatic gains in self-esteem, confidence, poise, and self-sufficiency. They enjoy greater intimacy as a result of bonds that were forged under magical and sometimes adverse circumstances. They become more fearless risk takers, better problem solvers, and far more adaptable to everchanging circumstances. They become more knowledgeable about the world, its fascinating customs, and its diverse people. Finally, travel teaches you most about yourself—about what you miss when you are gone and what you don't, about what you are capable of doing in strange circumstances, about what you really want that you don't yet have. Regardless of what exactly you are looking for, and where you hope to find it, travel may change your life for the better.[33]

BREAKING BREAD

When someone faces constraints to travel, no matter the disadvantage, the results are greater social exclusion and lower self-rated well-being.[34] The social aspect partly reflects a tendency for travel to help create rituals and common memories.

For instance, as one of the few national CVI organizations working in multiple cities, Advance Peace intentionally brings together staff and Fellows from different cities to share travel experiences. When street outreach workers travel to the same places together, they build solidarity, share their own and new life experiences, and learn from one another about how to be effective in the work. Similarly, Fellows get to meet peers from other cities, build friendships, and plan future gatherings. Advance Peace intentionally organizes these national gatherings in places where the entire organization can learn and grow.

As part of these gatherings, Advance Peace includes specific rituals for just about every trip. One ritual is that the entire group must eat together and visit one of the best restaurants in that new place. Our Fellows (or NCAs) have rarely had the opportunity to engage in the luxury and privilege of being served at a fine dining establishment, and often struggle to find their next meal at home. We treat them like the important VIPs they are in regard to ending the cycles of urban gun violence.

On one trip to see the play *Hamilton* in San Francisco, the cultural experience got subsumed by the restaurant experience. Before the show, we took the Fellows to an old-school, famous steak and seafood restaurant. It was the kind of place where all the famous people who had eaten there had their pictures on the wall. Before they sat us in a white-tableclothed section where Truman Capote, Steve Jobs, and George Lucas were regulars (not that any of the Fellows had heard of those people), they required our Fellows to borrow a sport coat. They had to meet the dress code. While most complained at first, the Fellows were taken aback when the waiters, in their white coats and black ties, talked to them like VIPs. The Fellows weren't used to men in suits calling them "sir" and asking if they "needed anything else." After we explained what all the silverware meant, the Fellows were utterly confused by the menu. The names of different cuts of steak and fish were like a foreign language.

"Let's all order the surf and turf," suggested one of the NCAs. "So we can order steak and lobster?" asked most of the Fellows. The Fellows learned they could order anything off the menu. Despite all the selection, they all ordered the same thing, which also happened to be the most expensive item on the menu: the Black Angus filet mignon and Maine lobster tail. The Fellows ate well! Then the bill came, and they couldn't believe how much Advance Peace was spending on their food.

The Fellows were more interested in taking pictures of the receipt than all the famous people on the walls. They were all posting about the steak and lobster, bragging to their crew how they were going to treat "their girl" to something like that someday. Through actions like this, Advance Peace sends a message to them that they are important and deserve to share in the rituals mostly elites only get to experience, while seeking to have them dream that this too can be their reality. Mission accomplished, although those "borrowed" blazers also somehow made it into the car. We still had some mentoring to do.

On another trip to a San Francisco 49ers game, Fellows and NCAs from multiple Advance Peace cities came together. This was a unique moment because this was the first time Advance Peace had ever created a space for multiple Advance Peace teams and Fellows to be together. On this excursion, there were Fellows and staff from Sacramento, Stockton, and Fresno at the game, all meeting one another and making new friendships. This was a new and important dynamic for the Advance Peace transformative travel experience in that Fellows from different cities got to meet each other in a neutral setting, have fun, and expand their networks to new people also involved in peacemaking.

Right before the game kickoff, the crowd was on its feet roaring for the home team. A Fellow turned to his buddy and said, "This sounds just like *Madden*!" He was referencing the video game. For this Fellow, "real life" while being in a stadium of eighty thousand people sounded like the *Madden* video game, not the other way around. He gained a new perspective to help with transformative thinking while in a community that supported these experiences.

"THAT'S MY SUCKA PARTNA"

The conditions for traveling with Advance Peace out of a Fellow's home state or the country are that they have been enrolled in the program for at least six months, have a LifeMAP, are making regular progress on LifeMAP goals and actions, are in contact with their assigned NCA daily, are attending group life skills classes, and are willing to travel with a rival. Of course, only Fellows who have shown progress toward more peacefully resolving conflicts and a commitment to their own healing would even consider traveling with a rival. It means sitting in the same vehicle with them, eating meals together, navigating an unknown place together, going out at night, unarmed, in a place with both known and unknown gangs, and sometimes even sharing a hotel room with a rival.

Before one group trip to Washington, DC, and New York City, what Advance Peace calls its East Coast swing, each Fellow was taken to the tailor for a new, custom-fitted suit. Since the Fellows were going to visit politicians and attend a conference, Advance Peace wanted each of them to "look" like they belonged in those spaces. It was in DC, on the way to the Capitol, that the Fellows' NCA mentor noticed that the rivals were "still in the feeling-out period," meaning they weren't exactly bonding or even talking to one another. Passing though the metal detectors seems to trigger something in the Fellows. It was just them together, in an unknown place, unarmed. As their NCA mentor watched the dynamic, he reflected on what was happening. "Once they realized, 'We in DC now, and the closest thing to Richmond that I know is this dude right here from my rival neighborhood,' that conflict from back home, they just left it behind."

The rivalries were made even less significant after they visited Howard University. They were transposed to a new reality on a campus where people their same age who looked just like them (well, except for the gold teeth) seemed to all be getting along and were having fun. Standing on the quad in their suits, some coeds approached the Fellows. They asked the Fellows what they were doing there and where they were from.

"Richmond," the Fellows all responded in unison. The female students replied, "Like, Richmond, Virginia?" The Fellows, now a little surer and prouder of themselves, responded back, "Nah, Richmond . . . California." The Howard students shook their heads and quickly said, "Never heard of it." They turned away, wishing the Fellows a good time.

The Fellows' NCA mentors were standing behind them, smiling and trying not to laugh. The Fellows, dressed to the nines, thought they were going to impress the college students, but the women didn't even care and had never heard of Richmond. This was the same place they were killing one another over to defend. Over dinner that night (at the Capital Grille), the Fellows could be heard talking to their hometown rivals and agreeing with one another that "those college women weren't all that anyway." There were a lot of "you right" and a subtle recognition that they were more alike than different.

As their NCA mentor described the experience, "No one trip is going to solve all the problems that exist. But I believe they crossed a real threshold when they started acknowledging one another not for where they from but [instead] from how they are. The reconciliation has begun."

HEALING THROUGH UNCOMMON HISTORY

Travel can bring us to places and experiences to learn about shared history. This can be moving but also empowering, especially when learning about an aspect of one's history that had been ignored or written out of most narratives. This is one reason why the Advance Peace travel experiences to DC always bring Fellows to both the National Museum of African American History and Culture and the Holocaust Memorial Museum.

The African American Museum is a powerful reminder of the brutality Black people have faced throughout our history, but also celebrates much that Black folks have contributed to society. The Advance Peace staff and Fellows that are African American always appear to learn something new about themselves there. This is why we do it on every trip. Just a short walk across the National Mall is the Holocaust Memorial. The similarities and differences between the experiences of these two groups always stimulates insights from our staff and Fellows.

The horrors of the Holocaust are rarely known by our staff or Fellows. The brutality and visceral experiences that both museums offer always move us to tears. Many express feeling the common dehumanization experienced by many groups. And after one NCA reflected that when he and his Fellows learned about an all-Black army tank regiment that was the first to liberate people in the Nazi gas chambers, it contrasted with the stories about gun violence. He stated, "There's lots of groups suffering out there, but when our people do something brave, we don't get no recognition for it. It's only when we are violent are they paying attention."

This is one of many examples where Advance Peace's transformative travel approach aims to educate and stimulate self-reflection about human nature, the impacts that our actions have on the lives of others, what unifies us as a community, and how hatred attempts to deny our universal humanity.

Another historical site visit has become a mandatory destination for all Advance Peace Fellows. One year the national meeting was held in Montgomery, Alabama, and the event was organized around visits to the Legacy Museum and National Memorial for Peace and Justice, informally known as the National Lynching Museum. Few staff or Fellows had previously been familiar with that city's role in the slave trade and the civil rights movement. The group learned about and was visited by staff members who created the museum and memorial from the Equal Justice Initiative (which is led by attorney and *Just Mercy* author Bryan Stevenson). Both the museum and memorial were more than transformative for staff and Fellows. As Advance Peace staff and Fellows meandered through the lynching memorial and the hanging column-like "coffins," many saw their families' names etched in the steel. Most were shocked to encounter the "grave site" of a long forgotten or unknown family member.

One Fellow reflected in a group debrief, "I was like, whoa, hold up, that's my family! I knew we was from Arkansas, but I ain't never heard nobody in my family talk about something like that happening to us. Of course,

7.1 Staff and Fellows in Alabama experiencing transformative travel.

there was probably others with the same name, but to see your name as part of the remembrance of those who were lynched, it broke me."

The museum proved equally powerful as most of the group had been incarcerated and involved in the type of violence the Legacy Museum highlights that is part of a deliberate continuum of dehumanization of Black folks, stretching from the Middle Passage, to slavery and lynching, to Jim Crow and mass incarceration. One Fellow described how during a moment in the exhibit where you encounter holograms of actual inmates accused of crimes they didn't commit, he saw himself in that figure:

Slavery today is doin' time. Jim Crow is what our neighborhoods still look like. The more shit changes, the more shit don't change. I mean, everything I seen in the museum and the "who in jail" part, I did that. I was a pawn in their game. We doin' their work for them. If dude stepped on my sneakers, that was reason enough for me to shoot 'em. Now that I seen that, I'm gonna look the other way. I'm not shootin' no n** in the streets for them.

An NCA described how the entire experience gave him new language and examples to bring back to his work with Fellows, stating, "I'm a fifty-year-old Black man and nobody never exposed me to that part of our history. You think, oh, I'm in California, we all aware and shit. F* that. Now I got more knowledge about what we as a people doing to ourselves and how this is about our liberation as a people, not just a gun violence prevention strategy."

FAMILY IS WHERE I FEEL SAFE

When traveling is truly transformative, we come home feeling a little different. There is a greater bounce in our step, and we are often refreshed. Traveling with Advance Peace is intended to give staff and Fellows a sense that they are part of a family, and even when returning home, that family is still going to be there for them. That family is also expecting them to stay alive and healthy so they can travel again to the next Advance Peace gathering. As one Fellow described it, "I'm part of a big family now and it mean something to me to be accepted the way they did me. They said we might be going to New Orleans next. I gotta make it! I think I will. Just gonna keep my head down and keep grinding."

A trip can allow someone to find new passions and purpose for life as well as contribute to realizing their true potential.[35] As Kottler put it when ending his earlier statement, "Travel teaches you most about yourself—about what you miss when you are gone and what you don't, about what you are capable of doing in strange circumstances, about what you really want that you don't yet have."[36]

Staff and Fellows face a challenge, though, when they return home transformed while their communities and those around them are not. Advance Peace helps prepare them to navigate this difficult dynamic, with Fellows describing the tension of heading back home and putting back on the "armor" needed to navigate "this shit," as D called it.

Yet our Fellows (and staff) frequently come home to a crew that wants to know more about their experience, and we often hear from the Fellows' friends, "How can I go on that?" All the videos, pictures, and live postings the Fellows made while showing off their travel can make their crews envious. Added to that, it's not uncommon for a Fellow to "hear it" from their crew at home when they are taking pictures and hanging out with a rival. They often have to field calls from back home asking, "What you doing hanging out with that sucka?"

Fellows work with their NCAs to develop a response and prepare for that pushback when they get home. For example, one Fellow and his NCA crafted a response to a barrage of text messages about spending time with a rival: "I told 'em we cool now, like we 'backstreet cool.' I got his number, and I can call him anytime if we run into people."

Another Fellow explained how he had just been making "snow angels" with a rival whom he'd spent ten days with. Then he got a call on the ride home from the airport from someone in his crew that one of his family members had been shot. It hit him hard. He sank into his seat and stared out the window. His NCA mentor looked at him from the front of the car and knew that look. Something bad had happened. The Fellow's phone was now "blowing up" with messages. His crew was asking him what they should do? They were "in the car" ready to go.

The NCA also got some messages on his phone and quickly realized what was happening. He turned toward the Fellow in the back seat. The Fellow and his rival (whose crew was likely responsible for the shooting) had just spent days living, learning, and laughing together. The NCA

TRAVEL AS HEALING THERAPY

listened for the Fellow to give the go-ahead and instruct his crew to take one of their rivals out. It couldn't wait until he got there, they were telling the Fellow. They wanted to retaliate now.

The Fellow finally picked up the phone, and the NCA turned around and looked away. All he heard from behind him was a quiet, "Let him go. Stand-down." The Fellow stayed silent the rest of the ride home.

The NCA remembered thinking how this was a product of the work. The trip had helped transform the Fellow's decision-making and the new choice for the safety of his community. His Fellow decided to save a life. Somebody else was also going home alive that night.

8

THE IMPACTS OF ADVANCE PEACE

If they alive and free, we winning.
—Kevin Yarborough, former ONS NCA

Data keeps the lights on.
—Advance Peace NCA

In June 2019, the Fresno City Council was on the verge of working with and supporting a coalition of community activists dedicated to ending that city's gun violence epidemic.[1] Although the council had authorized $200,000 to fund the Advance Peace program, then mayor Lee Brand vetoed the proposal, citing a lack of scientific evidence that it works.[2] Yet that October, the *American Journal of Public Health* released a study showing that the Advance Peace's Peacemaker Fellowship in Richmond was responsible for a 55% reduction in firearm violence in that city.[3]

The Fresno mayor's office responded by stating, "Although the results of this study are not definitive, they are promising and they will help guide our efforts to develop efforts tailored to the realities of Fresno." The mayor's office declined to specify why the findings were not definitive. Fresno City Council member Miguel Arias pushed back and stated, "The mayor made it clear he was vetoing Advance Peace based on the lack of scientific research. Now that the research has been published, and shows the program is effective. The mayor needs to reconsider."[4]

The City of Fresno eventually decided to allocate the $200,000 to the EOC, a large community action agency providing services that was founded through the 1964 National Economic Opportunity Act. The Fresno EOC began working with the Advance Peace's national office to hire and train outreach staff for the launch of Advance Peace Fresno.

Toward the end of 2021, the Fresno City Council was again debating whether to fund Advance Peace. The city was now considering pledging an additional $950,000 as a onetime infusion of federal, American Rescue Plan Act dollars, but began to waffle. Meanwhile, Fresno had already spent $36.6 million of its 2020 federal Coronavirus Aid, Relief and Economic Security Act funds on the police department, or about 40% of all of Fresno's funds from that act.[5] According to the *Guardian*, that amounted to the city spending "more than double of its CARES money on police than it did to COVID testing, contact tracing, small business grants, childcare vouchers and transitional housing combined."[6]

New mayor Jerry Dyer, the former Fresno police chief, was refusing to reauthorize funding for Advance Peace after one year of outreach work. So by the middle of 2022, Advance Peace Fresno still hadn't received any additional funds from the city. At a budget hearing, a community resident testified, saying, "They've stopped shootings. They've curbed a possible race riot. They've made Southwest Fresno safer, something our city has yet to be able to do in all of these years."[7] The mayor claimed there were "trust issues" between the program and the city. Yet the mayor publicly proclaimed during the meeting that "Advance Peace intervention specialists have done some great work out there. I know for a fact they've stopped shootings. I know that for a fact."[8] Fresno police chief Paco Balderama also stated that programs such as Advance Peace are a necessary complement to police work, claiming,

I am very supportive of violence prevention programs which add to the efforts of what police are trying to do, which is to prevent violent crime. I am hesitant on moving forward with a partnership with Advance Peace until accountability and output measures are established and implemented. In speaking with EOC, [Advance Peace], and the City Manager's Office, I'm hopeful this is a possibility. The police can't solve every social issue or do it alone, we need these types of programs in existence.[9]

That statement came despite data from the University of California at Berkeley evaluation team that was presented at the hearing. The data showed that the Advance Peace Fresno program had already interrupted over 270 community conflicts and 76 imminent gun conflicts in just twelve months, and that firearm homicides and nonfatal shootings had declined by 10% citywide as well as over 26% in the most impoverished and violent Southwest area.

But before approving the funding, Arias had more lukewarm support, saying that he wanted more evidence that Advance Peace was working: "We can't simply settle on the perception of safety. There has to be actual safety. There has to be an actual reduction in crime, and I find it very hard to dismiss a program that may not be working to my expectations and simply walk away from it."[10]

SHOULD WE MEASURE VIOLENCE OR PEACE?

The debates in Fresno reflect what similar cities across the United States have wrestled with when considering adopting CVI. Concerns center on how to know if a program works and whether the numbers obtained speak for themselves.

Evaluating the efficacy, influences, and impacts of Advance Peace is a challenge. Of course, one goal must be ending gun violence. Yet that will not happen overnight in most cities that already have a gun violence issue, as was hoped for by some in the Fresno debates. Even if an initiative like Advance Peace could reduce gun violence significantly in a city in a year or two, it would be insufficient to end the epidemic. Why? Because the traumas that are contributing to those impacted from using guns will still be there. Ending the epidemic of urban gun violence means ensuring the "bleeding stops" today, tomorrow, and into the future. This means we must help heal those at the heart of violence, prevent the next generation from engaging in this activity, and change the social conditions that contribute to urban gun violence.

That healing process is not as easy to peg on charts. We will share evidence of Advance Peace impacts later in this chapter, but first it helps to have context on why data sometimes muddies the waters instead.

THE CHALLENGES OF MEASURING PROGRAM IMPACTS

One factor that makes traditional crime data challenging to work with is that the quality of it varies. For example, the FBI's Uniform Crime Reporting system is supposed to be the definitive record of local crime data, but the quality of firearm incident data is highly segmented. Some cities do not keep track of firearm homicides in a timely way, and when they do, often subjectively label these as "gang involved."[11] As a result, some researchers are forced to use all homicide data as a "proxy" for firearm homicides, often noting that about 75 to 80% of urban homicides are committed with a firearm.[12] For nonfatal shootings, cities may not specify which caused an injury, and which were just shots fired into a car or building.

Further complicating firearm shooting data is that police departments in different jurisdictions can code a shooting incident differently and there is no national definition of a nonfatal shooting incident, nor a repository of these data.[13]

Perhaps even more disturbing is that some city police departments manipulate data on homicides and shootings to make it look like crime is declining or increasing to serve their political needs. Reporters at *Chicago* magazine uncovered dozens of missing homicides and other manipulations of crime data during a 2014 investigation that made it appear statistically that crime was declining in that city when in fact it wasn't.[14] More recently, in Oakland, California, the police department was found to be publishing inaccurate crime data.[15]

Data related to violence also has been used to perpetuate narratives around public safety that are often racist. As Khalil Gibran Muhammad reminds us in his 2010 book *The Condemnation of Blackness: Race, Crime, and the Making of Modern Urban America*, while Black crime data are frequently cited to justify (or stymie) action and policy, "white crime statistics are virtually invisible, except when used to dramatize the excessive criminality of African Americans. Although the statistical language of black criminality often means different things to different people, it is the glue that binds race to crime today as in the past." Muhammad highlights how intellectuals, politicians, and the state used statistical methods as well as data to treat Black criminality, "alongside disease and intelligence, as a fundamental measure of black inferiority."[16]

Not only can crime data be biased, but it fundamentally fails to capture the human harms that can result from policing along with increased cases of arrests and incarceration. These include increased fear, adverse impacts on mental health, and the social and economic costs of removing people from what are often Black and Brown communities. Data also rarely gets used to ask questions that community members want answered, such as whether people who have experienced violent, racist dehumanization have had their humanity restored, repaired, and respected.

What all of this means is that it can be difficult and costly to "prove"—using just crime data—that a gun violence reduction and prevention strategy that doesn't rely on law enforcement is working. Rates of firearm homicides and nonfatal shootings shouldn't be the only measures of whether a community-driven gun violence prevention strategy is effective. Moreover, gun crime data are just measuring violence, albeit a type we want to eliminate. We must be seeking true peace in our communities, and the absence of violence is not the presence of peace, which is both a state of mind and the "presence of justice."[17]

At the same time, we recognize that data and evidence have always been central to supporting policies. So with the caveats above in mind, here are the ways we have been considering metrics for Advance Peace as well as defining its costs and benefits.

TRAUMA-INFORMED ADVANCE PEACE DATA

While crime outcomes are important, they do not give us any insights into *how* a program might be working, what, if any, influence it is having on those at the center of gun violence, and whether the root causes of violence—from individual and community traumas, to neighborhood disinvestment, to institutional neglect and racism—are changing? We suggest that without showing data about the participants in the gun violence initiative (e.g., who are they and what happens to them), and the specific interventions and investments delivered to these people aimed at helping end gun violence, we are missing key indicators about whether an intervention is working, and if it is racially and socially just. Judging the influences and impacts of an intervention like Advance Peace should always include data on what happens to the participants, what specific supports and interventions are needed to help people heal and change behaviors in the short as well as medium terms, and broader indicators of community safety, peace, and prosperity.

Previous chapters covered some data about the complexities of outreach workers and participants, along with their individual stories and community influences. We prioritized that "data" because too often the voices of intervention participants and mentors are ignored or minimized in presentations of crime statistics. But as shared, most Fellows in Advance Peace want to change as they enter the program (albeit some remain committed to using a firearm to solve street conflict), and most have assets and skills to build on to help them change. Advance Peace data also revealed that about 60% of our Fellows enter the program with four or more childhood traumas (ACEs) that—when left unaddressed—can adversely impact the brain, the ability to decipher right from wrong, and impulse control as well as producing other mental and physical health issues.

In addition, we highlighted that the daily mentoring and engagements by our NCAs, services and supports, and group life skills and travel opportunities—the entire Peacemaker Fellowship—foster healing from those unaddressed traumas. This is what we call neurourbanism: the street outreach and consistent presence of healthy and loving adults that helps to rewire the brain, heal the body, and develop entire communities.[18]

Through the direct support and service provider access of the Peacemaker Fellowship, Fellows get help to understand, disrupt, and overcome the traumatic impacts of childhood ACEs, including prior abuse. Neurourbanism is fundamentally about promoting healthy human development and post-traumatic growth, which is the process of turning traumatic experiences into positive outcomes.[19] Indicators of post-traumatic growth often include increased self-awareness and recognition of personal strengths, improved relationships and comfort with intimacy, a greater appreciation of life, and openness to discovering new possibilities.[20]

We know that finding positives out of chronic adversity is neither easy nor inevitable; so Advance Peace staff document the number of engagements and time spent with each Fellow, or what we call the "dosage" of the work. This allows us to better understand what it takes to help a Fellow heal and become a peacemaker.[21]

Below we present data on Fellows after eighteen or twenty-four months in the program, while recognizing that even these metrics are early milestones in a long healing process.

THE DOSAGE AND INFLUENCES

The Peacemaker Fellowship delivers a suite of supports and services to our Fellows. In the thirty-month period from July 2021 through December 2023, across ten Advance Peace cities (as mentioned before, Antioch, Fresno, Pomona, Richmond, Stockton, and Vallejo in California, along with Lansing, Fort Worth, Rochester, and Orlando in other states), we captured the dosage or percent of Fellows that received specific supports from NCAs and/or service providers (for definitions of the specific supports and services, see chapter 5). More than half of our Fellows received five or more different services.

Note that every percentage here would likely be zero if Advance Peace wasn't in these cities courting, chasing, counseling, and catering to active firearm offenders. We know this because at intake in the Peacemaker Fellowship, only about 16% of the Fellows were receiving any social services.

During those thirty months across all of these Advance Peace cities, the average age of our 627 Fellows was twenty-three; 17% were under eighteen; 45% were eighteen to twenty-five; 21% were twenty-six to thirty-four; and 16% were thirty-five or older. In terms of other statistics, 90% of our Fellows were male and 10% were female; 73% were Black, 20% were Latino, and 6% were Asian, white, or didn't specify their ethnicity.

- *85% received individualized life coaching* sessions from an NCA
- *68% attended life skills classes* with other Fellows
- *72% received cognitive behavioral therapy* from their NCA
- *63% received social service navigations* from their NCA
- *61% received culturally responsive counseling* from an NCA
- *31% received internships*
- *30% attended elder circles* led by community members
- *33% received job readiness* supports from an NCA
- *56% of participated in excursions and/or transformative travel*

Because the NCAs cannot deliver all the supports a Fellow needs, Advance Peace partners with service providers to deliver specific supports, ranging from mental health and anger management counseling, to family and child custody guidance, to navigating the DMV, Section 8 housing vouchers, and food supports. Usually, an Advance Peace NCA will not only accompany the Fellow to the service but also sit with them to ensure they are treated fairly and get the services they deserve.

The most frequent referral is taking a Fellow to get their driver's license, ID, and Social Security card. As shown in table 8.1, family counseling comes next, which can include things like child support and improving relations with family members; this service actually takes up the largest number of hours per referral. Getting Fellows basic needs, including housing and food, are also typical referrals. Working on avoiding conflict, managing emotions and anger, and getting with mental health care are some of the referrals that take a large time commitment from each Fellow. Referrals also include group healing work, such as restorative justice practices.

CONFRONTING TIME POVERTY

As the table on referrals highlights, certain supports demand more time, such as counseling and mental health care. The University of California at Berkeley evaluation team asked whether time, versus just the amount or type of engagements, mattered for not only Fellow outcomes but also impacting gun violence in each city with the Peacemaker Fellowship. Remember that each Fellow gets unique supports tailored to their needs as defined in the LifeMAP.

What we found was that no matter the types of interventions during the Peacemaker Fellowship, the more time staff spent with Fellows, the better their outcomes and the greater the percentage reduction in gun crime outcomes (firearm homicides and nonfatal shootings). Jason's team calculated the mean number of hours spent per Fellow in each of the cities that had a complete eighteen-month Fellowship and for cities that we had gun crime data. The change in combined firearm homicides and nonfatal shootings was calculated using the counts for the eighteen-month period before the Fellowship and during the Peacemaker Fellowship period. We then computed the percentage of Fellows who had any "negative outcome" in that city, which includes a death, gun injury, and any arrest, and compared the mean number of hours for Fellows who had a negative outcome to those who did not.

Table 8.1 Advance Peace, All Cities, July 2021–December 2023: Social Service Referral
Counts and Hours

Referrals	Percentage of Fellows receiving	Mean number of hours spent per Fellow
DMV / license / Social Security card	54.0	5.3
Family support and counseling	41.0	10.5
Housing supports	44.0	8.3
Internship / work readiness	35.0	5.5
Violence avoidance / social emotional learning	30.0	7.8
Anger management counseling	27.0	4.5
Restorative justice practices	25.0	6.1
Mental health care	20.0	8.5
Court legal supports	17.0	6.6
Food assistance	15.0	4.0
Education vocational training	15.0	2.1
GED classes	12.0	3.5
Probation support	10.0	8.8
Prosocial leadership skills and activities	10.0	6.8
Substance abuse / addiction services	9.0	3.4
Health care	7.1	4.0
Parole support	5.8	6.3

For example, in Rochester and Fresno, the mean number of hours an NCA spent with a Fellow during the Fellowship period was 393 and 388, respectively. During the Fellowship period, 26% of Fellows had a negative outcome in these two cities. Compared to the eighteen-months before the Advance Peace intervention, Rochester had a 24% reduction in firearm homicides and shootings after the Peacemaker Fellowship, and Fresno experienced a 30% reduction. In Stockton, there was an average of 301 hours per Fellow during the Fellowship period, 32% of Fellows had a negative outcome, and that city experienced a 9% reduction in firearm homicides and injury shootings after the Advance Peace intervention compared to the preintervention period. While the Advance Peace program in Stockton is helping to reduce gun violence and negative outcomes for Fellows, it had less success than cities that invested more time into their Fellows. Our data suggest is that time is a hidden currency; the more time we spend with Fellows, the more likely we are to get them a positive result, and their city seems to benefit too.

DOES PAYING SHOOTERS STOP THEM FROM SHOOTING?

A unique component of the Peacemaker Fellowship is the LifeMAP milestone allowance. A Fellow becomes milestone allowance eligible, as noted earlier, only after they have cocreated a LifeMAP with their mentor, are actively participating in all aspects of the Fellowship for at least six months, are regularly attending life skills classes and social services referrals, and have made progress on at least 65% of their LifeMAP actions. These are not easy thresholds. Thus only 36% of the Fellows received a milestone allowance during the Peacemaker Fellowship period from July 2021 through December 2023. The average amount the milestone allowance recipients received during the Peacemaker Fellowship was $3,000. Since a Fellow must be active and meeting the criteria for the allowance for the first six months of the Fellowship, this means that a Fellow received an average of about $125 per month.

What we also found during the same Fellowship period described above was that 9% of the Fellows who received an allowance had a negative outcome (i.e., death, gun injury, or any arrest) while 25% of the Fellows who did not receive an allowance had one of these outcomes. The allowance seems to also support the healing of our Fellows, as 82% of those who received an allowance reported improved basic needs (i.e., food, housing, and clothing) and 87% reported improved mental health, compared to 69% reporting improved basic needs and 72% reporting improved mental health of those not receiving an allowance.

HELPING FELLOWS HEAL FROM TRAUMA AND MAKE BETTER DECISIONS

Throughout the Fellowship, each NCA tracks weekly if their Fellow is alive, injured by a gun, arrested, or arrested on a gun charge. Across all

Advance Peace cities from June 2021 to December 2023, of the 627 Fellows, 31 tragically died, but 95% were alive. Of those alive, only 1 was injured by gunshot during this period and 97.6% of alive Fellows had not been arrested on a new gun charge while in the Fellowship.

The NCAs also track if their Fellow is using guns to resolve conflicts, their self-rated mental health, if they feel safer in their community, if they have improved anger/conflict management skills, whether they have improved basic needs including food and housing, and if they have a trusted adult in their lives to talk to about difficult issues. Many of these questions get asked at intake, such as Fellows' self-rated mental health along with whether they have stable housing and secure food. We know many of these factors contribute to stress, anxiety, and anger, which can lead someone to pick up a gun.

Of those 627 Fellows who completed the program or were enrolled at least twelve or more months, 83% reported an improved mental health / outlook on life, 74% reported improved anger management skills, 68% felt safer in their communities, 50% reported being employed or having new job skills, 84% reported no longer using a gun to resolve conflicts, 82% reported peacefully resolving a conflict that previously might have resulted in gun use, and 92% reported having a trusted adult in their lives to talk to in times of crisis or solve daily challenges.

These are healing-centered accomplishments. Remember, most Fellows entered the program with a high degree of unaddressed trauma: 57% with four or more ACEs, and almost 50% with both four ACEs and two or more gun violence exposures. Most important, the Fellows are alive, free, and making better life decisions. We are confident these influences of the program contribute to reductions in shootings and firearm homicides—something we discuss below.

SAVING COMMUNITY LIVES AND TAX DOLLARS

Advance Peace both mentors and helps heal active firearm offenders *and* interrupt conflicts in communities. This is a testament to the broad trust the NCAs build. Frequently, NCAs will get calls from concerned parents and community members to act as the *first* responder to a potential or actual conflict. During the thirty-month period of July 2021 through

December 2023, across ten active Advance Peace cities, NCAs mediated over two thousand conflicts and invested almost 5,450 hours conducting these mediations.

Advance Peace trains NCAs to define the specific type of conflict they are mediating. As we described in the NCA chapter, general conflicts differ from a shooting response, which often differs from social media conflict mediations. The most critical type of mediation that NCAs confront is the *cyclical and retaliatory gun violence interruption* or CRGVI, when an NCA interrupts a situation where guns are, or are suspected to be, present and likely to be used. These situations are usually gun-involved conflicts between rivals who are known to be "at war" in each community or city. These disputes are the most likely to perpetuate urban gun violence, and resemble cancers that spread senseless killing and retaliation, often for generations.

The CRGVIs never make it to the city's police database. These are frequently conflicts that only the mediator (in this case, the NCA), those involved in the conflict, or the community member(s) who hipped Advance Peace to it knows about, or at least formally documents having occurred. Few CVI programs that we know of are explicitly training their outreach staff to identify and count these interruptions, although we are sure many must mediate them.

Looking at the thirty-month period from July 2021 to December 2023, across the same ten Advance Peace cities mentioned above, there were 361 CRGVIs for 1,262.5 hours. This means that Advance Peace likely saved 361 lives if each of these were not mediated and resulted in a firearm homicide. If they didn't result in a homicide, those 361 mediations likely prevented a nonfatal gun injury—injuries that could have contributed to lifelong disability and trauma for the victim, adverse impacts to their family, and increased fear, anxiety, and other uncertainty across the community. Everyone benefits through CRGVIs.

There is also an economic cost to gun violence. We would never place a dollar figure on a human life—injured or lost. The costs, however, to families, taxpayers, and local governments from urban gun violence has been well-documented. The estimates include the direct costs of a gunshot injury or homicide, such as criminal justice services like court and public prosecution, jail and prison incarceration, police and EMT responses, and medical care and victim supports. The indirect costs include those employers lose from work absence and tax revenues lost by local governments. The nonprofit group Everytown for Gun Safety estimated that every gun death costs US taxpayers about $274,000, and each nonfatal gun injury about $25,000, but acknowledges these costs vary widely by state and locality.[22] The National Institute for Criminal Justice Reform (NICJR) has calculated the cost of gun violence to cities around the country, and estimated that a single gun homicide costs about $1.2 million and each nonfatal injury shooting about $700,000.[23] Using the NICJR cost figures and number of CRGVIs (361) performed by NCAs with Advance Peace, the program likely saved taxpayers between $252 and $433 million, or about $842,000 to $1.4 million per month, per city.[24]

Imagine now that each Peacemaker Fellowship cost about $1 million per year to operate. Over thirty months, this would be about $2.5 million in expenses for the Peacemaker Fellowship. This means that after 3 CRGVIs, the funding for this Peacemaker Fellowship would easily pay for itself. If we calculate a cost-benefit ratio for ten cities by dividing the estimated benefits ($252 or $433 million) by the time period costs (about $25 million for all ten cities), we get $252/$2.5 million = $10.08 and $433/2.5 million = $17.32. Thus we estimate that for every dollar spent on Advance Peace, there is a social return of $10 to $17. We know this is a great return on an investment, especially for social policy.

THE GUN VIOLENCE DATA

Before we present data on firearm homicides and nonfatal shootings in the cities where Advance Peace operates, we want to remind you that each Advance Peace city has an average of ten NCAs, with some as few as four. A program with limited staff cannot be responsible for reducing citywide gun crime, particularly while striving to engage select people, most of whom happen to be young Black and Brown men under thirty-five years old. Remember, Advance Peace is hyperfocused on those involved in cyclic and retaliatory gun violence, meaning not everyone who might be using a gun. But this initiative and CVI programs more generally are frequently held to an extremely high, unrealistic standard by officials in their cities: Are you responsible for reducing gun crime in our city in the few years and few neighborhoods where you work?

With these limitations in mind, we will start with a look at Richmond, the longest-running Peacemaker Fellowship, and compare firearm homicides and assaults across San Francisco Bay Area cities.

Despite California having some of the most stringent gun access laws in the United States, some cities and communities in that state remain disproportionately burdened by gun violence.[25] California's gun homicide rate was 3.8 deaths per 100,000 people in 2012 and 5.0 in 2021, averaging 3.9 over the past decade.[26] The victims have also remained the same in California, with African Americans comprising 21% of firearm homicide victims and Latinos 4.7% in 2021.

Compared to the largest cities in the Bay Area, none except Richmond have significantly *reduced* and *sustained* any reductions in their firearm homicide rates over the past twenty years. For example, Oakland, a city once recognized for its innovative firearm homicide reduction program between 2013 and 2018, saw its firearm homicides return to 2012 rates by 2020.[27] In fact, since 2003, Oakland's firearm homicide rate has remained steady at about 25 deaths per 100,000 population. San Jose's gun homicide rate, while low at about 3.4 deaths per 100,000 population, has remained unchanged in the twenty years from 2003 to 2022. San Francisco has seen about a 25% reduction in its firearm homicide rate from 2002 to 2022, going from a peak of around 13.3 in 2007 to about 7 out of 100,000 in 2022, which was equivalent to 56 firearm homicides.

Of all of these cities, only Richmond has achieved and maintained significant reductions in firearm homicides over the last twenty years. Richmond reached a 56% year-over-year reduction in firearm homicides over the period 2008 (when the ONS outreach apparatus was launched) through 2023. In 2007, there were 47 firearm homicides, and 8 in 2023–a remarkable 83% decrease. Injury shootings in Richmond have decreased during this period too, going from an annual average of 180 prior to the ONS to 69 after the implementation of the Peacemaker Fellowship (of note is that shootings have averaged 42 per year since 2020, and there were 37 in 2023). While firearm homicide rates and injury shootings do not tell the entire story, we know of no other US city that has reduced and maintained reductions in firearm homicides as well as injury shootings over this fifteen-plus-year period (including during COVID-19) like Richmond.

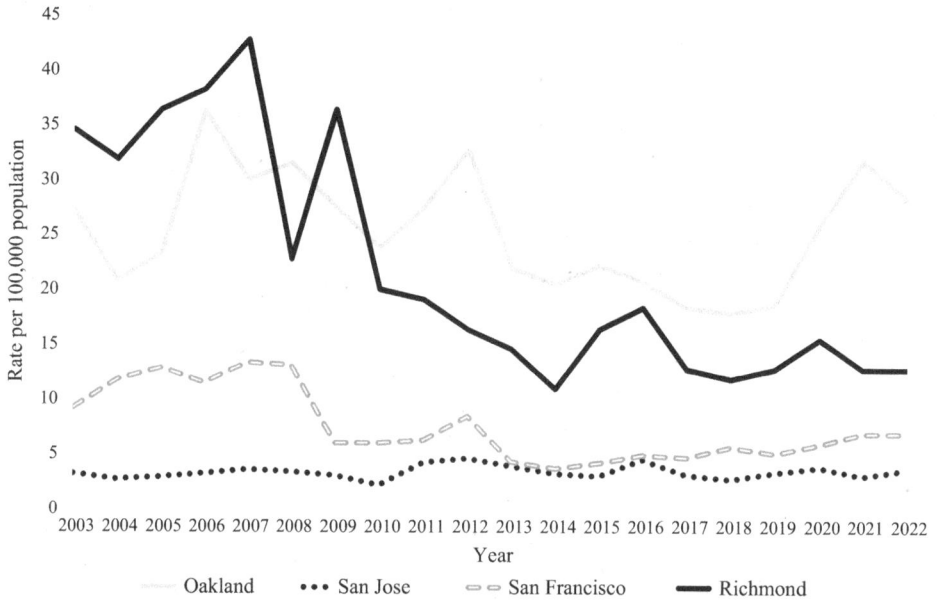

8.1 Firearm homicide rates for Oakland, San Francisco, San Jose, and Richmond, California, per 100,000 people.

We also looked at the impacts on firearm crime just in the neighborhoods where Advance Peace focuses its work in four cities—Fresno, Richmond, Sacramento, and Stockton. We concentrated on the COVID-19 pandemic period when many cities experienced a spike in gun homicides and shootings. What we found was that in these four cities in every Advance Peace target neighborhood, there was a reduction in firearm homicides in the 2020–2021 period compared to the 2018–2019 period. For example, Stockton's Advance Peace zones averaged 15 firearm homicides during the 2018–2019 period but only 10 during the 2019–2020 period—a 33% reduction. In Sacramento, the Advance Peace intervention neighborhoods of Oak Park, Del Paso Heights, and South Sacramento experienced a 5% reduction in the percentage of citywide firearm homicides during 2020–2021 compared to the prepandemic 2018–2019 period. These data run counter to the narrative that gun violence increased everywhere during the COVID-19 period. As important, during the initial pandemic period (2020 and 2021), fewer gun homicide victims were Black men under thirty-five years old compared to the previous two years; and there were 22% fewer young Black gun homicide victims in Fresno, 3% fewer in Stockton, and 18% fewer in Richmond.

Furthermore, in Sacramento, Advance Peace delivered significant reductions in firearm homicides and assaults during an eighteen-month Peacemaker Fellowship from July 2018 to December 2019. The Advance Peace "target zones" are neighborhoods with the highest poverty rates, percent people of color, and violent crime rates. They were selected by the city's Office of Gang Prevention as the areas to direct the Advance Peace intervention. During the Peacemaker Fellowship, the Sacramento intervention zones or neighborhoods, mentioned above, experienced an 18.2% reduction in gun homicides and assaults ($n = 203$) compared to the gun crime mean of the prior fifty-four months ($n = 249$). In areas only outside the Advance Peace zones, Sacramento experienced an 8.7% *increase* in firearm homicides and assaults ($n = 147$ versus $n = 159$) during the Peacemaker Fellowship. For the entire city of Sacramento (including outside targeted Advance Peace zones), there was an 8.3% reduction in firearm homicides and assaults ($n = 395$ versus $n = 362$).

What these data suggest is that Advance Peace is reducing firearm homicides in the neighborhoods where gun violence is greatest and among the young, Black male population, the group most victimized by gun violence. For us, this means Advance Peace seems to be chipping away at the urban gun violence epidemic in the United States.

When we drill down further into these Advance Peace cities, the data are even more compelling about the impacts that the strategy is having toward eliminating the epidemic of urban gun violence.

In Fresno, we found there was a 30% reduction in firearm homicides and assaults in the July 2021 to June 2023 Peacemaker Fellowship period compared to the trends from 2014 through 2021 (figure 8.2). Also in Fresno, there was a 41.4% reduction in Black male firearm homicide victims between the ages of zero and thirty-four during this same Peacemaker Fellowship period, and a 77.8% reduction in firearm homicides among Black men under thirty-five years old living in the city's Southwest area, the most segregated and gun violent neighborhood.

The data analysis presented for Fresno includes using a statistical model called an interrupted time series. The goal of this analysis is to

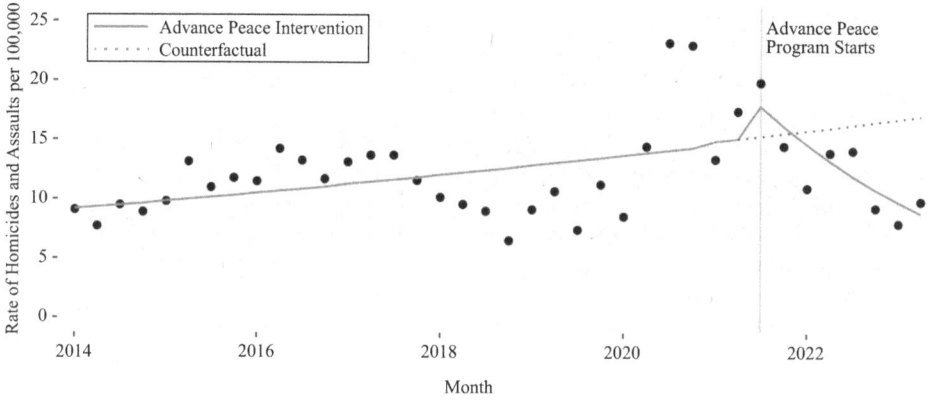

8.2 Interrupted time series analyses of Fresno gun homicides and assaults, 2014–2019.

evaluate whether there is a change in the level or trend of an outcome following an interruption. The study design is called an interrupted time series because the intervention is expected to "interrupt" the level or trend of the time series. The Fresno analysis above compares the trend in firearm homicides and assaults after the intervention with the projected trends, or the counterfactual. This is what the model predicts would happen should there be no interruption, or in this case, the Peacemaker Fellowship. The dots in figure 8.2 are the monthly rates of gun crimes, the solid line is the mean of these rates, and the dashed line is the counterfactual. The difference between the slope of the dashed and solid lines is the likely impact of the Peacemaker Fellowship.

We can also look at gun crime in Fresno by area along with Peacemaker Fellowship conflict mediations and street outreach engagements (figures 8.3 and 8.4). The heat maps below highlight the density of firearm homicides and nonfatal shootings in Southwest Fresno for the eighteen months before and eighteen months of the Peacemaker Fellowship. What these maps suggest is that gun violence is no longer highly concentrated in the segregated, largely Black Southwest neighborhood.

A CONCRETE PEACE IN RICHMOND

Richmond's Peacemaker Fellowship, which began in 2010, has contributed to a sustained low rate of firearm homicides and injury shootings, with a thirty-year low recorded in 2023 of 8 firearm homicides and 37

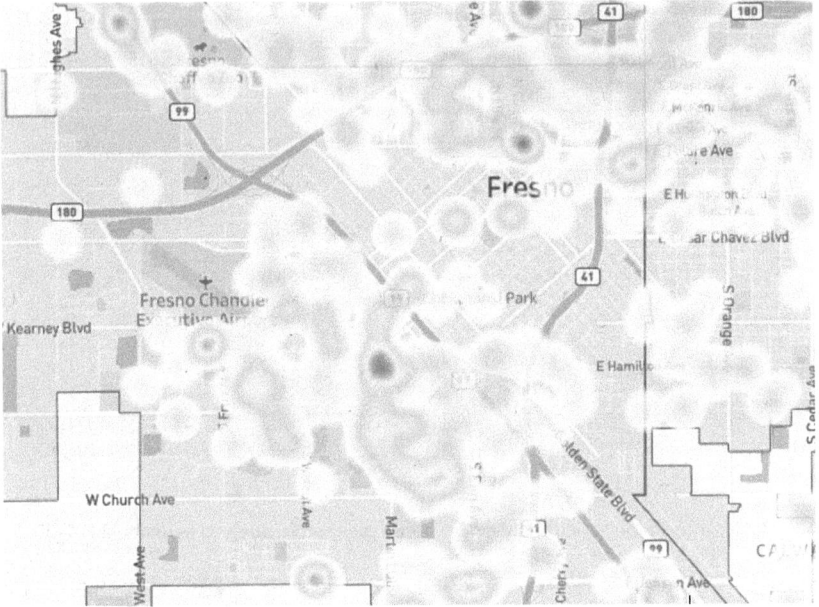

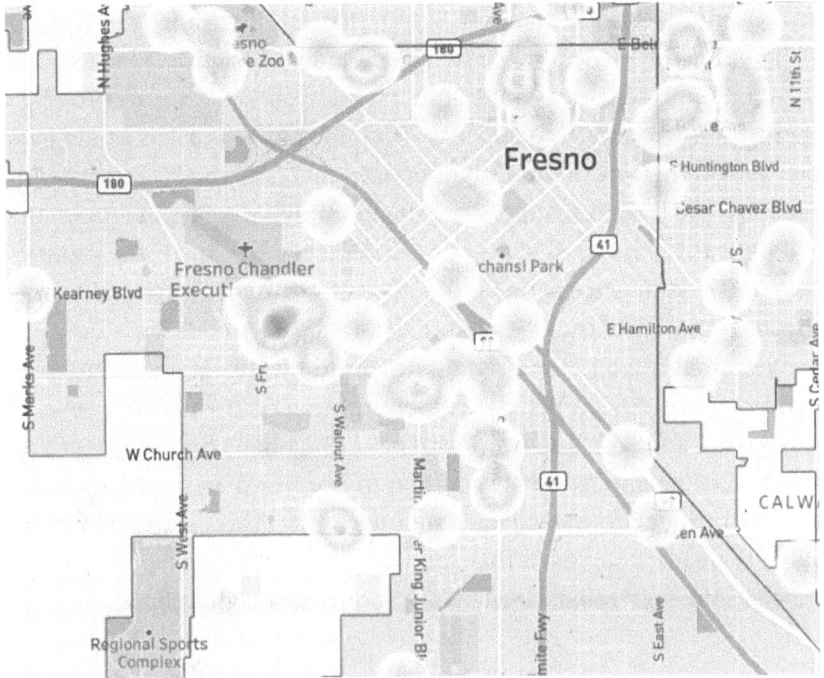

8.3 Southwest Fresno "heat map" of the density of gun violence before (2019–2020, above) and after the Peacemaker Fellowship (2021–2023, below).

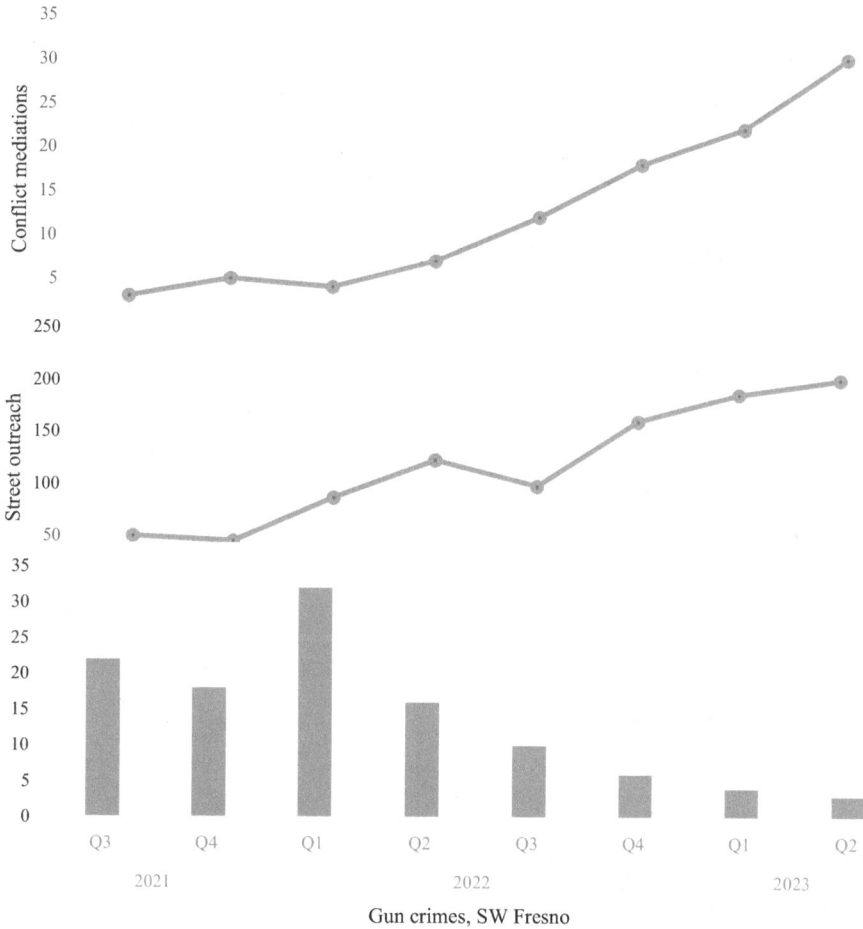

8.4 Peacemaker Fellowship quarterly street conflict mediations (top line), number of street outreach engagements (middle line,) and gun crimes (bottom bar chart) in Southwest Fresno, July 2021–June 2023.

shootings. From July 2016 through December 2023, Richmond has gone from averaging 5 firearm homicides a quarter to less than 2, a 60% reduction, and from averaging 34 shootings with an injury a quarter to averaging 11, a 74.6% reduction. During its most recent twenty-four-month Peacemaker Fellowship (July 2021–June 2023), Richmond had a 25% reduction in firearm homicides (24 versus 32) and a 12.5% reduction in injury shootings (140 versus 160) compared to the prior twenty-four

8.5 Richmond, California, density of firearm homicides, July 2019–June 2021 (above) and July 2021–June 2023 (below).

months (July 2019–June 2021). Moreover, 34.5% fewer men and 66.7% fewer women as well as 31.5% fewer Blacks and 50% fewer Latinos were killed by a firearm during this period, compared to the previous twenty-four months. Among the Peacemaker Fellowship's target population of eighteen- to twenty-four-year-olds, there was a 66.7% reduction in firearm homicides and 25% reduction in injury shootings. During this Peacemaker Fellowship, firearm homicides were cut by more than half, and about a third of the injury shootings occurred in the once most violent Richmond district, Central (figure 8.5).

What we are suggesting is that over a roughly fifteen-year period, the Peacemaker Fellowship in Richmond continues to reduce gun violence across the city in the most hard-hit neighborhoods and among the most impacted groups. It does not seem to have displaced gun crime to another part of the city. Over this same period, Richmond's overall life expectancy increased by almost eight years, poverty rates declined, and neighborhoods like Central, also called the Iron Triangle, saw a new influx of public and private sector development. Schools were rebuilt, parks and trees were planted, businesses opened, and housing values increased. How the Peacemaker Fellowship may have contributed to this "concrete peace" is what we explore in the next chapter.

9

HEALING PEOPLE TO HEAL PLACES

Brandon grew up in central Richmond. He was a good student and wanted to give back to his community. He found a job at a local community center with a program called Opportunity West. He didn't imagine working there for too long, but his plans changed one afternoon near the Nevin Center. A car drove by and gunfire rang out. Brandon was shot in the leg. He was bleeding badly and there was no time to waste. His friends picked him up off the street and drove him to the best trauma center, which is over twenty minutes away. In the emergency room, the surgeon told him that if he had arrived a minute or two later, he would have been dead.

As soon as Brandon got home from the hospital, NCAs from Richmond's ONS, visited him. They suspected he might be thinking of retaliating or be a target again by a crew from North Richmond that was "at war" with those from the Central neighborhood. Not long after, another young Black man from Central was shot and killed. Tensions were high, and Brandon settled into a job working at another nonprofit called Pogo Park, which focuses on community revitalization and at the time was redeveloping a park right next door to his house.

As Brandon was working at Pogo Park, one of his neighbors, Markel, returned to Richmond. Markel had left the neighborhood to avoid the violence, and as soon as he got back, the ONS also engaged with him, knowing he too had a target on his back and was close to Brandon. Soon

Markel was even busier than Brandon, working at Pogo Park during the mornings and going to ONS life skills classes in the evenings. He also worked with an NCA to get counseling and work on his job skills.

Months passed, and Brandon and Markel stayed out of harm's way. Still, an NCA from the ONS would roll by Elm Playlot where they were working and check in on them. If they needed anything or any conflicts arose, the NCAs let them know they were only a phone call away.

It's now more than seven years since Markel returned to Richmond. Both he and Brandon are still working full-time at the nonprofit Pogo Park. The park where they work has not only helped them but been revitalized by residents throughout the neighborhood as well. The peace that Brandon and Markel helped keep—along with their NCA mentors—has enabled dozens of residents to also work on revitalizing their neighborhood, particularly through Pogo Park. They redesigned the space, helped rebuild the park, and now program and maintain it. Their success has helped attract millions of reinvestment dollars to the community. Affordable housing for the elderly and a new school were built. Hundreds of homes have received free rooftop solar and energy efficiency upgrades, reducing their energy bills to zero. Many new community gardens have taken root along a former railway that is now the Richmond Greenway, and community residents work their land and grow food.

None of this would have happened if Brandon, Markel, and the north versus central Richmond turf war had escalated. As the former city manager of Richmond told us, "There is no doubt in my mind that as the city became more peaceful . . . community economic development and revitalization slowly took hold. When it was violent, we couldn't attract any investment and we were in significant debt. As it's been said, the peacekeepers of the ONS have helped deliver an economic 'peace dividend' to this city that is immeasurable."

A local media outlet described the change in Richmond as a "renaissance," stating,

A new spirit in city government has helped transform industry, the quality of life in the city, and Richmond's grim reputation. The city has undergone a facelift. Citizens are attending community meetings and events in unprecedented numbers, and new businesses—many of them green—are bringing economic opportunities back to town.

While other cities are desperately contending with debilitating budget deficits and struggling to maintain public safety and other basic services . . . the combined efforts of city departments and community members have resulted in meaningful reductions in violent crime. And the city has completed numerous civic and neighborhood revitalization projects that have given Richmond a new air of vitality and community health.[1]

THE PLACE EFFECTS OF VIOLENCE

Gun violence not only harms people but it kills the public realm too. When people live in fear, they do not bring their children to parks, they avoid civic life, and they turn their backs on neighbors. The lack of civic life can reverberate outside the community, especially when the media and real estate agents characterize a place as dangerous. A city's bond rating can go down, making it more expensive or impossible to borrow money that is essential to maintain life-supporting infrastructure. Roads and sidewalks do not get repaired, parks aren't maintained, and police, fire, and emergency medical services can be slower to respond or fear responding to some neighborhoods. Private sector investment, particularly small businesses, working-class jobs, and affordable housing, look for sites elsewhere.

At the same time, a community rife with gun violence will attract excessive policing and surveillance. Local police may ask their county, state, and federal agency partners to increase their presence as well as bring heavy-handed enforcement. Urban residents then not only lose civic life and economic opportunities but also tend to "gain" military-style policing along with racist strategies such as "broken windows" policing—which criminalizes small infractions like loitering and graffiti—and "stop-and-frisk" targeting.[2] Residents afraid of random gunfire then also deal with the fear of overzealous policing.

This was the case for Richmond in the early 2000s. Richmond was the ninth most violent city in the United States (in terms of gun homicides) in 2005, and had the highest prevalence of chronic illness and lowest life expectancy of any city in the San Francisco Bay Area at that time.[3] Life expectancy in Richmond's most impoverished neighborhood, called the Iron Triangle, was 71.2 years compared to an average of 80.3 in the Bay Area.[4] By 2010, 16.4% of Richmond's residents lived in poverty and the median household income was $54,012. That year in

Richmond's Iron Triangle neighborhood, 30% of Black residents were living in poverty and the median housing value was $154,618, less than half of that for the city as a whole. The health status of Richmond and Iron Triangle residents was also some of the worst in the Bay Area. According to the Contra Costa County Health Service agency in 2010, 22% of African American children in Richmond were hospitalized for asthma compared with less than 9% of white children; 32% of adults aged twenty to forty-four were obese, compared with 21% of similar Californians; and over 28% of residents reported their health as fair or poor, compared with only 16% of similar Californians.[5]

URBAN ACUPUNCTURE

How does a violent city like Richmond create peace and rebuild itself into a healthier place? We can look to Medellín, Colombia—once the world's most deadly cities for gun violence—for some insights. Medellín today is revered as a transformed city, not as the murder capital of the world. How did Medellín shift? In some ways, the same way Richmond has, through combining investments in people and places. Both Richmond and Medellín have focused in on the "hot people" and "underresourced" areas. We can think of these as the "pain points" in a city, or the people and challenging community issues that stymie human potential.

Brazilian architect Jaime Lerner called this approach to urbanism—where city and community together attempt to address the pain points, "urban acupuncture." Urban acupuncture is an idea practiced by Latin American architects and urbanists who were interested in ending the violence plaguing their cities.[6] These architects and planners mobilized both city leaders and community residents to cocreate solutions to the violence. The idea was that to "stop the pain," the city needed to prioritize the people and places hurting and suffering the most. Lerner described urban acupuncture as a way for cities and communities to heal, explaining,

I believe that some of the magic of medicine can and should be applied to cities, as many are sick and some nearly terminal. Just as good medicine depends on the interaction between doctor and patient, successful urban planning involves triggering healthy responses within the city, probing here and there to stimulate improvements and positive chain reactions. Intervention is all about revitalization, an indispensable way of making an organism function and change.[7]

Yet the city couldn't act alone, according to practitioners of urban acupuncture. Community members themselves, those experiencing the pains, needed to be leaders in identifying the projects as well as interventions that would be most helpful and healing.

Instead of large-scale redevelopment strategies, urban acupuncture focuses on a large number of small-scale interventions. These interventions can and must be done by local people, and they should be compensated for the interventions. Just like the needles used in acupuncture are targeted at specific points to relieve stress on the entire body and stimulate healing, a series of small-scale urban pins were proposed to change the violence in cities like Medellín.

Urban acupuncture was possible because in Medellín, like Richmond and many cities, the gun violence was highly concentrated among a small group of people and in certain neighborhoods, or *comunas* as they are called in Medellín. For example, in Comuna 1, also called Popular, residents dreamed of having a new library, an office that could incubate local businesses, and transportation that could travel up and down its steep hillsides. In another Medellín neighborhood, Comuna 13, or San Javier, youths wanted to use street art, music, and culture to reclaim the streets. They converted a water storage facility into a community center and came up with the idea of installing escalators to traverse the neighborhood's hills. Even neighborhood gangs, groups known as a *combo*, which were blamed for the gun violence were invited to generate so-called acupuncture projects. The city opened an office of planning and community development in these neighborhoods.

These ideas not only turned into actions. The mayor Medellín, Sergio Fajardo, also ran his campaign on a platform called "social urbanism." A key commitment of social urbanism was to not only invest in urban acupuncture projects but ensure they were the most beautiful and functional projects within the city too. Instead of new libraries, museums, schools, community centers, gardens, and other spaces being built in the downtown, Fajardo committed to placing them in the poorest, most violent communities. This idea became known as the "ethics of aesthetics." Medellín showed its poor and those suffering from violence that they mattered by not only listening to them but building its most beautiful projects in their communities as well.[8] One result of these efforts was that the murder rate plummeted in Medellín, and the city is no longer a place known for its gun violence.[9]

Richmond, without using the terms "urban acupuncture" and "social urbanism," took a similar path as Medellín toward peace and greater prosperity. Neither Medellín nor Richmond have eliminated gun violence, poverty, or inequality, as they are both works in progress. Nevertheless, there are lessons from Richmond for how cities and communities everywhere can turn people-focused peacemaking into a concrete peace of prosperity for all.

REORIENTING THE "FACE" OF CITY GOVERNMENT

Perhaps the first lesson from Richmond is the importance of rebuilding trust in local government. In gun-violent Richmond, residents had lost faith in the city's ability to deliver services, respond to their needs, and rein in a racist police department (as we described in chapter 2). There was no built environment project that could repair this trust. People needed to be placed into positions of power that were accountable to the community and responsive to their concerns. This is exactly what the ONS accomplished.

As a city office staffed by formerly incarcerated Black and Brown people from Richmond's neighborhoods, the ONS has literally reoriented the face of local government. Until the ONS was established and committed to hiring homegrown street outreach workers, most residents in Richmond's Black and Brown neighborhoods experienced only a dehumanizing, racist police department, or an unresponsive city council largely captured by big industry (Chevron operates a large petrochemical refinery in the city).[10] The ONS single-handedly changed who was seen as part of local government. Suddenly, familiar Black and Brown people were driving city-owned vehicles and presenting at city council meetings as staff, not just outside activists.

Residents started calling ONS staff when they had a question about a city service, not just a violence issue. Why? These were trusted and respected members of the community. NCAs have shared that families would even call them to accompany a young person walking to school or going to doctors' appointments. Residents trusted NCAs to keep the peace at local sporting events or barbecues. The ubiquitous presence and high-quality service that the ONS delivered changed how Richmond's residents viewed their own government, helping to stimulate a renewed interest by many who had written off the city as uninterested in their issues or neighborhoods.

This is a crucial and often overlooked step in revitalizing places: local government must reestablish its credibility with residents who have been ignored for far too long. Building fences, installing new lighting, or revitalizing a park without first rebuilding institutional credibility will not sustainably transform neighborhoods. This is because the place-based interventions will not be seen as by and with the community, and city institutions must be present to ensure these interventions are maintained for and beneficial to residents.

REBUILDING SAFETY WITH A PEOPLE-FIRST FOCUS

A violence intervention program is just one part of restoring the broader community. One of the first urban acupuncture programs in Richmond revolved around creating a new job pipeline for young people, most of whom had never participated in the workforce. In 2007, the city created a green jobs training program called RichmondBUILD. It was described as a complement to the work of the ONS since it would rely on some Peacemaker Fellows who were being mentored by the ONS to populate the program.[11]

Sal Vaca, the former director of the RichmondBUILD program, told us, "Nothing stops a bullet like a job." While we aren't convinced it is this simple, it was important that RichmondBUILD intentionally wanted to recruit and train justice-impacted young people from Richmond.[12] As Vaca put it,

Most of our students come from public housing or are formerly incarcerated. They are dealing with the same violence [that the] ONS encounters, but we can't handle the shooters like they can. Sure, our students have trauma, but we couldn't enroll guys who would come in here with guns. It threatened everybody. So without the ONS, we wouldn't be able to serve as many high-risk, formerly incarcerated people.

By 2022, RichmondBUILD had won numerous awards, and been recognized by organizations from the FBI to the US Green Building Council as a model program for helping to reduce violence and ensure low-income people of color get high-quality jobs along with access to the emerging green economy. Over a thousand people have graduated the program since it began, and 95% are receiving union-level wages, full benefits, and a pension. As one former participant shared,

My probation officer basically pointed me to this program. I'm from Central and never heard of it before. I like going there 'cause it is more peaceful than my neighborhood. I like the skills too, but for me it was learning about how to start a small business that got me. After the fires in Santa Rosa, we started a company repairing houses, fixing the community. Now I own a business, not just working for somebody else.

ATTRACTING CAPITAL AND JOBS

Former Richmond city manager Bill Lindsay reflected that one of his tasks when he took the position was to right a "sinking ship" in terms of Richmond's budget and tax base. A neighboring city called Vallejo became a national symbol of urban mismanagement when it declared bankruptcy, and Lindsay was committed to avoiding that scenario. He knew he needed to build the tax base and attract well-paying jobs, explaining,

I saw this city on the waterfront, with great infrastructure "bones" and a manufacturing history, in critical decline. The thing we had that few others in the Bay Area did was land near rail, highway, and port infrastructure. Yet our violent reputation was scaring investors away. What we also heard from residents was that we weren't capitalizing on the regions "foodie" culture.

A solution came from residents eager for jobs in the growing health food industry: create a special district near underutilized infrastructure and warehouses that incentivized food manufacturing and distribution. The city manager's office and planning department established a new land use district for food production and distribution. The food company Nutiva was one of the first to move in and develop a large food production facility. Others followed, and Richmond became the Bay Area's home to numerous industrial kitchens producing energy bars, cookies, and other products. The Artisan Kitchen company opened a commercial cooperative kitchen where caterers and cooking start-ups could come to use its facilities without the need for individual permits along with other challenges for food businesses. Blue Apron, which creates meal kits in a box and delivers them to households, moved into a Richmond warehouse in 2013, eventually hiring over a thousand employees.

Richmond's Rubicon Programs, a job training, placement, and housing support organization, was a leader in recruiting residents to access these new jobs. Rubicon also opened the Reentry Success Center in 2015 in the Iron Triangle neighborhood. This center aids folks coming home from incarceration with wraparound supports for housing, family services, employment, financial planning, mental health care, and legal aide. Ken Street, a former career coach at Rubicon, told us,

When ya'll [the ONS] started, say [in] 2006, businesses didn't want a Richmond address. Even if it was cheap rent and access, they didn't want Richmond on their letterhead. By 2014–2015, we were placing like three to four hundred people a year after these new companies "took a chance" and moved to Richmond. Then they heard from others it was safe and your employees wouldn't get shot.

By 2017, the special district had attracted over five thousand new, well-paying jobs, and included such companies as Galaxy Deserts, Urban Remedy, Blue Apron, Hello Fresh, UPS, Whole Foods, and Amazon.[13]

REBUILDING A ONCE DEADLY NEIGHBORHOOD

Urban acupuncture in Richmond also included resident-led redevelopment. Brandon's mother, Carmen, and his Aunt Tonie were tired of the bloodshed in their neighborhood, especially in a park next to their house in the Iron Triangle called Elm Playlot. The playground was overrun with drug dealers and violence. Carmen and Tonie pulled together other neighbors, such as Ms. Mason and Eddie, to form the Elm Playlot Action Committee. They surveyed residents, took pictures of boarded-up housing and the dilapidated park, and pressured the city to help them. They were joined by newcomer Toody Maher, and together they founded a new nonprofit called Pogo Park. The mission of Pogo Park was to create safe, beautiful, and function public space in the Iron Triangle.[14]

The Pogo Park group used its own resources to take back Elm Playlot. The participants occupied it day and night. They built new play structures and spaces with input from other residents. Pogo Park employee James Anderson, who lives across the street from Elm Playlot, remarked that "we needed to see and feel what the new space might be like. When people said they wanted a tree somewhere, we went out and got a tree in a five-gallon bucket and put it there. We wanted to see what it might be like before we finalized the plan."

Pogo Park started working with the city to obtain resources and permission to redesign the public park. Residents wanted things city planners had never told them could occur in an urban park, like a zip line, healing garden, petting zoo for kids, kitchen, and public bathroom. The city had never built or contracted to build any public parks with these amenities. Pogo Park did not balk. The group worked with the city to gain permission to build the park the way residents wanted it. Members wrote grants with the city's support for resources and obtained private donations. Pogo Park also convinced local artists, most of whom had never met residents and remained behind locked doors for many years, to open up their studios to the neighborhood.

Moreover, a partnership was built between the nonprofit, local businesses, and studios to train residents in construction and design skills. This way, local people would be able to not just design their new park but build and maintain it too. A few ONS Fellows such as Markel were even hired by Pogo Park as part of its teen "All Stars" team. Still an employee today, Markel helped survey other youths about needed park amenities and learned construction skills as a teen All Star.

Anderson and other Iron Triangle residents began reconstructing Elm Playlot, including building the play equipment, a fence, and wooden benches, and welding a new climbing structure. Maher underscored that "this is a one-of-a-kind place. Local people designed and built it. Its beauty is in the materials, and that people see themselves in this park and their labor, every day. They also earned living wages and continue to earn as we maintain and build out the park."

Pogo Park eventually built a small office on-site at Elm Playlot, which included that bathroom and kitchen. Today, Pogo Park has daily programming for kids and adults, and distributes over nine thousand free meals each year to residents. Over fifteen thousand children visit Elm Playlot each year, with about twice as many adults as either chaperones or visitors themselves.

As one marker of how safe people felt in this new space, Lee stated that parents started just "dropping their kids off at the park since they trusted us so much to take care of them. That was unheard of before we did all of this." Pogo Park employed about 120 residents for some period of time between 2009 and 2019. The now full-time staff of twelve people make over $20 per hour with full health and other benefits. According to Maher, Pogo Park had paid out over $1.5 million in total wages and small contracts all to community residents during this time.

One youth account of the park revealed the complementary roles the ONS and Pogo Park can play in supporting healing. The young person's photo and accompanying narrative about it appear below:

I see a picture of the creek in the park. It symbolizes peacefulness, and it shows that there is a place in the community just to sit down, chill, and take a breath. This is important to me because everyone needs a space to just sit and think, or to relax in peacefulness; even if it's not being used, it's good to know it's there. This is like this because the Pogo Park team was thinking of others who might be stressed or would just need a spot to relax. If I was in charge, I would make more spaces like this for people to relax in with more shade.

Lindsay reflected,

We had no idea that the transformation of that little park in the Iron Triangle could lead to such a big change there and across the city. We had more parents from there coming to meetings, more people demanding policy changes. Young people from there went on to be leaders. People from around the region, even

9.1 Picture of Elm Playlot, Richmond, California.

the country, come to see Pogo Park now because the transformation of the place and people has been nothing short of remarkable.

Projects like Pogo Park were possible because Brandon, Markel, and others—working with the ONS—helped keep the peace. There are and continue to be shootings in central Richmond, even near Pogo Park. The Iron Triangle neighborhood, however, is increasingly recognized for its innovative park and how it is helping residents heal from stress, not just for its violent past.[15] Peace work there and in other Richmond neighborhoods has also indirectly spurred on added city as well as state support.

INVESTING FROM THE INSIDE OUT

Urban acupuncture projects in the Iron Triangle and elsewhere have attracted new investment from outside the city. The California Endowment, the state's largest foundation, selected Richmond as one site for its Building Healthy Communities program. Dozens of Richmond's community groups and the city received about $50 million over ten years from the TCE program.[16]

A new youth-focused community group was also created in response to the violence in Richmond and has played an important role as a partner in keeping the peace in the city. The RYSE youth center opened in 2008 to aid young people who were looking for trauma supports in response to gun violence near Richmond High School.[17] RYSE quickly grew from just offering a safe space for youths to providing them with professional counseling, building youth leadership, and a nationally recognized arts and media program.

The RYSE approach to community development is much like the ideal of urban acupuncture in that it is healing focused, centered on those experiencing trauma to help them become leaders and transforming the city through transforming young people. RYSE claims,

We envision strong, healthy, united communities where equity is the norm and violence is neither desired nor required, creating a strong foundation for future generations to thrive. A time and place where youth have opportunities to lead, to dream, and to love. Towards this vision, RYSE creates safe spaces grounded in social justice for young people to love, learn, educate, heal, and transform lives and communities.[18]

RYSE and the ONS continue to collaborate with and complement one another. Their most recent joint project is investing in what they call building "beloved community" in the spirit of MLK. Yet the presence of the ONS remains instrumental in their success, and we would argue, many social and built environment initiatives in Richmond. As RYSE cofounder and executive director Kanwarpal Daliwal put it,

> If they [the ONS] didn't exist, we would be dealing with the police more regularly and working more on helping young people avoid being system impacted. We have the counselors who know how to relate to these young people and even the ONS outreach workers. But there are just some youths who we aren't prepared to or don't have the lived experience on staff to deal with. They [the ONS] are crucial for supporting those folks. If they didn't, none of this would be possible. Some of these projects, parks, and programs wouldn't likely be here, or might be shut down by now.

A FORMAL CITY COMMITMENT TO HEALING

In 2014, with the support of numerous community groups, Richmond became the first city in the United States to adopt a Health in All Policies ordinance.[19] This law committed every city agency to include programs focused on promoting greater health equity and healing into their budget as well as daily work. The city manager described it as "city services through the prism of health." The local ordinance made explicit that the city and its community-based partners were dedicated to institutionalizing a healing approach to health and community improvement.

Health in All Policies includes specific strategies for reducing and eliminating community-based toxic stressors while tracking progress toward stress reduction. The strategy guides the city's partnerships with community groups, and created an interdepartmental group within the city manager's office to coordinate healing and wellness within the city.[20] This is unique because Richmond does not have a health department. The city relies on the county for its public health services. Yet the city's Health in All Policies ordinance identifies how local government can be a leader in promoting community health, healing, and public safety.

TOWARD A HEALTHIER CITY

Walking down the Richmond Greenway near a new park project called Harbour-8, Brandon reflected on his journey and changes in his neighborhood:

I mean before, I wouldn't even be seen walkin' here. I'd likely be dead. If gun violence doesn't go down, this park, this garden, this playground, that new school and clinic, none of it is here today. I remember they installed new street-lights on Macdonald Ave to create a new vibe, like it was an old downtown or something. What happened there? Nothing. Why? Because nobody from around here was involved. It was like they say, "Puttin' lipstick on a pig."

What you see here, my life today, is possible because this city invested first in making peace with the kids who were pushing the violence. I mean some of 'em were my friends back in the day. It don't just matter what the data say, Black people who left this neighborhood want to come back every day. They want to have their kids play here. They be coming from Antioch just for that. That don't happen if the shootings didn't stop.

10

URBAN GUN VIOLENCE PREVENTION POLICY

It isn't enough to talk about peace. One must believe in it. And it isn't enough to believe in it. One must work at it.
—Eleanor Roosevelt

As long as we refuse to address fully the place of love in struggles for liberation we will not be able to create a culture of conversion where there is a mass turning away from an ethic of domination.
—bell hooks, "Love as the Practice of Freedom"

On Friday, September 22, 2023, President Joe Biden established and launched the first ever White House Office of *Gun* Violence Prevention.[1] This new office is aimed at implementing executive and legislative action, including the historic bipartisan Safer Communities Act signed by Biden to end the scourge of gun violence in the United States. We are excited about the promise that this office holds in helping to reduce gun violence in our most impacted communities. We are also cautiously optimistic that this new tool is more than a political consideration. For this office to achieve its full promise, it must provide an equal amount of attention and resources to the retaliatory gun violence happening in Black and Brown communities in the United States as it will surely provide for those impacted by mass shootings in this country.

Signs of federal interest had already occurred. In June 2021, DeVone spent about ninety minutes with Biden at the White House. It was an intimate affair in the Roosevelt Room with some on the White House Domestic Policy Council staff, Attorney General Merrick Garland, and about five or six other government and CVI leaders. The president appeared to be genuinely interested in knowing what it would take strategically to significantly reduce gun violence beyond the traditional policing approach in urban communities. At the same time, however, POTUS was committed to making sure more resources were available for policing. In fact, some in the administration were concerned about an interview request that DeVone had received from Dana Bash of CNN just before the meeting. The worry was over his potential public reaction to how much money would be earmarked for policing in communities of color to address the gun violence happening there with these new resources.

The president and his administration would be strongly encouraging states, counties, and city governments to use the millions of America Rescue Plan Act resources he'd helped bring to the table for policing and CVI services. The challenge for most of us within the CVI space was not that police would be included in the funding allocations but instead the gross disparity of the proposed investment between the two avenues. We weren't surprised by the administration's approach, though. There hasn't been a single president in our lifetime who hasn't invested big money into the institution of policing.

Many in the public hoped that because of the impact of the "Ferguson Effect" and murder of George Floyd, things would be different.[2] The social justice momentum from these experiences generated the "Defund the Police" mantra, which had many believing that a tipping point moment in US history around policing investment was near.[3] Albeit as important and impactful as these experiences and voices proved to be during that period, they weren't strong enough to reduce the policing investment footprint. We believe that law enforcement is a crucial part of local and national communities. Yet strategies revolving around law enforcement do not represent CVI, even if a significant reengineering and reimagination of the institution's roles and functions in Black and Brown communities impacted by gun violence is necessary for CVI to ultimately thrive as well as survive.

To say that overhauling policing within our most impacted communities should happen would be an understatement. Year after year, investments in policing are a robust portion of the city's budget in those cities where gun violence is most prevalent. And year after year, gun violence takes the lives of many Black and Brown bodies in the same small pockets within the same communities in those cities. In these same communities, clearance rates for gun crimes are often low—under 40%. That means someone has over a 60% chance of escaping prosecution for a suspected act of gun violence. Under these circumstances, victims may feel incentivized to enact street justice toward their enemies as a way of holding a shooter accountable. In other words, law enforcement doesn't do much to prevent gun violence when it comes to deterring our most active offenders. As an institution, it lacks the requisite cache of extensive positive relationships, trust, cultural competence, integrity, and legitimate authority within these communities, particularly with those at the center of gun violence.

It was during this meeting at the White House and thereafter at dinner with some of the White House staff where we began to hear concerns the administration had about the hard fights to come from both sides of the political aisle to get the proposed as well as additional resources approved, out the door, and into the impacted communities. One concern was about CVI programs and organizations. Most inside and outside the CVI field understood that the community-based infrastructure to work with the proposed federal resources was limited. The Biden administration was worried that if it secured the resources, the dollars might not be effectively harnessed by CVI organizations and practitioners. The fact is that today, the CVI field remains far from where we need it to be to successfully administer billions in federal resources and be effective in doing so. But the catch-22 is that these very federal resources are critical to further establish and expand the field, and achieve the promise that the Advance Peace initiative has experienced. In addition, such funds would allow local governments (city and county) to create and nurture new offices of peacemaking within their jurisdictions, rather than within law enforcement, increasing accountability to the public as a regular function of municipal practice.

URBAN OFFICES OF GUN VIOLENCE PREVENTION

There are now more than sixty OVPs inside local and/or county governments around the country employing over 550 staff members.[4] As with the new White House office, most developed because of American Recovery Plan Act funds along with local community demand that something more and different be done to reduce the gun violence terrorizing its poorest neighborhoods.

Among the positives are that few OVPs exist within police departments, typically residing instead in the mayor's office or other government departments; this creates an infrastructure geared toward public safety that uses less invasive interventions, promotes prevention, and emphasizes healthy behaviors and communities. This is also a win because the work of CVI is too important, too difficult to sustain, and too essential for reparative justice for it to solely sit in a nonprofit organization. OVPs can be overly reliant on private philanthropy for their survival, despite the numerous challenges faced by a violence intervention program within local government.

As cofounder and now cochair of the National Office of Violence Prevention Network, DeVone has a bird's-eye view of these government-housed CVIs. Some of the challenges we are concerned about include that most new OVPs are being asked to prevent and intervene on all types of violence, not just on the gun violence for which most were created to address. Most OVPs are not being provided the requisite resources needed to meet the demands of these broad mandates, and our concern is that gun violence prevention may get lost or at best become a tertiary objective.

Having the word "gun" within the White House description of its violence prevention focus is smart, providing a clear mandate along with a clear path to evaluate its effectiveness. Local OVPs that have come into existence because of enduring gun violence should follow this course. And cities that consider establishing an OVP should include such a concerted effort within their local public safety policy, plan, and budget. Beyond including the word "gun" in the OVP's name, cities must make it policy to adopt similar approaches to what we have described here for Advance Peace: hiring formerly incarcerated community residents as violence interrupters and credible mentors, focusing on shooters as well as offering them wraparound healing supports and social services, and many other Peacemaker Fellowship components. This work should receive dedicated annual resources from a city's general fund and be viewed as a permanent addition to city governance, much like we now do with law enforcement, fire, public works, and parks and recreation.

CONSIDERING MORE THAN (JUST) GUN RESTRICTION POLICIES

The 2022 US Supreme Court *Bruen* ruling overturned a long-standing restriction on the public's ability to carry a firearm in New York State. This case seems to be casting doubt on local gun control laws across the United States, as an analysis in a 2023 *Duke Law Journal* article suggests.[5] The backlash could involve greater restrictions on who can carry firearms. While we support policies that take guns out of the hands of those who are unstable and mentally ill, increasingly restrictive gun access policies are unlikely to do much to reduce urban gun violence in Black and Brown communities.

Our home state of California is a case in point. *Everytown for Gun Safety* ranked California as number one in the country for gun law strength in 2022, and the state had the eighth-lowest rate of gun deaths and sixth-lowest rate of gun ownership.[6] Yet 30.6% of homicide victims in California were Black in 2013, and this was the same percentage in 2022.[7] The number of white homicide victims decreased from 21.2% in 2013 to 16.6% in 2022. In Oakland, a city with a large proportion of African Americans, gun homicide rates have remained relatively unchanged for over twenty years from 2003 to 2022. In fact, Oakland's most significant reductions in gun violence over the last twenty years were between 2013 to 2018, and are widely attributed to an intensive community-driven gun violence interruption strategy, not gun access laws.[8]

Some gun access restriction laws, however, do seem to be working in already violent neighborhoods. Extreme risk protection order laws, intended to keep guns away from people who demonstrate threatening behaviors and have violated laws related to firearm use, are largely aimed at preventing suicides and mass shooting.[9] In California, extreme risk protection orders are called gun violence restraining orders, and they authorize civil courts to temporarily prohibit the purchase as well as possession of firearms and ammunition by persons who exhibit dangerous or threatening behaviors, have or could have access to a firearm, and are not subject to an existing firearm prohibition.[10] While California's gun violence restraining order law has been in effect for almost a decade and nineteen states now have similar policies, implementation has been slow. More to the point, recent studies suggest that these restrictions are barely reducing suicides while increasing arrests of existing gun owners, and not having *any* impact on urban gun violence.[11]

If the concern is with what cities and counties can do to reduce and eliminate gun violence, consider that cities tend to spend a majority of their budgets on "public safety," which turns out to be mostly policing. In some cities, more than half of the budget goes to policing. As we've argued here, those expenditures tend to hire more cops and add more military-style weapons to the officers, despite little evidence that this reduces gun homicides in urban communities of color. There is ample evidence, though, that overpolicing disproportionately arrests and incarcerates Blacks, which only exacerbates racist inequities, trauma, and bodily dehumanization, which in turn can lead to more gun violence.

WHY PEACEMAKING AND PEACEKEEPING WITHIN LOCAL GOVERNMENT?

Today, a model like Advance Peace can only be sustained when it is institutionalized into city or county government as another natural part of the public safety, planning, and community health promotion toolbox. The pathway to greater community peace is using a public health approach to healing that also catalyzes community development. This is our model of neurourbanism. We recognize the many potential challenges institutionalizing CVI in local government will face—from empowering leadership, to political, economic, cultural acceptance, and more issues. Among the upsides are an opportunity to create a new policy field that will increase the professionalization, accountability, and ultimately impact of CVI.

A dual opportunity and challenge is defining what CVI ought to look like inside city government but outside law enforcement. There are promising models in addition to Advance Peace that have demonstrated a commitment to helping heal those at the center of gun violence, and they are working in multiple communities, including the Health Alliance for Violence Intervention, Cure Violence, Community Based Public Safety Collective, Newark Community Street Team, Brotherhood United for Independent Leadership through Discipline, and Roca.[12] A review of CVI by Cities United suggested that a combination of street violence interruption, cognitive behavioral support, youth/perpetrator mentorship and service delivery, hospital-based violence intervention, and place-based investments could be combined in an urban policy to prevent gun violence.[13]

A similar review of research on programs known to reduce community violence without relying on police pointed to seven strategies that ought to be integrated into policy, including place-based interventions, strengthening antiviolence social norms and peer relationships, engaging and supporting youths, reducing substance abuse, mitigating financial stress, reducing the harmful effects of the justice process, and reducing access to guns.[14] These reports also underscore that policies must be multipronged and integrate strategies, rather than lacking discernment in their approach to gun violence prevention.

PROFESSIONALIZATION AND THERAPY SUPPORT OF STREET OUTREACH

A second challenge is to develop a way of demonstrating the competence of violence intervention outreach workers. That would involve a mechanism to certify/license and professionalize the credible messenger / street outreach worker / violence interrupter job, so cities know who to hire, how to train them, and how to support their personal and professional development. A select few in the CVI space are receiving any professional certification along with ongoing credentialing credits/education. We suggest there is a need to further develop and professionalize this workforce, identifying pathways for formerly incarcerated people to return to their communities as wounded healers and continue to acquire the skills to interrupt gun violence while also delivering healing-centered supports to traumatized folks in their communities to prevent gun violence.

It's clear from NCAs that many understand this need. Take the current head of Richmond's ONS, Sam, who shared that he "wanted to soak up every new opportunity and skill the organization was throwing at me." He continued,

I was always like, "How different would my life be if I had something like this at the age where I was going through pain and suffering?" We all flowers, just some of us didn't get watered or worse got pissed on. Every single youngster who we working with, what they got and dealing with, we got the same shit inside us. Every one of us. Seeing yourself in that youngster, that is motivation. You go out there every day not knowing, but hoping, you gonna make a difference.

Furthermore, professionalization within the CVI space will help keep the public safe by establishing clear accountability standards and guidelines for gun violence interruption work. This should include the development of codes of conduct, ethical guidelines, and protocols to ensure responsible and accountable interventions. CVI must create certification opportunities within this process that will enable the workforce to demonstrate its competence and adherence to professional standards.

This will also demand an expansion of programs within prisons for self-discovery, healing, and conflict resolution, such as the VOEG, run by the Insight Prison Project that James Houston and others took advantage of while in San Quentin prison. There is a need for more of these programs, and more of them that are directly connected to community-based violence prevention efforts, as part of the suite of reentry services that should be offered to those coming home.[15]

We have shared previously that street outreach workers can be retraumatized themselves in this work, so the professionalization needs to be attentive to and include support for them too.[16] Folks returning home from prison (and jail) may have more trauma than when they went in, even while acquiring violence de-escalation, cognitive behavioral therapy, and mentoring skills. A local CVI policy must commit to supporting the entire reentry process for those they might hire, from housing to family supports. As the field becomes more professionalized, and CVI training becomes more learner centered and performance based, the outreach workers must be fairly and justly compensated for their work as well as have opportunities for professional advancement. This includes the same or greater benefits offered to other civil service job titles, from medical benefits for the worker and their family, to employment protections offered by unions, to disability and retirement programs. As cities create gun violence prevention policies, they will need a steady and highly skilled workforce to fill those jobs, and those workers must be compensated and offered traditional supports, such as long-term benefits and continuing education opportunities.

SECURITY OF AND QUALITY EMPLOYMENT

In order to hire street savvy outreach workers, employment policies and norms in cities that restrict the hiring of former felons must be eliminated. Most of the credible messengers needed for this workforce are people who have been convicted of crimes and spent years in prison, but did important self-healing work while incarcerated. Too many governments refuse to hire those with a record. Some local governments have adopted "ban-the-box" policies that do not require former felons to check a box indicating their prior convictions; we are suggesting that this information should be viewed as an asset in the first place rather than a liability.

Instead of making job requirements based on years of formal education, degrees, and prior work experience, local governments will need to create job classifications that reward, for example, in-prison received certifications, knowledge of or experience in street groups, experience navigating juvenile hall, and having been a recipient of certain social services.

NCAs, though, are often aware of the resistance to their presence in traditional civic spaces. ONS leader Sam, whose training included early certification through a violence interruption class at a Richmond community college, shared some of what he's experienced:

Some of those classes and D really, brought us into spaces we'd never been or thought we'd ever go. We were talking to the city manager, attorney, and police chief. We were in rooms we probably didn't belong in, but we were there. We listened and learned. We shared our experience. That exposure was critical for learning that this shit is as much political as anything else. City leaders likely don't value you, where you came from, or maybe what you do, but they got to see something different. You learn that street work needs to be supported from within government and not undermined by it, especially by the police, which was what was happening.

TRANSPARENCY AND ACCOUNTABILITY

As alluded to earlier, creating a local policy that institutionalizes CVI into government will increase its transparency and public accountability.

When CVI sits only in nonprofits, volunteer, or philanthropy-funded initiatives, there are fewer demands and requirements of public transparency. When DeVone ran the ONS and a shooting occurred, for instance, he would hear almost immediately from community residents, the city manager, elected officials, and the local media, and would have to respond publicly as to why this was still occurring. The public scrutiny by citizens and regular skeptics on the city council kept him and his team constantly working to improve their craft, remain curious, stay accountable, be disciplined, and remain on task. Nonprofit community-based organizations and programs do not, and most likely never will, face the same level of scrutiny and accountability checks.

A BUDGET LINE ITEM

If CVI within government is going to be scrutinized and held accountable, then it must also be allowed time to achieve the results, which we have demonstrated can take years. The Richmond ONS is successful in large part because the city did not shut it down after a spike in gun crime in the second and third year of its existence. Once a city commits to this work, it must see it through for at least a decade. This is a reasonable, minimal commitment, especially after the decades of disinvestment and neglect by local government that have contributed to our gun violence epidemic. This means creating a line item in the annual budget, funding an adequate number of outreach and support staff, and ensuring there are resources for the supports, services, referrals, and other essential elements of the strategy for participants as well as outreach staff.

Long-term hiring and pay could be linked to ongoing professional development criteria, much like other professions have continuing education credit requirements. This will create a demand for qualified trainers and even the creation of academic-based training.

PARTNERSHIPS AND SERVICE PROVIDERS

Adequately supporting violence intervention work requires expanding a city's local partnerships, including with schools and credible service providers. CVI should be invited into primary, middle, and high schools impacted by gun violence, while being viewed as an integral part of behavioral and community health systems. A city's CVI program should also be partnered with organizations that support inclusive and healthy urban planning, parks and recreation, housing, and more, all committed to rebuilding the social and physical infrastructure that can help maintain true peace. CVI in government may more easily get into public settings where we can reach and engage a potential "future Fellow" before they fit the criteria for the Fellowship. In government, moreover, CVI can leverage its influence to hold service providers and supportive programs accountable in ways a nonprofit cannot. Contracting with a service provider for the Fellows using government procurement practices will demand more from those claiming to offer supportive services. As the outreach workers become more professionalized as well as recognized professions, they may be able to more easily connect and collaborate with other certified professionals, be they social workers, counselors, teachers, coaches, CHWs, and others.

We also recognize that there are incredibly skilled and effective counselors, educators, healers, and antiviolence practitioners who may never choose to pursue the demands of working within a government setting. Yet these folks are essential for some of the strategies, referrals, and services included within the Peacemaker Fellowship. Thus even when embedded within government, CVI must have the flexibility to secure services, training, and counseling from unconventional providers often grounded in the local community, and not be solely bound by the rules of government procurement This can ensure that CVI programs can utilize all available locally and culturally competent supports for their "unconventional" clientele.

EVALUATION AND EVIDENCE BUILDING

Having CVI within government means it will be subject to increased reporting, evaluation, and monitoring of intervention impacts. Currently, there is inconsistency among CVI programs about whether and how to evaluate participants, limited reporting of the dosage or services clients receive, almost no evaluation of what happens to outreach workers throughout the intervention, and scant attention to following participants after exiting the program. There is no agreed-on method for evaluating the impacts of CVI on gun homicides and injury shootings either, making it difficult to refine processes in this field of intervention.

Some CVI programs do not use longitudinal gun crime data, and instead have relied on general homicide and violent crime incidents as more readily available indicators to track. Other programs measure impacts by comparing districts or neighborhoods that received the intervention with those that did not. Still others use statistical models to generate a control group if one does not exist or wasn't designed into the intervention strategy. And other evaluations aim to measure the influence of their program on gun violence among "group-involved" people, otherwise known as gangs, or community perceptions of safety.

Not only is there no agreement within the field of CVI over what the "correct" way is to evaluate these initiatives, few include the voices of the participants or outreach staff. As we hope you now understand, these qualitative data can be as or more important for understanding the influences as well as impacts of a CVI initiative, and could be required by government programs.

POLICE ACCOUNTABILITY TOO

While we hope government institutionalization will help clarify the types of evidence that provide a holistic accounting of the impacts of CVI, we also think this process can contribute to increased accountability for police departments when reporting on their role in reducing gun crime. Police are rarely, if ever, held accountable to prove their impact or even produce evaluations showing causal "evidence" in the ways CVI programs are now expected to do. Police rarely quantitatively demonstrate that what they did was in part or more often solely responsible for any change in gun crime.

We experienced this firsthand during our evaluation of Advance Peace, including its Fresno strategy. The team at the University of California at Berkeley generated a data-sharing agreement in 2019 with the Fresno Police Department, specifying exactly which criminal codes and data fields were needed for gun crime analysis. After this agreement was signed, the police department began sharing monthly gun crime data.

Only after a few months did the University of California team start notic-
ing that there were regular errors and omissions in the data the police
were sharing, such as leaving off victim information or address loca-
tion. In some cases, there were repeat entries for shootings. We asked
the Fresno Police Department for clarification, but were rarely given any
explanation. We were frequently left to analyze these data with many
outstanding uncertainties.

After the first year of the Advance Peace Fresno intervention, gun crime
had declined from previous years. Our analysis also showed a significant
reduction in Black male gun homicide victims, particularly in the racially
segregated Southwest district of Fresno. When our research team released
these draft findings, the Fresno police requested a private meeting with the
Advance Peace Fresno team. There, the police disputed our findings and
distributed a paper version of their own analyses of firearm homicides in
the city, including the number of Black male victims. The police, however,
didn't let anyone in the meeting leave with a copy of this paper report.

The Advance Peace Fresno staff proceeded to file a Freedom of Information Act request with the city to obtain the police department's paper
report. Before the city responded to the request, there was a city council
meeting and our research team presented specific examples to the public of how the Fresno police had omitted information in the data they
shared and these data seemed to be riddled with errors too. The next day,
the Fresno deputy police chief drove to our office at the University of
California at Berkeley to share their paper report with us. We reconciled
the missing data and reran our analyses.

The data dispute made clear to elected officials and members of the
public that they rarely had any information that could hold the police
accountable when they presented their crime findings. When we showed
the police's sloppy data sharing on a slide for the public and media to
review, the police quickly realized they were now subject to a new type
of accountability. The data the Fresno Police Department shared after the
meeting with us was on time and accurate, and the police began reporting more regularly to the public about shootings and how many firearm
homicide cases had been closed.

DIVERSIFIED FUNDING SOURCES

Finally, when local governments create CVI infrastructure, there will be greater opportunities for state and federal funding. The Biden administration strongly encouraged state, county, and local governments to use millions of approved American Recovery Plan Act resources for CVI along with $5 million within the proposed Build Back Better Act for CVI.[17] Nevertheless, little of the American Recovery Plan Act money went to CVI and instead went to police departments.[18] The $5 billion promised for community gun violence prevention in the Build Back Better Policy never materialized.[19]

In 2025, the future of federal funding for Community Violence Intervention (CVI) remains uncertain. We imagine private philanthropy will need to play a much larger role re-investing their wealth into community peacemaking. While CVI has been chronically under-funded given its vital role in public safety, a set of diverse programs over the previous few years reveal the types of public financial supports that are necessary. For example, in 2023, Department of Justice grant programs for CVI allocated over $76 million to thirty-three different projects through the Office of Justice Programs Community Based Violence Intervention and Prevention Initiative.[20] The state of California has one of the largest sources of annual public dollars for implementing CVI at the local level (not exclusively for governments) through its Violence Intervention and Prevention program of the Board of State and Community Corrections.[21] This program issues approximately $9 million per year to cities, counties, and nonprofits across the state, and in 2021 alone provided $200 million. Recently, the California legislature passed a tax on ammunition sales that will also go toward permanently funding CVI programs.[22] And the potential for paying violence interrupters and mentors as part of Medicaid is an increasing possibility. Hurdles will include certifying these community outreach workers, getting a clinician to refer their clients, and "proving" that their interventions deliver specified health services.[23]

A NEW CIVIC FACE TO REBUILD PUBLIC TRUST

Another important step is building community awareness of the CVI apparatus that a city puts in place. Doing so can help reorient the face of government for those in Black communities whose previous engagements with government have only been through the police, or overwhelmed and underfunded welfare agencies. It is no small thing to have community members see people from their own community driving city-owned vehicles and doing positive, uplifting things for the most disconnected people. Through these credible government actors, we may be able to rebuild trust in local government as well as the process of reinvigorating government to truly be by and for the people.

11

SUSTAINING URBAN PEACE

This book has been about how to end urban gun violence through the healing of those traumatized and investing in a new permanent workforce of peacekeepers. We have offered our experience and evidence of the Advance Peace's CVI strategy. We are driven by the reality that the absence of violence is not the presence of peace. We seek peace for all of our urban communities impacted for far too long by gun violence. Here, we summarize what we believe is necessary to not just deliver urban peace but sustain it too, along with the specific needs and roles for CVI. We suggest twelve related strategies that are essential for advancing peace.

1. DECLARE AND RESOURCE A NATIONAL COMMITMENT TO ENDING URBAN GUN VIOLENCE

The United States' gun violence problem is multidimensional, and each dimension should be given explicit attention. Ending the gun violence impacting young Black and Brown men of color must be prioritized as well as resourced in ways that it hasn't been in our country's history. Biden's White House Office of Gun Violence Prevention, the Department of Justice's investment in CVIs, and the Centers for Disease Control and health departments seeing this issue as a public health crisis is a good start. Yet a sustained all-hands-on-deck that includes significantly more resource investments from our states, counties, and city general fund coffers, like those made with federal American Recovery Plan Act resources in cities such as Baltimore and Indianapolis, is a step that must be taken, and taken again and again until we meet the moment. A national and sustained communications campaign centered on reducing gun violence in the United States is essential.

Part of this outreach can help address the fact that little is known about CVI among communities that most need this strategy, not to mention most of the voting population. A broader public must become aware of this important work along with its demonstrated power and effectiveness to reduce gun violence.

We believe that such a campaign must be national in scope, and could embody the cadence of the tobacco-free and seat belt campaigns of the past, which included strategic media messaging, public education, legislation, lawsuits, research, community advocacy, pressure on the private sector, and use of emerging technologies. These campaigns took the long game and built a strategic approach with those most impacted. We suggest that a similar, integrated, well-resourced, long-term, public, and private sector set of strategies are needed to end the urban gun violence that happens in poor Black and Brown communities.

The narrow agendas of a few well-resourced philanthropies that are shaping much of the national gun violence discourse and prevention strategies is not serving the healing as well as redevelopment needs of the most impacted urban communities. We need a more inclusive strategy that is led by those who were and are at the center of this epidemic.

This campaign must saturate the mainstream while proactively and constantly lifting up CVI infrastructure as a crucial and viable community / public safety tool, noble profession, and essential answer to our gun violence problem in impacted urban communities.

2. REPAIR BEGINS WITH THOSE WHO ARE PULLING THE TRIGGERS

We must better ensure that whatever supports, services, opportunities, and/or resources secured for ending urban gun violence reach and meet those at the center of it. As noted throughout this book, an estimated 80% or more of those suspected of being involved in past and recurrent gun violence who have not been held accountable by the justice system are also not being engaged by any public or community-based system of care. This cannot be their reality or ours if we are serious about ending gun violence in the urban United States. Yet most mainstream and well-established public and/or community-based social services providers lack the required capacity to support these individuals in optimal ways. Local CVI must ensure that potentially lethal actors from each side of the conflict are benefiting from the same life supports and life-giving messaging too. They must be provided opportunities to experience each other's humanity in trusted, safe environments.

The voice, input, and vision of the "shooter" should be considered when conceptualizing what the work ought to look like. The Peacemaker Fellowship grew from the reflections of the youth interns hired in Richmond, and evolves constantly based on feedback from and with Fellows. A great amount of cultural humility must be the pretext for those of us who will be assistive and collaborative in our efforts to support as well as partner with these few, but influential, neighborhood stakeholders. If our efforts are not attractive, legitimate, and/or credible to our client partners, we will not successfully deliver the most optimal outcomes to the impacted communities. When its by them and for them, CVI strategies keep participants engaged longer and more meaningfully, increasing the likelihood they will stay alive and out of street conflicts, and in turn, keeping them and all of us safer.

3. BUILD AND LEARN FROM PAST BLACK LIBERATION MOVEMENTS

We must learn from as well as build on successful strategies for safety and peace led by African Americans throughout history. We discussed the important role leaders such as Ida B. Wells played in confronting the white terror of lynching. The victims of lynching were primarily Black men, and so too are the victims of urban gun violence. Black history has taught us that we will need leaders like Wells accompanied by strong social movements like the Afro-American Council and NAACP. By pressuring local governments along with working to change laws and criminal justice institutions, they mostly ended lynching by the 1940s.

History has taught us that practical solutions came when Black leaders worked with and employed those who were suffering, such as through the Black settlement houses and Black Panther Party. These movements offer insights and a road map for implementing peacemaking and peacekeeping with, not for, Black folks that can also improve our long-term wellness.

CVI alone can't be expected to solve all the root causes of gun violence. We also know there will be resistance and dissent, and in the age of social media and the 24/7 news cycles, challenges to building such movements. Yet, urgent action on urban gun violence is needed and possible now, although we agree that major social upheavals are necessary to redress the legacies of segregation, economic discrimination, and institutional dehumanization that contribute to today's urban gun violence epidemic. Stopping the "bleeding" shouldn't be ignored while we mobilize for larger structural changes.

4. IDENTIFY, HIRE, AND SUPPORT FORMERLY INCARCERATED COMMUNITY ASSETS

Highly qualified folks are present or returning to impacted communities soon, and share a common lived experience with today's shooters and victims of gun violence. We must capitalize on the often untapped assets and talents among these individuals, who grew up and remain in and/or have strong family names within these communities; many of them will be formerly incarcerated people from these communities with gun charges in their histories. We should also look to hire former military personnel who have navigated post-traumatic stress disorder successfully and can also return as wounded healers to their communities.

Regardless of their particulars, the credible messengers / street outreach workers / violence interrupters will be people who deeply care, are capable of self-love, possess deep awareness and confidence, and are nonjudgmental, unafraid, and humble enough to be trained to continue to work on themselves and serve others. They must be committed to and supported through post-traumatic growth, the positive psychological change that can come from struggling with trauma and extremely challenging experiences. Even with these skills, being credible, trustworthy, and having a "license to operate" in the streets is earned, not given by those on the streets. These outreach workers might seem like unicorns, but we are confident they are out there since we work with them every day.

Moreover, this will mean focusing on the pipeline of the potential CVI workforce while people are still incarcerated. It means partnering with prison education and other programs to provide more folks with the baseline skills of self-awareness, conflict resolution, anger management, and other tools that are essential for effective street credible messengers. It means working with reentry programs to recruit and identify people coming out, and getting them the support, additional training, and economic stability they need to enter the CVI profession.

Once hired, the personal as well as professional development and training of the CVI professional is critical to their success along with the success of this work. As we noted, most CVI workers are still healing themselves, and some of this is what makes them effective wounded healers with their clients. Yet they also run the daily risk of retraumatization from being around trauma, anger, gun violence, injury, and death far too often. Gun violence outreach workers are first responders, CHWs, and social workers, all wrapped into one. Many still only work part-time, however, and need side jobs to pay the bills. These assets to all of our communities need to be properly compensated, trained, supported, and given the security of employment that any civil servant deserves. Professional academies, associations, and societies for the CVI professional are necessary, and should be developed and maintained.

5. INSTITUTIONALIZING PEACEMAKING INSIDE GOVERNMENT

As we noted in earlier chapters, urban gun violence isn't stopped through volunteers, faith-based work, or nonprofits alone; government must be on board and have financial skin in the game. The sustained achievements in gun violence reductions and related community benefits in Richmond over the life course of the ONS are powerful evidence of what is possible with this type of institutionalization. Similarly, the often fleeting reductions in urban gun violence that other cities have seen from CVI reinforce to us the limits of nonprofit-based strategies absent sustained public sector supports.

As we described, this work must be held in local government outside the police department, and needs a singular focus on reducing and eliminating gun violence—instead of trying to address all violent crime, end gangs, stop the drug trade, and engage all at-risk youths. The impacted community benefits by having an accountable, trusted, stable, consistent, and constant presence of people who aren't law enforcement, and instead are trained to mediate and interrupt conflict nonviolently. The CVI professional gains job stability, government compensation and benefits, professional development, growth opportunities, and improved generational upward mobility trajectory.

Civic organizations and communities benefit from this approach as well. Government-employed CVI peacemaking professionals will raise the bar of competence and accountability because they will be scrutinized rigorously by the public as well as municipal officials in ways nonprofit actors never are. The entire government benefits by this investment in CVI since it can reorient how disinvested in and dehumanized communities see the state, and rebuild trust, credibility, and legitimacy with its most vulnerable and disenfranchised populations. Plus the CVI field will benefit because government is where the resources are, where there will be demands for ongoing certification and codification, and where there will likely be new and ongoing demands for training and professional development.

While institutionalizing this work inside government is crucial, there will remain a critical role for CVI organizations and specialists outside government. They will provide much-needed specialized training and support services beyond internal offerings. Further, private philanthropy will need to fill funding gaps left by meager city budgets and support aspects of CVI that may be harder to sustain with public expenditures, such as the Peacemaker Fellowship elements of transformative travel and LifeMAP milestone allowances. We must also get to a place where these kinds of expenditures are publicly acceptable, particularly when we see reductions in gun violence and vivid evidence of their lifesaving value.

6. PREVENTING THE NEXT GENERATION OF SHOOTERS

We have argued that Advance Peace means seeing the humanity, harm done to, and healing potential of active firearm offenders. Yet we don't want to be on a treadmill of response where we fail to also prevent the next generation of shooters from emerging. We are seeing this in our work as older Fellows are influencing the younger generation in a positive way by no longer engaging in shooting. Yet we don't want to rely on this osmosis of peacekeeping. We know the traumas, temptations, and triggers for gun conflict remain in too many of our neighborhoods. And we have seen children as young as ten engage in retaliatory gunfire in some of our cities. We need to get to these youngsters before they become shooters, because the healthier relationships that they have, the less likely they will engage in future violence.

The Advance Peace teams in each city regularly tell us who the next Fellows will be if nothing or no one gets to them. As a small organization, we rarely have the resources to get to them on a regular basis, but we are doing more to engage them through a "junior" Peacemaker Fellowship. It focuses on youths who may not yet be shooters but instead present a variety of risk factors, suggesting that without healthy engagements and supports, they have a high probability of becoming one. Despite the limited staff, time, and money of Advance Peace and many other CVI efforts, we know this outreach needs to involve getting into schools, not just the streets. We also acknowledge that CVI strategies, including Advance Peace, have not done a good enough job engaging with women who have proximity to and influence over a potential firearm offender.

Advance Peace is hiring female outreach workers too, and building networks of them to support one another and their Fellows. We know girls and young women can have a different set of traumas than boys, such as from intimate partner violence and sex trafficking, and these can lead to gun violence. The women NCAs who work for Advance Peace are connecting to a population we previously did not reach, while extending our work supporting boys who could be the next shooter. They are nurturing fellows in ways our male NCAs cannot and acting as big sis, big auntie, or even mother, as well as mentor. They are helping women say no to straw purchasing, hiding, carrying, or holding guns for a partner who can't legally have a gun. We are excited about CVI models being specifically developed for and by young women.

7. PREPARE AND IMPROVE LOCAL SYSTEMS OF CARE

As noted, about 17% of the population considered to be the most likely to use guns in a community are supported by our current public or community-based system of care. Society cannot stop or reduce gun violence if the healing work required isn't being done where and with those whom it is most needed. Our public and private systems of care are not reaching the people who have the greatest influence on whether gun violence in Black and Brown communities stops. We must build and create new capacity to effectively support a population of individuals who are completely disconnected, want to remain anonymous, or are isolated, angry, and navigating life with heavy loads of unaddressed past and chronic trauma.

The Advance Peace approach brings most supports and services *to* the population most disconnected and in need, not inviting those people to an unfamiliar and often unwelcoming place. This is a well-known approach to care that "meets people where they are at," and is known to work as demonstrated by the neighborhood health center movement and strategies previously used by the Black Panthers, among others. Yet the care systems and providers also need to change to serve our population of traumatized shooters.

For instance, they need to have more Black and Brown practitioners with the lived experience of the clientele, eliminate barriers to entry, and focus more on community healing and lifting up assets rather than just the clinical treatment of challenges.

8. PLACE MATTERS, BUT PEOPLE MAKE PLACES AND THE POLICIES THAT SHAPE THEM

If trauma is collectively experienced, this means that we must consider the environmental context that caused the harm in the first place. By only treating the individual, we only address part of the equation, leaving the toxic systems, policies, and practices neatly intact.

We know that Advance Peace can't continue to support and help heal our Fellows, and then send them back into the living conditions that are contributing to their trauma and violence. Our places matter, and influence our opportunities for being safe as well as accessing the basic needs of shelter, food, and other life-affirming resources—from quality schools and green spaces to more libraries than liquor stores. As we showed in various chapters, a set of policies that contributed to the disinvestment and abandonment of urban neighborhoods and extracted resources from Black folks, accompanied with a policy regime of punishing poor Black people for being poor and Black, have been major contributors to the conditions for urban gun violence today. More needs to be done to address those factors, while acknowledging that Advance Peace and other CVIs alone should not be expected to change the violent conditions of our communities that are centuries in the making. It is just a starting point to invest in the traumatized people perpetuating gun violence right now.

How environmental improvements are handled also matters in terms of not being a band-aid approach applied from outside communities. One of our NCAs described how their city wanted to improve community safety by improving the street sewers and creating new bicycle lanes. He told us that the community wanted the city to first "stop the blood of our kids from flowing into those sewers" and that "nobody was going to ride a bike if they are afraid of being shot." The reminder in this story is that people and policies make places; a space becomes a place as it gets an identity and gains meaning as people work, name, interpret, feel, and change it over time. You must invest first in the people who give places meaning and value.

Thus if we want to change the ways places influence people's behaviors and opportunity structures, we must invest in the people and change the policies that shape our places. One-off, pilot, or boutique place-based interventions—whether upgrading vacant lots and parks, building affordable housing, or improving streetlighting—are not going to succeed long-term in helping to reduce urban gun violence unless they meaningfully involve active shooters along with impacted community members in their design, construction, and maintenance. These are policy choices, and we suggest place-based changes must be accompanied by an intensive street outreach and mentoring effort like that of Advance Peace. This is what we witnessed with the Pogo Park project in Richmond—a community-led redevelopment where residents built the space, and now maintain and program it. Yet as Sam from the ONS reminds us, the work changing the systems and institutions that shape both people's opportunities and the qualities of our places need to be changed:

We still not changing the culture. It is still broke. The policing, the poverty, those responsible not willing to change if it threatens their power. We still believe in something that is unbelievable to most. We still in it, still in the flow, but how much longer can we keep swimming upstream? Wealthy communities never stop investing in their schools, in their youth programs, in their infrastructure, in the people who make that place go. They know this work never ends, and you don't wait until a crisis to try and address the issues. So not only will we never not be needed but we are also needed everywhere. Show me a place that doesn't need more loving in their community, more caring for young people, more people fulfilling the obligations of healthy adults. We should never go away. Never!

9. GREATER POLICE AND LEGAL SYSTEM ACCOUNTABILITY

Long-standing mistreatment by police along with hostility between them and residents have contributed to an alienation where many people in low-income communities of color see themselves as outside the purview of the laws, while also being on their own, unprotected by the state and not considered full citizens in their city. We have argued against the dominant police and criminal justice system methods for dealing with urban violence in this country, which includes aggressive policing, intensive surveillance, and mass incarceration. As shared, these methods have created an enormous amount of harm and trauma by themselves, removing people from their families and neighborhoods, and even contributing to making Black people not feel welcome in their own communities.

In too many of our neighborhoods, the first responders to conflict and violence are police and parole officers, not parents or coaches. While we might agree that a greater (accountable) police presence in neighborhoods helps reduce crime, the psychological distress of being heavily surveilled, stopped and frisked, and aggressively policed weighs on our young people's minds and bodies. More policing and punishment do not build healthier people, stronger communities, or reduce extreme inequality. We need new ways of policing, enforcement, and "punishment" that communicate that gun violence is unacceptable, there is a serious consequence if you perpetrate such violence, and your separation will be spent doing the personal development and healing-centered work required to return to society at large.

As we've noted, clearance (prosecution) rates for gun crimes in our most impacted cities are disgracefully low. As such, most who commit these crimes will never reap a consequence for it; while remaining in the community as is, they can shoot again or become a victim of gun violence themselves. In urban neighborhoods where gun violence is prevalent, victims have had a long history of experiencing the failure of accountability for the one doing the harm too. This experience incentivizes the harmed to go about getting justice on their own terms, and in a timely manner. These activities having gone unchecked over several generations, getting us to where we are today—more and more gun violence. To change this debilitating reality, better ways must be developed for law enforcement and the legal system to work with other social service institutions to hold perpetrators of gun violence in Black and Brown (and white) communities accountable, while investing equally in prevention.

10. DEPLETING URBAN NEIGHBORHOODS OF ILLEGAL GUNS

Tackling whether or how laws restricting access to firearms might help reduce urban gun violence has not been our focus, because we have seen little evidence that these well-intended laws have reduced, or will do so, near-term gunfire in urban neighborhoods currently impacted by cyclic and retaliatory gun violence. We are also skeptical of laws that aim to keep firearms out of the hands of law-abiding citizens who have completed every legal requirement to obtain and own a registered firearm.

What we are concerned about are the thousands of illegal firearms that flood the streets where we work. The guns used by Fellows aren't purchased legally in their communities. States like California with stronger gun-purchasing requirements do have lower gun death rates than states with more lax purchasing requirements. This suggests that we need every state, or rather federal legislation, to help reduce illegal guns from reaching urban areas by requiring such things as prepurchasing permits and background checks. It shouldn't be easier and cheaper to obtain an illegal gun in many of the communities where Advance Peace operates than it is to get a phone or computer. In addition, we need to eliminate easy access to guns with high-capacity clips, license sales of large amounts and dangerous types of ammunition, and regulate "ghost guns," which are firearms made from legal mail-order kits and parts obtained at gun shows that do not have serial numbers (making them unregistered, untraceable, and available without a background check).

We are not naive in thinking that the illegal gun supply will dry up. Our community members don't feel safe or trust public safety institutions, so one logical response might be to obtain a gun for protection. Yet we must do a far better job at enforcing a ceasefire in illegal firearm trafficking in urban neighborhoods. If firearm traffickers buy guns and ammunition in bulk in states with lax firearm-purchasing laws and illegally sell these in the underground street market, then prosecutorial approaches must track down and punish these suppliers. Gun shops that knowingly sell large caches of weapons that have been found on the streets of our cities must also be held accountable.

Consider this for a comparison: when the opioid epidemic exploded into white communities, legislators and law enforcement eventually prosecuted doctors who were overprescribing drugs, and went after and held the pharmaceutical industry liable. The question is, will law enforcement and the legal system be willing to invest the same or more resources into preventing the epidemic of illegal gun trafficking in predominantly minority urban areas?

11. FUNDING AND THE PEACE DIVIDEND

The reasons the multipronged work of CVI must be one of the key functions of municipal government were covered in the fifth point above. As is true with local law enforcement, state and federal government investments will be crucial to the success of local CVI efforts. The federal Safer Communities Act signed by President Biden in June 2021 includes $750 million to help states implement and run crisis intervention programs like CVI. We also believe that federal resources now directed toward militarizing police should end and be redirected toward community peacemaking that doesn't involve law enforcement.

Local governments can use creative mechanisms to ensure there are budgetary resources for peacemaking and peacekeeping. For example, local ballot measures in California, like the Oakland Fund for Children and Youth and Oakland's Measure Z, the 2014 Oakland Public Safety and Services Violence Prevention Act, have provided lasting resources to help communities invest in healing and violence prevention. The Oakland Fund for Children and Youth committed 2% of Oakland's annual budget to youth programs and includes a youth council to help direct where those resources are needed most. Measure Z authorized the city to use property and parking taxes to support both police staffing and community violence prevention/intervention programs too.

At the state level, an example is the Gun Violence Prevention and School Safety Act recently passed in California; it will impose an excise tax in the amount of 11% on licensed firearms dealers and ammunition vendors to fund programs that address gun violence. In 2022, California also added violence prevention services under CHW benefits covered under the Medical Assistance Program, which is the state's implementation of the federal Medicaid health insurance program serving low-income individuals and families. The National Uniform Claims Committee has already recognized violence prevention professionals as reimbursable health care providers. We now need private and other health insurers as well as Medicaid to pay for these services.

During one of DeVone's final meetings as the neighborhood safety director with City Manager Lindsay in Richmond, he let me know that he felt that the work we were doing at the ONS had significantly contributed to gun violence reduction. He stated that because gun violence had decreased significantly and the reductions were being sustained, he felt that he owed the ONS a "peace dividend." As a finance-trained administrator, Bill believed that there could be a way to determine what the savings were from our efforts at the ONS that contributed to gun violence reduction. He thought that whatever that number was should be reinvested back into the ONS as a supplement to existing general fund contributions to the office. We too believe that cities must identify ways to monetize gun violence reduction efforts and reinvest those resources back into CVI accordingly.

12. A NEW URBAN SCIENCE OF GUN VIOLENCE PREVENTION

Measuring the work of community gun violence intervention and prevention will demand a new approach to the science of evaluation. As we've emphasized here, Advance Peace enlists the expertise of its street outreach worker and Fellows in defining what to measure along with how to do it. This form of "citizen science" is a crucial aspect of the metrics of urban gun violence prevention. The participants and communities impacted must see themselves in the data, own it, and use it for their betterment.

Too much of CVI today is measured only on rates of firearm homicides and injury shootings, although the absence of gun violence doesn't necessarily mean the presence of peace. We need new ways to document the healing effects of community-driven CVI strategies on those involved in gun violence and those around them—families, friends, neighbors, and entire communities. As people and communities heal from toxic stress, we need to measure which services, supports, and experiences contribute to positive personal growth while sustaining community peace. This new urban science should also measure how peacemaking and peacekeeping can help rewire our brains in beneficial ways, and which interventions are contributing to what we call neurourbanism.

Ending the epidemic of gun violence that severely impacts Black and Brown people in our most violent US neighborhoods can be accomplished. It is a choice that we can make where we as a society commit to thinking and doing differently. To continue the path that has gotten us here today and resulted in almost no change in urban gun violence for Black folks over multiple decades is a form of societal malpractice! We will also need to connect to our siblings around the world in marginalized neighborhoods who are similarly struggling with gun violence—from Rio to Kingston to Johannesburg—and create a CVI world community.

By joining forces on a global scale, we can learn together, advocate together, develop solutions together, improve practices together, and identify and secure resources together. Advance Peace is a global call to action and commitment to offer leadership to make this happen. We can and must be victorious. We must choose to act together.

NOTES

CHAPTER 1

1. Amber K. Goodwin and T. J. Grayson, "Investing in the Frontlines: Why Trusting and Supporting Communities of Color Will Help Address Gun Violence," *Journal of Law, Medicine & Ethics* 48, no. S4 (2020): 164–171, https://doi.org/10.1177/1073110520979418.

2. Andre Gobbo, "The Economic Costs of Gun Violence in the United States," Washington Center for Equitable Growth, 2023, https://equitablegrowth.org/the-economic-costs-of-gun-violence-in-the-united-states/#:~:text=It%20is%20near%20impossible%20to,go%20into%20making%20these%20calculations.

3. Kristen Hwang and Nigel Duara, "As California Closes Prisons, the Cost of Locking Someone up Hits New Record at $132,860," *CalMatters*, January 23, 2024, http://calmatters.org/justice/2024/01/california-prison-cost-per-inmate/.

4. Yasemin Irvin-Erickson, Mathew Lynch, Annie Gurvis, Edward Mohr, and Bing Bai, "Gun Violence Affects the Economic Health of Communities," Urban Institute, June 2017, https://www.urban.org/sites/default/files/publication/90666/eigv_brief_3.pdf.

5. Susan Heavey and Doina Chiacu, "Gun Violence Is a Public Health Crisis, US Surgeon General Declares," Reuters, June 26, 2024, https://www.reuters.com/world/us/us-surgeon-general-declares-firearm-violence-public-health-crisis-2024-06-25.

6. Elliott Currie, *A Peculiar Indifference: The Neglected Toll of Violence on Black America* (New York: Metropolitan Books, 2020); Khalil Gibran Muhammad, *The Condemnation of Blackness: Race, Crime, and the Making of Modern Urban America* (Cambridge, MA: Harvard University Press, 2010).

7. Ari Davis, Rose Kim, and Cassandra Crifasi, *U.S. Gun Violence in 2021: An Accounting of a Public Health Crisis* (Johns Hopkins Center for Gun Violence Solutions, June

2023), https://publichealth.jhu.edu/sites/default/files/2023-06/2023-june-cgvs-u-s -gun-violence-in-2021.pdf.

8. John A. Rich and Courtney M. Grey, "Pathways to Recurrent Trauma Among Young Black Men: Traumatic Stress, Substance Use, and the 'Code of the Street,'" *American Journal of Public Health* 95, no. 5 (May 2005): 816–824, https://doi.org/10 .2105/AJPH.2004.044560.

9. Eugenio Weigend Vargas and Rukmani Bhatia, "No Shots Fired," Center for American Progress, October 20, 2020, https://www.americanprogress.org/article/no-shots -fired.

10. "2020 Saw Surge in Gun Deaths, Especially in Big Cities," Big Cities Health Coalition, 2020, https://www.bigcitieshealth.org/2020-gun-deaths-big-cities-data/.

11 Aliza Aufrichtig, Lois Beckett, Jan Diehm, and Jamiles Lartey, "Want to Fix Gun Violence in America? Go Local," *Guardian*, January 9, 2017, https://www .theguardian.com/us-news/ng-interactive/2017/jan/09/special-report-fixing-gun -violence-in-america.

12. Lois Beckett, "How the Gun Control Debate Ignores Black Lives," *ProPublica*, November 24, 2015, https://www.propublica.org/article/how-the-gun-control -debate-ignores-black-lives.

13. Andrew V. Papachristos, Christopher Wildeman, and Elizabeth Roberto, "Tragic, but Not Random: The Social Contagion of Nonfatal Gunshot Injuries," *Social Science & Medicine* 125 (January 2015): 139–150, https://doi.org/10.1016/j.socscimed.2014.01 .056.

14. Anthony A. Braga, Andrew V. Papachristos, and David M. Hureau, "The Concentration and Stability of Gun Violence at Micro Places in Boston, 1980–2008," *Journal of Quantitative Criminology* 26, no. 1 (March 2010): 33–53, https://doi.org/10 .1007/s10940-009-9082-x.

15. Sara F. Jacoby, Beidi Dong, Jessica H. Beard, Douglas J. Wiebe, and Christopher N. Morrison, "The Enduring Impact of Historical and Structural Racism on Urban Violence in Philadelphia," *Social Science & Medicine* 199 (February 2018): 87–95, https://doi.org/10.1016/j.socscimed.2017.05.038.

16. Kayla Holloway, Gina Cahill, Tiffany Tieu, and Wanjikũ Njoroge, "Reviewing the Literature on the Impact of Gun Violence on Early Childhood Development," *Current Psychiatry Reports* 25, no. 7 (July 2023): 273–281, https://doi.org/10.1007 /s11920-023-01428-6; Katherine P. Theall, Elizabeth A. Shirtcliff, Andrew R. Dismukes, Maeve Wallace, and Stacy S. Drury, "Association Between Neighborhood Violence and Biological Stress in Children," *JAMA Pediatrics* 171, no. 1 (January 1, 2017): 53, https://doi.org/10.1001/jamapediatrics.2016.2321.

17. Mazda Adli, Maximilian Berger, Eva-Lotta Brakemeier, Ludwig Engel, Joerg Fingerhut, Ana Gomez-Carrillo, Rainer Hehl, et al., "Neurourbanism: Towards a New Discipline," *Lancet Psychiatry* 4, no. 3 (March 2017): 183–185, https://doi.org/10 .1016/S2215-0366(16)30371-6.

18. Ben Senkler, Julius Freymueller, Susanne Lopez Lumbi, Claudia Hornberg, Hannah-Lea Schmid, Kristina Hennig-Fast, Gernot Horstmann, and Timothy McCall,

"Urbanicity—Perspectives from Neuroscience and Public Health: A Scoping Review," *International Journal of Environmental Research and Public Health* 20, no. 1 (December 30, 2022): 688, https://doi.org/10.3390/ijerph20010688.

19. James A. Reavis, Jan Looman, Kristina A. Franco, and Briana Rojas, "Adverse Childhood Experiences and Adult Criminality: How Long Must We Live Before We Possess Our Own Lives?," *Permanente Journal* 17, no. 2 (June 2013): 44–48, https://doi.org/10.7812/TPP/12-072.

20. Megan Ranney, Rebecca Karb, Peter Ehrlich, Kira Bromwich, Rebecca Cunningham, Rinad S. Beidas, and FACTS Consortium, "What Are the Long-Term Consequences of Youth Exposure to Firearm Injury, and How Do We Prevent Them? A Scoping Review," *Journal of Behavioral Medicine* 42, no. 4 (August 2019): 724–740, https://doi.org/10.1007/s10865-019-00035-2; James Garbarino, "The War-Zone Mentality—Mental Health Effects of Gun Violence in U.S. Children and Adolescents," *New England Journal of Medicine* 387, no. 13 (September 29, 2022): 1149–1151, https://doi.org/10.1056/NEJMp2209422; Benjamin P. Comer and Eric J. Connolly, "Exposure to Gun Violence and Handgun Carrying from Adolescence to Adulthood," *Social Science & Medicine* 328 (July 2023): 115984, https://doi.org/10.1016/j.socscimed.2023.115984.

21 Bessel van der Kolk, *The Body Keeps the Score: Brain, Mind, and Body in the Healing of Trauma* (New York: Penguin Books, 2015), 227, 39.

22. Hillary Franke, "Toxic Stress: Effects, Prevention and Treatment," *Children* 1, no. 3 (November 3, 2014): 390–402, https://doi.org/10.3390/children1030390.

23. Arianna M. Gard, Jeanne Brooks-Gunn, Sara S. McLanahan, Colter Mitchell, Christopher S. Monk, and Luke W. Hyde, "Deadly Gun Violence, Neighborhood Collective Efficacy, and Adolescent Neurobehavioral Outcomes," ed. Jay Van Bavel, *PNAS Nexus* 1, no. 3 (July 1, 2022): pgac061, https://doi.org/10.1093/pnasnexus/pgac061; Ijeoma Opara, David T. Lardier, Isha Metzger, Andriana Herrera, Leshelle Franklin, Pauline Garcia-Reid, and Robert J. Reid, "'Bullets Have No Names': A Qualitative Exploration of Community Trauma Among Black and Latinx Youth," *Journal of Child and Family Studies* 29, no. 8 (August 2020): 2117–2129, https://doi.org/10.1007/s10826-020-01764-8.

24. Daniel P. Moynihan, "Memorandum for the President," White House, January 16, 1970, https://www.nixonlibrary.gov/sites/default/files/virtuallibrary/documents/jul10/53.pdf.

25. Deborah Wallace and Rodrick Wallace, "Benign Neglect and Planned Shrinkage," *Verso*, March 25, 2017, https://www.versobooks.com/blogs/news/3145-benign-neglect-and-planned-shrinkage.

26. Nathalie M. Dumornay, Lauren A. M. Lebois, Kerry J. Ressler, and Nathaniel G. Harnett, "Racial Disparities in Adversity During Childhood and the False Appearance of Race-Related Differences in Brain Structure," *American Journal of Psychiatry* 180, no. 2 (February 1, 2023): 127–138, https://doi.org/10.1176/appi.ajp.21090961.

27. Haley Peckham, "Introducing the Neuroplastic Narrative: A Non-Pathologizing Biological Foundation for Trauma-Informed and Adverse Childhood Experience

Aware Approaches," *Frontiers in Psychiatry* 14 (May 22, 2023): 1103718, https://doi .org/10.3389/fpsyt.2023.1103718.

28. Bruce S. McEwen, "In Pursuit of Resilience: Stress, Epigenetics, and Brain Plasticity," *Annals of the New York Academy of Sciences* 1373, no. 1 (June 2016): 56–64, https://doi.org/10.1111/nyas.13020; Christina Bethell, Jennifer Jones, Narangerel Gombojav, Jeff Linkenbach, and Robert Sege, "Positive Childhood Experiences and Adult Mental and Relational Health in a Statewide Sample: Associations Across Adverse Childhood Experiences Levels," *JAMA Pediatrics* 173, no. 11 (November 4, 2019): e193007, https://doi.org/10.1001/jamapediatrics.2019.3007.

29. Thomas J. Schofield, Rosalyn D. Lee, and Melissa T. Merrick, "Safe, Stable, Nurturing Relationships as a Moderator of Intergenerational Continuity of Child Maltreatment: A Meta-Analysis," *Journal of Adolescent Health* 53, no. 4 (October 2013): S32–S38, https://doi.org/10.1016/j.jadohealth.2013.05.004.

30. Jack P. Shonkoff and Deborah A. Phillips, eds., *From Neurons to Neighborhoods: The Science of Early Childhood Development* (Washington, DC: National Academies Press, 2000), https://doi.org/10.17226/9824.

31. Kimberly G. Noble, Emma R. Hart, and Jessica F. Sperber, "Socioeconomic Disparities and Neuroplasticity: Moving Toward Adaptation, Intersectionality, and Inclusion," *American Psychologist* 76, no. 9 (December 2021): 1486–1495, https://doi .org/10.1037/amp0000934.

32. Julianne Holt-Lunstad, "Social Connection as a Public Health Issue: The Evidence and a Systemic Framework for Prioritizing the 'Social' in Social Determinants of Health," *Annual Review of Public Health* 43, no. 1 (April 5, 2022): 193–213, https:// doi.org/10.1146/annurev-publhealth-052020-110732; Dina Burstein, Chloe Yang, Kay Johnson, Jeff Linkenbach, and Robert Sege, "Transforming Practice with HOPE (Healthy Outcomes from Positive Experiences)," *Maternal and Child Health Journal* 25, no. 7 (July 2021): 1019–1024, https://doi.org/10.1007/s10995-021-03173-9.

33. Blair Paddock, "Homicide Clearance Rate Lower in Chicago's Black Communities: Report," WTTW News, February 3, 2023, https://news.wttw.com/2023/02/03 /homicide-clearance-rate-lower-chicago-s-black-communities-report.

34. Lakeidra Chavis and Geoff Hing, "The War on Gun Violence Has Failed. And Black Men Are Paying the Price," Marshall Project, March 23, 2023, https://www .themarshallproject.org/2023/03/23/gun-violence-possession-police-chicago.

35. The cities in California are Antioch, Fresno, Pomona, Richmond, Stockton, Woodland, and Vallejo. The other cities are Fort Worth (TX), Milwaukee (WI), Lansing (MI), Rochester (NY), and Orlando (FL).

36. Ellicott C. Matthay, Kriszta Farkas, Kara E. Rudolph, Scott Zimmerman, Melissa Barragan, Dana E. Goin, and Jennifer Ahern, "Firearm and Nonfirearm Violence After Operation Peacemaker Fellowship in Richmond, California, 1996–2016," *American Journal of Public Health* 109, no. 11 (November 2019): 1605–1611, https:// doi.org/10.2105/AJPH.2019.305288.

37. Jason Corburn, Yael Nidam, and Amanda Fukutome-Lopez, "The Art and Science of Urban Gun Violence Reduction: Evidence from the Advance Peace Program

in Sacramento, California," *Urban Science* 6, no. 1 (February 2, 2022): 6, https://doi.org/10.3390/urbansci6010006.

38. Martin Luther King Jr., "When Peace Becomes Obnoxious," Martin Luther King, Jr. Research and Education Institute, March 18, 1956[?], https://kinginstitute.stanford.edu/king-papers/documents/when-peace-becomes-obnoxious.

CHAPTER 2

1. Julia Lesnick, Laura S. Abrams, Kassandra Angel, and Elizabeth S. Barnert, "Credible Messenger Mentoring to Promote the Health of Youth Involved in the Juvenile Legal System: A Narrative Review," *Current Problems in Pediatric and Adolescent Health Care* 53, no. 6 (October 31, 2023): 101435, https://doi.org/10.1016/j.cppeds.2023.101435.

2. Oliver Rollins, *Conviction: The Making and Unmaking of the Violent Brain* (Stanford, CA: Stanford University Press, 2021).

3. Rachel Wamser-Nanney, John T. Nanney, Erich Conrad, and Joseph I. Constans, "Childhood Trauma Exposure and Gun Violence Risk Factors Among Victims of Gun Violence," *Psychological Trauma: Theory, Research, Practice, and Policy* 11, no. 1 (January 2019): 99–106, https://doi.org/10.1037/tra0000410.

4. Amanda J. Aubel, Angela Bruns, Xiaoya Zhang, Shani Buggs, and Nicole Kravitz-Wirtz, "Neighborhood Collective Efficacy and Environmental Exposure to Firearm Homicide Among a National Sample of Adolescents," *Injury Epidemiology* 10, no. 1 (June 9, 2023): 24, https://doi.org/10.1186/s40621-023-00435-8; Mudia Uzzi, Kyle T. Aune, Lea Marineau, Forrest K. Jones, Lorraine T. Dean, John W. Jackson, and Carl A. Latkin, "An Intersectional Analysis of Historical and Contemporary Structural Racism on Non-Fatal Shootings in Baltimore, Maryland," *Injury Prevention* 29, no. 1 (February 2023): 85–90, https://doi.org/10.1136/ip-2022-044700.

5. Joseph B. Richardson, Jerry Brown, and Michelle Van Brakle, "Pathways to Early Violent Death: The Voices of Serious Violent Youth Offenders," *American Journal of Public Health* 103, no. 7 (July 2013): e5–e16, https://doi.org/10.2105/AJPH.2012.301160.

6. Jocelyn R. Smith and Desmond U. Patton, "Posttraumatic Stress Symptoms in Context: Examining Trauma Responses to Violent Exposures and Homicide Death Among Black Males in Urban Neighborhoods," *American Journal of Orthopsychiatry* 86, no. 2 (2016): 212–223, https://doi.org/10.1037/ort0000101; James Garbarino, "The War-Zone Mentality—Mental Health Effects of Gun Violence in U.S. Children and Adolescents," *New England Journal of Medicine* 387, no. 13 (September 29, 2022): 1149–1151, https://doi.org/10.1056/NEJMp2209422.

7. Joseph B. Richardson, William Wical, Nipun Kottage, and Che Bullock, "Shook Ones: Understanding the Intersection of Nonfatal Violent Firearm Injury, Incarceration, and Traumatic Stress Among Young Black Men," *American Journal of Men's Health* 14, no. 6 (November 2020): 155798832098218, https://doi.org/10.1177/1557988320982181.

8. Allana T. Forde, Danielle M. Crookes, Shakira F. Suglia, and Ryan T. Demmer, "The Weathering Hypothesis as an Explanation for Racial Disparities in Health: A

Systematic Review," *Annals of Epidemiology* 33 (May 2019): 1–18.e3, https://doi.org /10.1016/j.annepidem.2019.02.011.

9. Dina Burstein, Chloe Yang, Kay Johnson, Jeff Linkenbach, and Robert Sege, "Transforming Practice with HOPE (Healthy Outcomes from Positive Experiences)," *Maternal and Child Health Journal* 25, no. 7 (July 2021): 1019–1024, https://doi.org /10.1007/s10995-021-03173-9; Cortland J. Dahl, Christine D. Wilson-Mendenhall, and Richard J. Davidson, "The Plasticity of Well-Being: A Training-Based Framework for the Cultivation of Human Flourishing," *Proceedings of the National Academy of Sciences* 117, no. 51 (December 22, 2020): 32197–32206, https://doi.org/10.1073/pnas .2014859117; Kimberly Freeman, Kelly Baek, Michelle Ngo, Veronica Kelley, Elaine Karas, Stephanie Citron, and Susanne Montgomery, "Exploring the Usability of a Community Resiliency Model Approach in a High Need / Low Resourced Traumatized Community," *Community Mental Health Journal* 58, no. 4 (May 2022): 679–688, https://doi.org/10.1007/s10597-021-00872-z.

10. Christina Bethell, Jennifer Jones, Narangerel Gombojav, Jeff Linkenbach, and Robert Sege, "Positive Childhood Experiences and Adult Mental and Relational Health in a Statewide Sample: Associations Across Adverse Childhood Experiences Levels," *JAMA Pediatrics* 173, no. 11 (November 4, 2019): e193007, https://doi.org /10.1001/jamapediatrics.2019.3007; Naomi I. Eisenberger and Steve W. Cole, "Social Neuroscience and Health: Neurophysiological Mechanisms Linking Social Ties with Physical Health," *Nature Neuroscience* 15, no. 5 (May 2012): 669–674, https://doi.org /10.1038/nn.3086.

11. Liliana Dell'Osso, Primo Lorenzi, Benedetta Nardi, Claudia Carmassi, and Barbara Carpita, "Post Traumatic Growth (PTG) in the Frame of Traumatic Experiences," *Clinical Neuropsychiatry* 19, no. 6 (December 2022): 390–393, https://doi.org /10.36131/cnfioritieditore20220606.

12. Shawn A. Ginwright, *The Four Pivots: Reimagining Justice, Reimagining Ourselves* (Berkeley, CA: North Atlantic Books, 2021).

13. Shawn A. Ginwright, *Hope and Healing in Urban Education: How Urban Activists and Teachers Are Reclaiming Matters of the Heart* (New York: Routledge, 2016), 121.

14. Bessel van der Kolk, *The Body Keeps the Score: Brain, Mind, and Body in the Healing of Trauma* (New York: Penguin Books, 2015), 113.

15. Tricia Hersey, *Rest Is Resistance: A Manifesto* (New York: Little, Brown Spark, 2022).

16. César Caraballo, Shiwani Mahajan, Javier Valero-Elizondo, Daisy Massey, Yuan Lu, Brita Roy, Carley Riley, et al., "Evaluation of Temporal Trends in Racial and Ethnic Disparities in Sleep Duration Among US Adults, 2004–2018," *JAMA Network Open* 5, no. 4 (April 7, 2022): e226385, https://doi.org/10.1001/jamanetworkopen .2022.6385.

17. Mia Bay, *Traveling Black: A Story of Race and Resistance* (Cambridge, MA: Belknap Press of Harvard University Press, 2021).

18. Claudia Cowan, "One California City Is Paying People Not to Commit Crimes," *Fox News*, August 24, 2016, https://www.foxnews.com/politics/one-california-city

-is-paying-people-not-to-commit-crimes; Wayne Drash Sambou and Tawanda Scott, "Paying Kids Not to Kill," CNN, May 19, 2016, https://www.cnn.com/2016/05/19 /health/cash-for-criminals-richmond-california/index.html.

19. Desmond Upton Patton, Kyle McGregor, and Gary Slutkin, "Youth Gun Violence Prevention in a Digital Age," *Pediatrics* 141, no. 4 (April 1, 2018): e20172438, https://doi.org/10.1542/peds.2017-2438.

20. Desmond Upton Patton, Robert D. Eschmann, and Dirk A. Butler, "Internet Banging: New Trends in Social Media, Gang Violence, Masculinity and Hip Hop," *Computers in Human Behavior* 29, no. 5 (September 2013): A54–A59, https://doi.org /10.1016/j.chb.2012.12.035.

21. Cited in Keosha Varela, "4 Ways to Fight Against Injustice," Aspen Institute, July 20, 2016, https://www.aspeninstitute.org/blog-posts/death-row-attorney-bryan -stevenson-4-ways-fight-injustice/. The notion of "infusing love" is drawn from Salima Koroma, "Hear What Cornell West Says Is His First Political Memory," *TIME*, October 2, 2014, https://time.com/3453821/cornel-west-first-political-memory/.

22. Quoted in Mariel Antonia Waloff and Rachel Mary Waldholz, "A Confused War," Berkeley Graduate School of Journalism, May 14, 2013, https://escholarship .org/uc/item/4tx1b29p.

23. Quoted in Steve Olson and National Academies of Sciences, Engineering, and Medicine, eds., *The Effects of Incarceration and Reentry on Community Health and Well-Being: Proceedings of a Workshop* (Washington, DC: National Academies Press, 2020), 40.

CHAPTER 3

1. Jim Herron Zamora, "Richmond: 4 on Council Call for a State of Emergency / The Idea Is to Raise $2 Million to Fight Violent Crime Wave," *SFGATE*, June 17, 2005, https://www.sfgate.com/bayarea/article/richmond-4-on-council-call-for-a-state-of -2627613.php.

2. Dennis J. Bernstein, "Fatal Errors, Part 3: Police Reformer—or Cover-Up Artist?," *WhoWhatWhy*, October 21, 2020, https://whowhatwhy.org/justice/criminal-justice /fatal-errors-part-3-police-reformer-or-cover-up-artist/.

3. Chip Johnson, "A Pandora's Box Opens in Richmond / Police Force Depleted by Several Scandals," *SFGATE*, May 26, 2003, https://www.sfgate.com/bayarea/johnson /article/a-pandora-s-box-opens-in-richmond-police-force-2645322.php.

4. Hilary Moore and James Tracy, "Anti-Fascism Versus the Police, 1980s-Style," *YES!*, August 27, 2024, https://www.yesmagazine.org/social-justice/2020/06/10/book-no -nazis.

5. Wallace Turner, "Antipolice Suit Focuses on a Town's Ills," *New York Times*, February 13, 1983, https://www.nytimes.com/1983/02/13/us/antipolice-suit-focuses-on -a-town-s-ills.html.

6. Turner, "Antipolice Suit."

7. Quoted in Turner, "Antipolice Suit," 22.

8. "A CBS-TV '60 Minutes' Segment on Civil Rights Problems," Archives, February 27, 1984, https://www.upi.com/Archives/1984/02/27/A-CBS-TV-60-Minutes-segment-on-civil-rights-problems/1427446706000.

9. Stacy Finz, "Fargo's Top Cop Ready for Richmond / He Expects He Can Handle the Weather and Also the Crime," *SFGATE*, December 17, 2005, https://www.sfgate.com/bayarea/article/Fargo-s-top-cop-ready-for-Richmond-He-expects-2588001.php.

10. Robert Rogers, "Inner Unrest," *Richmond Confidential*, March 26, 2010, https://richmondconfidential.org/2010/03/26/inner-unrest.

11. "Richmond Police Chief Prepares to Bid Farewell to City," *East Bay Times*, August 27, 2024, https://www.eastbaytimes.com/2015/11/18/richmond-police-chief-prepares-to-bid-farewell-to-city/.

12. Steve Spiker, Junious Williams, Rachel Diggs, Bill Heiser, and Nic Jay Aulston, *Violent Crime in Richmond*, Urban Strategies Council, February 26, 2007, https://www.ci.richmond.ca.us/DocumentCenter/View/2086/Violent-Crime-Report-Final-3-29-07.

13. *Sam Vaughn—Community Engagement and Productive Actions in Richmond, CA–CfA Summit (2015)*, YouTube, October 6, 2015, https://www.youtube.com/watch?v=rcmYwcTltds.

CHAPTER 4

1. Sara F. Jacoby, Beidi Dong, Jessica H. Beard, Douglas J. Wiebe, and Christopher N. Morrison, "The Enduring Impact of Historical and Structural Racism on Urban Violence in Philadelphia," *Social Science & Medicine* 199 (February 2018): 87–95, https://doi.org/10.1016/j.socscimed.2017.05.038.

2. "HPI Score (v3.0)," California Healthy Places Index, August 27, 2024, https://map.healthyplacesindex.org/?redirect=false.

3. Cornel West, *The Cornel West Reader* (New York: Basic Civitas Books, 1999).

4. Ruth Bobick, *Six Remarkable Hull-House Women* (Portsmouth, NH: Peter E. Randall Publisher, 2015).

5. Elisabeth Lasch-Quinn, *Black Neighbors: Race and the Limits of Reform in the American Settlement House Movement, 1890–1945* (Chapel Hill: University of North Carolina Press, 1993).

6. "The White Rose Home for Colored Working Girls Opens," African American Registry, August 27, 2024, https://aaregistry.org/story/a-safe-place-the-white-rose-home-for-colored-working-girls.

7. Jacqueline Anne Rouse, *Lugenia Burns Hope, Black Southern Reformer* (Athens: University of Georgia Press, 1989).

8. Louie Davis Shivery and and Hugh H. Smythe, "The Neighborhood Union: A Survey of the Beginnings of Social Welfare Movements Among Negroes in Atlanta," *Phylon* 3, no. 2 (1942): 149, https://doi.org/10.2307/271522.

9. Obie Clayton and June Gary Hopps, "Hope Arrives for Atlanta: Lugenia Burns Hope and the Role of Women in the Development of the Atlanta University School of Social Work," *Phylon* 57, no. 2 (2020): 41–55.

10. Jerome H. Schiele and M. Sebrena Jackson, "The Atlanta School of Social Work and the Professionalization of 'Race Work,'" *Phylon* 57, no. 2 (2020): 21–40.

11. Henry B. Leonard, "The Immigrants' Protective League of Chicago 1908–1921," *Journal of the Illinois State Historical Society* 66, no. 3 (1973): 271–284.

12. Iris Carlton-LaNey, "African American Social Work Pioneers' Response to Need," *Social Work* 44, no. 4 (July 1, 1999): 311–321, https://doi.org/10.1093/sw/44.4.311.

13. Aldon D. Morris, *The Origins of the Civil Rights Movement: Black Communities Organizing for Change* (New York: Free Press, 1986).

14. Jerome H. Schiele, *Human Services and the Afrocentric Paradigm* (New York: Haworth Press, 2000).

15. Elmer P. Martin and Joanne Mitchell Martin, *Spirituality and the Black Helping Tradition in Social Work* (Washington, DC: NASW Press, 2002); Charles Hounmenou, "Black Settlement Houses and Oppositional Consciousness," *Journal of Black Studies* 43, no. 6 (September 2012): 646–666, https://doi.org/10.1177/0021934712441203.

16. J. S. Adler, "Less Crime, More Punishment: Violence, Race, and Criminal Justice in Early Twentieth-Century America," *Journal of American History* 102, no. 1 (June 1, 2015): 34–46, https://doi.org/10.1093/jahist/jav173; Khalil Gibran Muhammad, "Where Did All the White Criminals Go?: Reconfiguring Race and Crime on the Road to Mass Incarceration," *Souls* 13, no. 1 (March 18, 2011): 72–90, https://doi.org/10.1080/10999949.2011.551478.

17. W. E. B. Du Bois, Elijah Anderson, and Isabel Eaton, *The Philadelphia Negro: A Social Study* (Philadelphia: University of Pennsylvania Press, 1996).

18. Khalil Gibran Muhammad, *The Condemnation of Blackness: Race, Crime, and the Making of Modern Urban America* (Cambridge, MA: Harvard University Press, 2010).

19. W. E. B. Du Bois, *The Crisis*, April 1932, 132:

There is absolutely no scientific proof, statistical, social or physical, to show that the American Negro is any more criminal than other elements in the American nation, if indeed as criminal. Moreover, even if he were, what is crime but disease, social or physical? In addition to this, every Negro knows that a frightful proportion of Negroes accused of crime are absolutely innocent. Nothing in the world is easier in the United States than to accuse a black man of crime. In the South, if any crime is committed, the first cry of the mob is, "Find the Negro!" And while they are finding him, the white criminal comfortably escapes.

20. Edwin Hardin Sutherland, Donald Ray Cressey, and David F. Luckenbill, *Principles of Criminology* (Dix Hills, NY: General Hall, 1992).

21. Muhammad, *The Condemnation of Blackness*, 4.

22. Kimberly Fain, "The Devastation of Black Wall Street," *JSTOR Daily*, July 5, 2017, https://daily.jstor.org/the-devastation-of-black-wall-street/.

23. Elizabeth Dale, *Criminal Justice in the United States, 1789–1939* (Cambridge: Cambridge University Press, 2011), https://doi.org/10.1017/CBO9780511920158.

24. Ira Katznelson, *When Affirmative Action Was White: An Untold History of Racial Inequality in Twentieth-Century America* (New York: W. W. Norton, 2006).

25. Richard Rothstein, *The Color of Law: A Forgotten History of How Our Government Segregated America* (New York: Liveright Publishing Corporation, 2017).

26. Carolyn Swope, "The Problematic Role of Public Health in Washington, DC's, Urban Renewal," *Public Health Reports* 133, no. 6 (November 2018): 707–714, https://doi.org/10.1177/0033354918794932.

27. W. Edward Orser, *Blockbusting in Baltimore: The Edmondson Village Story* (Lexington: University Press of Kentucky, 1994); Thomas J. Sugrue, *The Origins of the Urban Crisis: Race and Inequality in Postwar Detroit* (Princeton, NJ: Princeton University Press, 2014).

28. *Urban Renewal . . . Means Negro Removal. ~ James Baldwin (1963)*, YouTube, 2015, https://www.youtube.com/watch?v=T8Abhj17kYU.

29. Mindy Thompson Fullilove, *Root Shock: How Tearing up City Neighborhoods Hurts America, and What We Can Do About It* (New York: One World, 2004), 11.

30. Richard T. Sale, *The Blackstone Rangers: A Reporter's Account of Time Spent with the Street Gang on Chicago's South Side* (New York: Random House, 1972).

31. James Alan Fullilove, "Chicago's Blackstone Rangers," *Atlantic*, August 27, 2024, https://www.theatlantic.com/magazine/archive/1969/05/chicagos-blackstone-rangers-i/305741.

32. Charles Sklarsky, "Chicago's Loud Revolution: The Blackstone Rangers," *Harvard Crimson*, April 29, 1967, https://www.thecrimson.com/article/1967/4/29/chicagos-loud-revolution-the-blackstone-rangers.

33. Gwendolyn Brooks, "The Blackstone Rangers," Poetry Foundation, August 27, 2024, https://beta.poetryfoundation.org/poems/43323/the-blackstone-rangers.

34. Bill Sanders, *A Dictionary of Gangs* (Oxford: Oxford University Press, 2019).

35. Joshua Bloom and Waldo E. Martin, *Black Against Empire: The History and Politics of the Black Panther Party* (Oakland: University of California Press, 2016).

36. Alondra Nelson, *Body and Soul: The Black Panther Party and the Fight Against Medical Discrimination* (Minneapolis: University of Minnesota Press, 2011).

37. "Nixon Adviser Admits War on Drugs Was Designed to Criminalize Black People," Equal Justice Initiative, March 25, 2016, https://eji.org/news/nixon-war-on-drugs-designed-to-criminalize-black-people/.

38. *Promoting Health, Preventing Disease: Objectives for the Nation* (Washington, DC: US Department of Health and Human Services, 1980).

39. "Report of the Secretary's Task Force on Black & Minority Health," National Library of Medicine," accessed October 31, 2024, https://collections.nlm.nih.gov/catalog/nlm:nlmuid-8602912-mvset.

40. Mary Ann Fenley, Juarlyn L. Gaiter, Marcella Hammett, Leandris C. Liburd, James A. Mercy, Patrick W. O'Carroll, Chukwudi Onwuachi-Saunders, et al., *The Prevention of Youth Violence: A Framework for Community Action* (Atlanta, GA: Centers for Disease Control and Prevention, 1993), https://stacks.cdc.gov/view/cdc/27385.

41. Elizabeth Hinton, Julilly Kohler-Hausmann, and Vesla M. Weaver, "Did Blacks Really Endorse the 1994 Crime Bill?," *New York Times*, April 13, 2016, sec. Opinion, https://www.nytimes.com/2016/04/13/opinion/did-blacks-really-endorse-the-1994 -crime-bill.html.

42. "H.R.4017—Racial Justice Act," congress.gov, March 24, 1994, https://www .congress.gov/bill/103rd-congress/house-bill/4017.

43. David M. Kennedy, Anthony A. Braga, Anne M. Piehl, and Elin J. Waring, *Reducing Gun Violence: The Boston Gun Project's Operation Ceasefire* (Washington, DC: Office of Justice Programs, September 2001), https://www.ojp.gov/ncjrs/virtual-library /abstracts/reducing-gun-violence-boston-gun-projects-operation-ceasefire.

44. Anthony A. Braga and David L. Weisburd, "The Effects of 'Pulling Levers' Focused Deterrence Strategies on Crime," *Campbell Systematic Reviews* 8, no. 1 (January 2012): 1–90, https://doi.org/10.4073/csr.2012.6.

45. Quoted in Daniel Duane, "Straight Outta Boston," *Mother Jones*, February 2006, https://www.motherjones.com/politics/2006/01/straight-outta-boston/.

46. Forum on Global Violence Prevention, Board on Global Health, Institute of Medicine, and National Research Council, *Contagion of Violence: Workshop Summary* (Washington, DC: National Academies Press, 2013), http://www.ncbi.nlm.nih.gov /books/NBK190337/.

47. Quoted in Alex Kotlowitz, "Blocking the Transmission of Violence," *New York Times*, May 4, 2008, sec. Magazine, https://www.nytimes.com/2008/05/04/magazine /04health-t.html.

48. Jeffrey A. Butts, Caterina Gouvis Roman, Lindsay Bostwick, and Jeremy R. Porter, "Cure Violence: A Public Health Model to Reduce Gun Violence," *Annual Review of Public Health* 36, no. 1 (March 18, 2015): 41, https://doi.org/10.1146/annurev -publhealth-031914-122509.

49. Charles Ransford, Candice Kane, and Gary Slutkin, "Cure Violence: A Disease Control Approach to Reduce Violence and Change Behavior," in *Epidemiological Criminology: Theory to Practice*, ed. Eve Waltermaurer and Timothy Akers (London: Routledge, 2013), 232–242, https://www.taylorfrancis.com/books/edit/10.4324/97802 03083420/epidemiological-criminology-eve-waltermaurer-timothy-akers.

50. Butts et al., "Cure Violence."

51. Jeff Frazier, "How Networking and Video Can Disrupt Community Violence: Cure Violence Fuses Technology with Public Art, Health, and Safety to Help Eradicate Community Violence," *Public Manager* 39, no. 4 (2010): 70–72.

52. "FACT SHEET: More Details on the Biden-Harris Administration's Investments in Community Violence Interventions," White House, April 7, 2021, https://www

.whitehouse.gov/briefing-room/statements-releases/2021/04/07/fact-sheet-more
-details-on-the-biden-harris-administrations-investments-in-community-violence
-interventions/.

53. "Community Based Violence Intervention and Prevention Resources," Office of Justice Programs," accessed October 31, 2024, https://www.ojp.gov/topics/community -violence-intervention/resources.

54. "Oakland's Ceasefire Strategy," City of Oakland, accessed August 27, 2024, https://www.oaklandca.gov/topics/oaklands-ceasefire-strategy.

CHAPTER 5

1. Ted Alcorn, "Reporting for Work Where You Once Reported for Probation," *Atlantic*, December 13, 2019, https://www.theatlantic.com/politics/archive/2019/12 /credible-messengers-reform-criminal-justice-system/603514/; Ruben Austria and Julie Petersen, "Credible Messenger Mentoring for Justice-Involved Youth," Pinkerton Foundation, January 2017, https://www.thepinkertonfoundation.org/paper/credible -messenger-mentoring-justice-involved-youth.

2. David Sedgwick, *The Wounded Healer: Countertransference from a Jungian Perspective* (London: Routledge, 2016), https://doi.org/10.4324/9781315678771.

3. C. G. Jung, "Fundamental Questions of Psychotherapy," in *Collected Works of C. G. Jung, Volume 16* (Princeton, NJ: Princeton University Press, 2014), 116, https://doi .org/10.1515/9781400851003.111.

4. Thomas P. LeBel, Matt Richie, and Shadd Maruna, "Helping Others as a Response to Reconcile a Criminal Past: The Role of the Wounded Healer in Prisoner Reentry Programs," *Criminal Justice and Behavior* 42, no. 1 (January 2015): 108–120, https:// doi.org/10.1177/0093854814550029.

5. Tedeschi, Richard G. Balcazar, "Growth After Trauma," *Harvard Business Review*, July 1, 2020, https://hbr.org/2020/07/growth-after-trauma.

6. Liliana Dell'Osso, Primo Lorenzi, Benedetta Nardi, Claudia Carmassi, and Barbara Carpita, "Post Traumatic Growth (PTG) in the Frame of Traumatic Experiences," *Clinical Neuropsychiatry* 19, no. 6 (December 2022): 390–393, https://doi.org/10 .36131/cnfioritieditore20220606.

7. "What We Do," Cure Violence Global, accessed October 31, 2024, https://cvg.org /what-we-do/.

8. M. Scott Peck, *The Road Less Traveled: A New Psychology of Love, Traditional Values and Spiritual Growth* (New York: Touchstone, 2003).

9. Maladoma Patrice Somè, *The Healing Wisdom of Africa: Finding Life Purpose Through Nature, Ritual, and Community* (New York: TarcherPerigee, 1999), 101–102.

10. Hector Balcazar, E. Lee Rosenthal, J. Nell Brownstein, Carl H. Rush, Sergio Matos, and Lorenza Hernandez, "Community Health Workers Can Be a Public Health Force for Change in the United States: Three Actions for a New Paradigm," *American Journal of Public Health* 101, no. 12 (December 2011): 2199–2203, https://doi.org/10 .2105/AJPH.2011.300386.

11. Elmer P. Martin and Joanne Mitchell Martin, *Spirituality and the Black Helping Tradition in Social Work* (Washington, DC: NASW Press, 2002).

12. Michael E. Sherr, "The Afrocentric Paradigm: A Pragmatic Discourse About Social Work Practice with African Americans," *Journal of Human Behavior in the Social Environment* 13, no. 3 (July 13, 2006): 1–17, https://doi.org/10.1300/J137v13n03_01.

13. Jerome H. Schiele, "The Afrocentric Paradigm in Social Work: A Historical Perspective and Future Outlook," *Journal of Human Behavior in the Social Environment* 27, no. 1–2 (February 17, 2017): 15–26, https://doi.org/10.1080/10911359.2016.1252601.

14. National Uniform Claim Committee, accessed April 1, 2023, https://www.nucc.org/index.php?option=com_content&view=article&id=221:new-1-1-2016&catid=21:provider-taxonomy.

15. Kyle R. Fischer, Carnell Cooper, Anne Marks, and Gary Slutkin, "Prevention Professional for Violence Intervention: A Newly Recognized Health Care Provider for Population Health Programs," *Journal of Health Care for the Poor and Underserved* 31, no. 1 (2020): 25–34, https://doi.org/10.1353/hpu.2020.0005.

16. The American Public Health Association describes CHWs as "a trusted member of and/or has an unusually close understanding of the community served," and "this trusting relationship enables the worker to serve as a liaison, link, or intermediary between health/social services and the community to facilitate access to services and improve the quality and cultural competence of service delivery." "A Strategy to Address Systemic Racism and Violence as Public Health Priorities: Training and Supporting Community Health Workers to Advance Equity and Violence Prevention," American Public Health Association, November 8, 2022, https://www.apha.org/policies-and-advocacy/public-health-policy-statements/policy-database/2023/01/18/address-systemic-racism-and-violence; Colleen Barbero, Abdul Hafeedh Bin Abdullah, Noelle Wiggins, Mariana Garrettson, Dean Jones, Angie S. Guinn, Candace Girod, et al., "Community Health Worker Activities in Public Health Programs to Prevent Violence: Coding Roles and Scope," *American Journal of Public Health* 112, no. 8 (August 2022): 1191, https://doi.org/10.2105/AJPH.2022.306865.

17. "Victim Offender Education Group (VOEG)," Insight Prison Project, accessed October 31, 2024, http://www.insightprisonproject.org/victim-offender-education-group-voeg.html.

18. Miguel Basto-Pereira, Ana Miranda, Sofia Ribeiro, and Ângela Maiam, "Growing up with Adversity: From Juvenile Justice Involvement to Criminal Persistence and Psychosocial Problems in Young Adulthood," *Child Abuse & Neglect* 62 (December 2016): 63–75, https://doi.org/10.1016/j.chiabu.2016.10.011; Nathan Hughes, Michael Ungar, Abigail Fagan, Joseph Murray, Olayinka Atilola, Kitty Nichols, Joana Garcia, and Stuart Kinner, "Health Determinants of Adolescent Criminalisation," *Lancet Child & Adolescent Health* 4, no. 2 (February 2020): 151–162, https://doi.org/10.1016/S2352-4642(19)30347-5.

19. Heather Strang, Lawrence W. Sherman, Evan Mayo-Wilson, Daniel Woods, and Barak Ariel, "Restorative Justice Conferencing (RJC) Using Face-to-Face Meetings

of Offenders and Victims: Effects on Offender Recidivism and Victim Satisfaction. A Systematic Review," *Campbell Systematic Reviews* 9, no. 1 (January 2013): 1–59, https://doi.org/10.4073/csr.2013.12.

20. "Many Cities Are Putting Hopes in Violence Interrupters, but Few Understand Their Challenges," *NBC News*, May 10, 2022, https://www.nbcnews.com/news/us -news/many-cities-are-putting-hopes-violence-interrupters-understand-challen -rcna28118.

21. Emily Crane, "Social Media Is Fanning Violence and Transforming Chicago's Gang Culture with Members Regularly Engaging in Taunts Online That Spiral into Deathly Street Violence, New Report Finds," *Daily Mail*, June 13, 2018, https://www .dailymail.co.uk/news/article-5840453/Social-media-fanning-violence-Chicagos -gang-culture.html.

22. We want to emphasize here that rap music gets singled out for its links to violence when folk, country, and heavy metal music have long contained references to murder, guns, the killing of police, and domestic violence. Eric Clapton's popular cover of Bob Marley's song "I Shot the Sheriff" (1974), Woodie Guthrie's "Pretty Boy Floyd" (1987) in which a police officer is killed, and Johnny Cash's "Folson Prison Blues" (1968) describing a murderer who kills someone just to see him die are a few examples of violent lyrical content. Metallica's song t "No Remorse" includes the lyrics, "Only the strong survive / No one to save the weaker race / We are ready to kill all comers / Like a loaded gun right at your face." Metallica, "No Remorse. Kill 'emAll," 1983, http://www.encycmet.com/lyrics/lyr-kil7.shtml.

23. Desmond Upton Patton, Robert D. Eschmann, and Dirk A. Butler, "Internet Banging: New Trends in Social Media, Gang Violence, Masculinity and Hip Hop," *Computers in Human Behavior* 29, no. 5 (September 2013): A54–A59, https://doi.org /10.1016/j.chb.2012.12.035.

24. Jesus Trevino, Lum Rizvanolli, Morriam O. Yarrow, Errick L. Christian, Neeraj Chhabra, and Matthew J. Kaminsky, "Survey of Firearm Injury Victims Suggests a Role for Social Media in Violence Prevention Programs," *American Journal of Emergency Medicine* 59 (September 2022): 187–188, https://doi.org/10.1016/j.ajem.2022.05.006.

25. Jeffrey Lane and Forrest Stuart, "How Social Media Use Mitigates Urban Violence: Communication Visibility and Third-Party Intervention Processes in Digital Urban Contexts," *Qualitative Sociology* 45, no. 3 (September 2022): 457–475, https:// doi.org/10.1007/s11133-022-09510-w.

26. David M. Hureau, Theodore Wilson, Hilary M. Jackl, Jalon Arthur, Christopher Patterson, and Andrew V. Papachristos, "Exposure to Gun Violence Among the Population of Chicago Community Violence Interventionists." *Science Advances* 8, no. 51 (December 23, 2022): eabq7027, https://doi.org/10.1126/sciadv.abq7027.

27. David M. Hureau, Theodore Wilson, Wayne Rivera-Cuadrado, and Andrew V. Papachristos, "The Experience of Secondary Traumatic Stress Among Community Violence Interventionists in Chicago," *Preventive Medicine* 165 (December 2022): 107186, https://doi.org/10.1016/j.ypmed.2022.107186.

28. Charles R. Figley, *Compassion Fatigue: Coping with Secondary Traumatic Stress Disorder in Those Who Treat the Traumatized* (London: Psychology Press, 1995).

CHAPTER 6

1. "Killed, Ignored, Never Forgotten: Chicago's Unsolved Homicides," Live Free, January 26, 2023, https://livefreeusa.org/news/killed-ignored-never-forgotten-chicagos -unsolved-homicides/.

2. The ten ACEs questions include:

1. Did a parent or other adult in the household often or very often swear at you, insult you, put you down, or humiliate you? Or did a parent or adult in the household act in a way that made you afraid that you might be physically hurt?

2. Did a parent or other adult in the household often or very often push, grab, slap, or throw something at you, or ever hit you so hard that you had marks or were injured?

3. Did an adult or person at least five years older than you ever touch or fondle you, or have you touch their body in a sexual way? Or attempt or actually have oral, anal, or vaginal intercourse with you?

4. Did you often or very often feel that no one in your family loved you, or thought you were important or special? Or did your family not look out for each other, feel close to each other, or support each other?

5. Did you often or very often feel that you didn't have enough to eat, had to wear dirty clothes, and had no one to protect you? Or were your parents too drunk or high to take care of you, or take you to the doctor if you needed it?

6. Was a biological parent ever lost to you through divorce, abandonment, or other reason?

7. Was your mother or stepmother often or very often pushed, grabbed, slapped, or had something thrown at her? Or sometimes, often, or very often kicked, bitten, hit with a fist, or hit with something hard? Or ever repeatedly hit over at least a few minutes, or threatened with a gun or knife?

8. Did you live with anyone who was a problem drinker or alcoholic, or who used street drugs?

9. Was a household member depressed or mentally ill, or did a household member attempt suicide?

10. Did a household member go to prison?

3. Vincent J. Felitti, Robert F. Anda, Dale Nordenberg, David F. Williamson, Alison M. Spitz, Valerie Edwards, Mary P. Koss, and James S. Marks, "Relationship of Childhood Abuse and Household Dysfunction to Many of the Leading Causes of Death in Adults," *American Journal of Preventive Medicine* 14, no. 4 (May 1998): 245–258, https://doi.org/10.1016/S0749-3797(98)00017-8.

4. Cornelius van Niel, Lee M. Pachter, Roy Wade, Vincent J. Felitti, and Martin T. Stein, "Adverse Events in Children: Predictors of Adult Physical and Mental

Conditions," *Journal of Developmental & Behavioral Pediatrics* 35, no. 8 (October 2014): 549–551, https://doi.org/10.1097/DBP.0000000000000102.

5. L. Sergio Garduno, "How Influential Are Adverse Childhood Experiences (ACEs) on Youths?: Analyzing the Immediate and Lagged Effect of ACEs on Deviant Behaviors," *Journal of Child & Adolescent Trauma* 15, no. 3 (September 2022): 683–700, https://doi.org/10.1007/s40653-021-00423-4.

6. Michael T. Baglivio, Nathan Epps, Kimberly Swartz, Mona Sayedul Huq, Amy Sheer, and Nancy S. Hardt, "The Prevalence of Adverse Childhood Experiences (ACE) in the Lives of Juvenile Offenders," *Journal of Juvenile Justice* 3, no. 2 (2014), https://www.posttraumaticsociety.com/s/Prevalence_of_ACE.pdf.

7. Kelly E. O'Connor, Terri N. Sullivan, Katherine M. Ross, and Khiya J. Marshall, "'Hurt People Hurt People': Relations Between Adverse Experiences and Patterns of Cyber and In-Person Aggression and Victimization Among Urban Adolescents," *Aggressive Behavior* 47, no. 4 (July 2021): 483–492, https://doi.org/10.1002/ab.21966; Michael T. Baglivio, Kevin T. Wolff, Matt DeLisi, and Katherine Jackowski, "The Role of Adverse Childhood Experiences (ACEs) and Psychopathic Features on Juvenile Offending Criminal Careers to Age 18," *Youth Violence and Juvenile Justice* 18, no. 4 (October 2020): 337–364, https://doi.org/10.1177/1541204020927075.

8. Michael D. De Bellis, Andrew S. Baum, Boris Birmaher, Matcheri S. Keshavan, Clayton H. Eccard, Amy M. Boring, Frank J. Jenkins, and Neal D. Ryan, "Developmental Traumatology Part I: Biological Stress Systems," *Biological Psychiatry* 45, no. 10 (May 1999): 1259–1270, https://doi.org/10.1016/S0006-3223(99)00044-X.

9. Sonali Rajan, Charles C. Branas, Dawn Myers, and Nina Agrawal, "Youth Exposure to Violence Involving a Gun: Evidence for Adverse Childhood Experience Classification," *Journal of Behavioral Medicine* 42, no. 4 (August 2019): 646–657, https://doi.org/10.1007/s10865-019-00053-0.

10. Kayla Holloway, Gina Cahill, Tiffany Tieu, and Wanjikū Njoroge, "Reviewing the Literature on the Impact of Gun Violence on Early Childhood Development," *Current Psychiatry Reports* 25, no. 7 (July 2023): 273–281, https://doi.org/10.1007/s11920-023-01428-6.

11. L. Rowell Huesmann, Eric F. Dubow, Paul B. Boxer, Brad J. Bushman, Cathy S. Smith, Meagan A. Docherty, and Maureen J. O'Brien, "Longitudinal Predictions of Young Adults' Weapons Use and Criminal Behavior from Their Childhood Exposure to Violence," *Aggressive Behavior* 47, no. 6 (November 2021): 621–634, https://doi.org/10.1002/ab.21984; Heather A. Turner, Kimberly J. Mitchell, Lisa M. Jones, Sherry Hamby, Roy Wade, and Cheryl L. Beseler, "Gun Violence Exposure and Posttraumatic Symptoms Among Children and Youth," *Journal of Traumatic Stress* 32, no. 6 (December 2019): 881–889, https://doi.org/10.1002/jts.22466.

12. Kimberly J. Mitchell, Lisa M. Jones, Heather A. Turner, Cheryl L. Beseler, Sherry Hamby, and Roy Wade, "Understanding the Impact of Seeing Gun Violence and Hearing Gunshots in Public Places: Findings from the Youth Firearm Risk and Safety Study," *Journal of Interpersonal Violence* 36, no. 17–18 (September 2021): 8835–8851, https://doi.org/10.1177/0886260519853393.

13. Amanda J. Aubel, Rocco Pallin, Garen J. Wintemute, and Nicole Kravitz-Wirtz, "Exposure to Violence, Firearm Involvement, and Socioemotional Consequences Among California Adults," *Journal of Interpersonal Violence* 36, no. 23–24 (December 2021): 11822–11838, https://doi.org/10.1177/0886260520983924; Dana Charles McCoy, C. Cybele Raver, and Patrick Sharkey, "Children's Cognitive Performance and Selective Attention Following Recent Community Violence," *Journal of Health and Social Behavior* 56, no. 1 (March 2015): 19–36, https://doi.org/10.1177/0022146514567576.

14. Angela J. Narayan, Alicia F. Lieberman, and Ann S. Masten, "Intergenerational Transmission and Prevention of Adverse Childhood Experiences (ACEs)," *Clinical Psychology Review* 85 (April 2021): 101997, https://doi.org/10.1016/j.cpr.2021.101997.

15 .Kathryn Ashton, Alisha R. Davies, Karen Hughes, Kat Ford, Andrew Cotter-Roberts, and Mark A. Bellis, "Adult Support During Childhood: A Retrospective Study of Trusted Adult Relationships, Sources of Personal Adult Support and Their Association with Childhood Resilience Resources," *BMC Psychology* 9, no. 1 (December 2021): 101, https://doi.org/10.1186/s40359-021-00601-x; Christina Bethell, Jennifer Jones, Narangerel Gombojav, Jeff Linkenbach, and Robert Sege, "Positive Childhood Experiences and Adult Mental and Relational Health in a Statewide Sample: Associations Across Adverse Childhood Experiences Levels," *JAMA Pediatrics* 173, no. 11 (November 4, 2019): e193007, https://doi.org/10.1001/jamapediatrics.2019.3007.

CHAPTER 7

1. Carla Sosenko, "Hotels Take Sleep Tourism to the Next Level," *New York Times*, March 6, 2024, sec. C, 9, https://www.nytimes.com/2024/03/06/travel/sleep-tourism-hotels.html.

2. Julie A. Markham and William T. Greenough, "Experience-Driven Brain Plasticity: Beyond the Synapse," *Neuron Glia Biology* 1, no. 4 (November 2004): 351–363, https://doi.org/10.1017/S1740925X05000219.

3. Marian C. Diamond, Janet L. Hopson, Marian Diamond, and Janet Hopson, *Magic Trees of Mind: How to Nurture Your Child's Intelligence, Creativity, and Healthy Emotions from Birth Through Adolescence* (New York: Penguin, 1999).

4. Brooks B. Gump and Karen A. Matthews, "Are Vacations Good for Your Health? The 9-Year Mortality Experience After the Multiple Risk Factor Intervention Trial," *Psychosomatic Medicine* 62, no. 5 (September 2000): 608–612, https://doi.org/10.1097/00006842-200009000-00003.

5. Jamshid Faraji and Gerlinde A. S. Metz, "Toward Reframing Brain-Social Dynamics: Current Assumptions and Future Challenges," *Frontiers in Psychiatry* 14 (July 6, 2023): 1211442, https://doi.org/10.3389/fpsyt.2023.1211442; Josh Noel, "Travel as a Health Regimen," *Chicago Tribune*, May 10, 2019, sec. Travel, https://www.chicagotribune.com/2014/01/28/travel-as-a-health-regimen-3/.

6. Steven F. Philipp, "Race and Tourism Choice: A Legacy of Discrimination?," *Annals of Tourism Research* 21, no. 3 (January 1, 1994): 479–488, https://doi.org/10 .1016/0160-7383(94)90115-5.

7. Mimi Sheller, *Mobility Justice: The Politics of Movement in the Age of Extremes* (London: Verso, 2018); Alana Dillette and Stefanie Benjamin, "The Black Travel Movement: A Catalyst for Social Change," *Journal of Travel Research* 61, no. 3 (March 2022): 463–476, https://doi.org/10.1177/0047287521993549.

8. Joe R. Feagin, "The Continuing Significance of Race: Antiblack Discrimination in Public Places," *American Sociological Review* 56, no. 1 (February 1991): 101, https:// doi.org/10.2307/2095676.

9. Alana Dillette, "Roots Tourism: A Second Wave of Double Consciousness for African Americans," *Journal of Sustainable Tourism* 29, no. 2–3 (March 4, 2021): 412–427, https://doi.org/10.1080/09669582.2020.1727913.

10. Mia Bay, *Traveling Black: A Story of Race and Resistance* (Cambridge, MA: Belknap Press of Harvard University Press, 2021), 13.

11. Isabel Wilkerson, *The Warmth of Other Suns: The Epic Story of America's Great Migration* (New York: Vintage Books, 2011).

12. James W. Loewen, *Sundown Towns: A Hidden Dimension of American Racism* (New York: New Press, 2005. Hawthorne, California, had a sign at its city limits in the 1930s that said, "Nigger, Don't Let the Sun Set on YOU in Hawthorne."

13. "'Green Book' Helped African-Americans Travel Safely," *Talk of the Nation*, NPR, September 15, 2010, https://www.npr.org/2010/09/15/129885990/green-book -helped-african-americans-travel-safely.

14. Anne E. Brown, "Op-Ed: L.A.'s Taxi Industry Discriminates Against Black Riders. If We Don't Force Them to Change, They Won't," *Los Angeles Times*, August 12, 2018, https://www.latimes.com/opinion/livable-city/la-oe-brown-racism-taxi-uber -lyft-201812-story.html.

15. Bay, *Traveling Black*.

16. David A. Harris, "Driving While Black: Racial Profiling on Our Nation's Highways," American Civil Liberties Union, June 1999, https://www.aclu.org/publications /driving-while-black-racial-profiling-our-nations-highways.

17. Frank R. Baumgartner, Derek A. Epp, and Kelsey Shoub, *Suspect Citizens: What 20 Million Traffic Stops Tell Us About Policing and Race* (New York: Cambridge University Press, 2018), https://doi.org/10.1017/9781108553599; Magnus Lofstrom, Joseph Hayes, Brandon Martin, and Deepak Premkumar, "Racial Disparities in Traffic Stops," Public Policy Institute of California, August 27, 2024, https://www.ppic .org/publication/racial-disparities-in-traffic-stops/.

18. Rhonda Colvin, "Why Some Americans Are Afraid to Explore Their Own Country," *Washington Post*, accessed October 31, 2024, https://www.washingtonpost.com /news/national/wp/2018/01/26/feature/traveling-while-black-why-some-americans -are-afraid-to-explore-their-own-country/.

19. Roderick Nash, *Wilderness and the American Mind* (New Haven, CT: Yale University Press, 1982).

20. John Muir, *The Yosemite* (New York: Century, 1912), chapter 16.

21. Henry D. Thoreau, *Walden; or, Life in the Woods* (New York: Thomas Y. Crowell & Co., 1910), 53.

Escaping to nature was essential for enlightenment for the transcendentalists, as Emerson would write in chapter I of his classic essay "Nature":

> In the woods, we return to reason and faith. There I feel that nothing can befall me in life,—no disgrace, no calamity, (leaving me my eyes,) Note which nature cannot repair. Standing on the bare ground,—my head bathed by the blithe air, and uplifted into infinite space,—all mean egotism vanishes. I become a transparent eye-ball; I am nothing; I see all; the currents of the Universal Being circulate through me; I am part or particle of God.

See R. W. Emerson. *Nature* (Boston: James Munroe, 1849). Available as ebook, at https://www.gutenberg.org/files/29433/29433-h/29433-h.htm.

22. Dorceta E. Taylor, *The Environment and the People in American Cities, 1600–1900s: Disorder, Inequality, and Social Change* (Durham, NC: Duke University Press, 2009).

23. Rachel Kaplan, "The Role of Nature in the Context of the Workplace," *Landscape and Urban Planning* 26, no. 1–4 (October 1993): 193–201, https://doi.org/10.1016/0169-2046(93)90016-7.

24. Marc G. Berman, Ethan Kross, Katherine M. Krpan, Mary K. Askren, Aleah Burson, Patricia J. Deldin, Stephen Kaplan, et al., "Interacting with Nature Improves Cognition and Affect for Individuals with Depression," *Journal of Affective Disorders* 140, no. 3 (November 2012): 300–305, https://doi.org/10.1016/j.jad.2012.03.012; Andrea Faber Taylor and Frances E. Kuo, "Children with Attention Deficits Concentrate Better After Walk in the Park," *Journal of Attention Disorders* 12, no. 5 (March 2009): 402–409, https://doi.org/10.1177/1087054708323000.

25. Dorceta E. Taylor, "Racial and Ethnic Differences in Connectedness to Nature and Landscape Preferences Among College Students," *Environmental Justice* 11, no. 3 (June 2018): 118–136, https://doi.org/10.1089/env.2017.0040.

26. Jenny Rowland-Shea, Sahir Doshi, and Shanna Edberg, "The Nature Gap: Confronting Racial and Economic Disparities in the Destruction and Protection of Nature in America," Center for American Progress, July 21, 2020. https://www.americanprogress.org/article/the-nature-gap/.

27. Anna K. Touloumakos and Alexia Barrable, "Adverse Childhood Experiences: The Protective and Therapeutic Potential of Nature," *Frontiers in Psychology* 11 (November 26, 2020), https://doi.org/10.3389/fpsyg.2020.597935.

28. Gump and Matthews, "Are Vacations Good for Your Health?"; "Destination Aging: The Health Benefits of Travel," Senior Friendship Centers, June 17, 2019, https://friendshipcenters.org/destination-aging-the-health-benefits-of-travel/.

29. Christopher J. May, Brian D. Ostafin, and Evelien Snippe, "The Relative Impact of 15-Minutes of Meditation Compared to a Day of Vacation in Daily Life: An

Exploratory Analysis," *Journal of Positive Psychology* 15, no. 2 (March 3, 2020): 278–284, https://doi.org/10.1080/17439760.2019.1610480.

30. Bryce Hruska, Sarah D. Pressman, Kestutis Bendinskas, and Brooks B. Gump, "Vacation Frequency Is Associated with Metabolic Syndrome and Symptoms," *Psychology & Health* 35, no. 1 (January 2, 2020): 1–15, https://doi.org/10.1080/08870446.2019.1628962.

31. Chun-Chu Chen and James F. Petrick, "Health and Wellness Benefits of Travel Experiences: A Literature Review," *Journal of Travel Research* 52, no. 6 (November 2013): 709–719, https://doi.org/10.1177/0047287513496477.

32. Yongfeng Ma, Shuyan Chen, Aemal J. Khattak, Zheng Cao, Muhammad Zubair, Xue Han, and Xiaojian Hu, "What Affects Emotional Well-Being During Travel? Identifying the Factors by Maximal Information Coefficient," *International Journal of Environmental Research and Public Health* 19, no. 7 (April 4, 2022): 4326, https://doi.org/10.3390/ijerph19074326.

33. Jeffrey A. Kottler, *Travel That Can Change Your Life: How to Create a Transformative Experience* (San Francisco: Jossey-Bass, 1997), xi.

34. Paulo Anciaes and Paul Metcalfe, "Constraints to Travel Outside the Local Area: Effect on Social Participation and Self-Rated Health," *Journal of Transport & Health* 28 (January 2023): 101535, https://doi.org/10.1016/j.jth.2022.101535.

35. Jonas De Vos, Tim Schwanen, Veronique Van Acker, and Frank Witlox, "Travel and Subjective Well-Being: A Focus on Findings, Methods and Future Research Needs," *Transport Reviews* 33, no. 4 (July 2013): 421–442, https://doi.org/10.1080/01441647.2013.815665.

36 Kottler, *Travel That Can Change Your Life*, xi.

CHAPTER 8

1. "Despite Lack of City Funding, a Father's Quest to Lower Gun Violence in Fresno Gets Results," KVPR, October 18, 2019, https://www.kvpr.org/community/2019-10-18/despite-lack-of-city-funding-a-fathers-quest-to-lower-gun-violence-in-fresno-gets-results.

2. J. Brian Charles, "Advocates Push California City to Adopt Program That Pays People Who Don't Shoot," *Trace*, December 6, 2019, https://www.thetrace.org/2019/12/fresno-gun-violence-advocates-advance-peace/.

3. Ellicott C. Matthay, Kriszta Farkas, Kara E. Rudolph, Scott Zimmerman, Melissa Barragan, Dana E. Goin, and Jennifer Ahern, "Firearm and Nonfirearm Violence After Operation Peacemaker Fellowship in Richmond, California, 1996–2016," *American Journal of Public Health* 109, no. 11 (November 2019): 1605–1611, https://doi.org/10.2105/AJPH.2019.305288.

4. Quoted in Charles, "Advocates Push California City to Adopt Program That Pays People Who Don't Shoot."

5. Kelly McClure, "Public Records Show California Cities Funneled COVID Relief Funds into Police Coffer," *Salon*, April 7, 2022, https://www.salon.com/2022/04/07/public-records-show-california-cities-funneled-relief-funds-into-police-coffer/.

6. Sam Levin, "California Cities Spent Huge Share of Federal Covid Relief Funds on Police," *Guardian*, April 7, 2022, sec. US news, https://www.theguardian.com/us -news/2022/apr/07/covid-relief-funds-california-cities-police.

7. Quoted in "Advance Peace Moves Closer to Reduced Anti-Violence Funding from City of Fresno," ABC30, August 11, 2022, https://abc30.com/advance-peace-fresno -gun-violence-anti-violence-initiative-gang-member/12118481/.

8. Quoted in Jessica Harrington, "Fresno City Leaders Address Funding for Advance Peace, Mayor Says He Can't Support Current Model," ABC30, June 20, 2022, https:// abc30.com/advance-peace-fresno-gun-violence-gang-mayor/11982407/.

9. Quoted in "Advance Peace Moves Closer to Reduced Anti-Violence Funding from City of Fresno."

10. Quoted in Daniel Gligich, "Dyer Flips, Opening Taxpayer Funds for Gang Program Paying Off Shooters," *San Joaquin Valley Sun*, June 20, 2022, https://sjvsun .com/news/fresno/dyer-flips-opening-taxpayer-funds-for-gang-program-paying-off -shooters/.

11. John K. Roman and Philip Cook, "Improving Data Infrastructure to Reduce Firearms Violence," NORC at the University of Chicago, October 2021, https://www .norc.org/content/dam/norc-org/pdfs/Improving%20Data%20Infrastructure%20 to%20Reduce%20Firearms%20Violence_Final%20Report.pdf.

12. John Gramlich, "What the Data Says About Gun Deaths in the U.S.," Pew Research Center, April 26, 2023, https://www.pewresearch.org/short-reads/2023/04 /26/what-the-data-says-about-gun-deaths-in-the-u-s/.

13. Natalie Kroovand Hipple, "Towards a National Definition and Database for Nonfatal Shooting Incidents," *Journal of Urban Health* 99, no. 3 (June 2022): 361– 372, https://doi.org/10.1007/s11524-022-00638-2.

14. David Bernstein and Noah Isackson, "The Truth About Chicago's Crime Rates," *Chicago*, August 27, 2024, https://www.chicagomag.com/Chicago-Magazine/May -2014/Chicago-crime-rates/.

15. Rachel Swan and Dan Kopf, "Oakland Has Been Publishing Misleading Crime Data for Years," *San Francisco Chronicle*, July 10, 2024, https://www.sfchronicle.com /crime/article/oakland-police-data-reports-19545681.php.

16. Khalil Gibran Muhammad, *The Condemnation of Blackness: Race, Crime, and the Making of Modern Urban America* (Cambridge, MA: Harvard University Press, 2010), 1, 20.

17. Philosopher Baruch Spinoza, in his 1670 *Theologico-Political Treatise*, wrote, "Peace is not an absence of war, it is a virtue, a state of mind, a disposition for benevolence, confidence, justice." MLK Jr. reiterated that "true peace is not merely the absence of tension; it is the presence of justice." See his book *Stride Toward Freedom* (New York: Harper & Row, 1958), 27.

18. Mark A. Bellis, Katie Hardcastle, Kat Ford, Karen Hughes, Kathryn Ashton, Zara Quigg, and Nadia Butler, "Does Continuous Trusted Adult Support in Childhood Impart Life-Course Resilience Against Adverse Childhood Experiences—a Retrospective Study on Adult Health-Harming Behaviours and Mental Well-Being," *BMC*

Psychiatry 17, no. 1 (December 2017): 110, https://doi.org/10.1186/s12888-017-1260-z.

19. Sara R. Jaffee, Lucy Bowes, Isabelle Ouellet-Morin, Helen L. Fisher, Terrie E. Moffitt, Melissa T. Merrick, and Louise Arseneault, "Safe, Stable, Nurturing Relationships Break the Intergenerational Cycle of Abuse: A Prospective Nationally Representative Cohort of Children in the United Kingdom," *Journal of Adolescent Health* 53, no. 4 (October 2013): S4–S10, https://doi.org/10.1016/j.jadohealth.2013.04.007; Zhiyuan Yu, Lin Wang, Wenyi Chen, Juan Zhang, and Amie F. Bettencourt, "Positive Childhood Experiences Associate with Adult Flourishing Amidst Adversity: A Cross Sectional Survey Study with a National Sample of Young Adults," *International Journal of Environmental Research and Public Health* 19, no. 22 (November 13, 2022): 14956, https://doi.org/10.3390/ijerph192214956.

20. Liliana Dell'Osso, Primo Lorenzi, Benedetta Nardi, Claudia Carmassi, and Barbara Carpita, "Post Traumatic Growth (PTG) in the Frame of Traumatic Experiences," *Clinical Neuropsychiatry* 19, no. 6 (December 2022): 390–393, https://doi.org/10.36131/cnfioritieditore20220606.

21. Richard G. Tedeschi, *Posttraumatic Growth: Theory, Research and Applications* (New York: Routledge, 2018).

22. "The Economic Cost of Gun Violence," Everytown for Gun Safety, July 19, 2022, https://everytownresearch.org/report/the-economic-cost-of-gun-violence/.

23. "The National Cost of Gun Violence: The Price Tag for Taxpayers," National Institute for Criminal Justice Reform, January 2023, https://costofviolence.org/.

24. $361 \times \$700{,}000 = \$252.7$ million $\div 30$ months $= \$8.43$ million per month saved $\div 10$ cities $= \$842{,}333$; $361 \times \$1.2$ million $= \$433.2$ million $\div 30$ months $= \$14.4$ million per month saved $\div 10$ cities $= \$1.444$ million.0

25. "Experts Explain Why California Is Still Rife with Gun Violence Despite Some of the Most Stringent Gun Laws in the Country," *ABC News*, January 26, 2023, https://abcnews.go.com/US/experts-explain-california-rife-gun-violence-despite-stringent/story?id=96665000.

26. "Gun Violence Data and Research," State of California, Department of Justice, Office of the Attorney General, September 20, 2022, https://oag.ca.gov/ogvp/data.

27. Mike McLively and Brittany Nieto, "A Case Study in Hope: Lessons from Oakland's Remarkable Reduction in Gun Violence," Giffords Law Center to Prevent Gun Violence, April 23, 2019, https://giffords.org/lawcenter/report/a-case-study-in-hope-lessons-from-oaklands-remarkable-reduction-in-gun-violence/.

CHAPTER 9

1. John Geluardi, "The Man Behind Richmond's Renaissance," *East Bay Express*, May 18, 2011, https://eastbayexpress.com/the-man-behind-richmonds-renaissance-1/.

2. George L. Kelling and James Q. Wilson, "Broken Windows," *Atlantic*, March 1, 1982, https://www.theatlantic.com/magazine/archive/1982/03/broken-windows/304465/.

3. Suzanne Bohan and Sandy Kleffman, "Shortened Lives: Where You Live Matters," USC Center for Health Journalism, August 27, 2024, https://centerforhealthjournalism

.org/our-work/reporting/shortened-lives-where-you-live-matters; "Local Data," Contra Costa Health, accessed November 1, 2023, https://www.cchealth.org/health-and-safety -information/local-data.

4. "Life Expectancy," Vital Signs, accessed November 11, 2022, https://vitalsigns .mtc.ca.gov/.

5. "Contra Costa Health Atlas," Contra Costa Health, https://atlas.cchealth.org/.

6. Manuel De Solà-Morales, "The Strategy of Urban Acupuncture" (paper presented at the Structure Fabric and Topography conference, Nanjing University, 2004); Jaime Lerner, *Urban Acupuncture* (Washington, DC: Island Press, 2014).

7. Lerner, *Urban Acupuncture*, 1.

8. Jason Corburn, Marisa Ruiz Asari, Jorge Pérez Jamarillo, and Aníbal Gaviria, "The Transformation of Medellín into a 'City for Life': Insights for Healthy Cities," *Cities & Health* 4, no. 1 (January 2, 2020): 13–24, https://doi.org/10.1080/23748834.2019 .1592735.

9. Christopher Blattman, Donald P Green, Daniel Ortega, and Santiago Tobón, "Place-Based Interventions at Scale: The Direct and Spillover Effects of Policing and City Services on Crime," *Journal of the European Economic Association* 19, no. 4 (August 11, 2021): 2022–2051, https://doi.org/10.1093/jeea/jvab002.

10. Steve Early, *Refinery Town: Big Oil, Big Money, and the Remaking of an American City* (Boston: Beacon Press, 2017).

11. Heather Gilligan, "Green Collar Jobs Give Richmond Residents Hope," *Richmond Confidential*, October 13, 2009, https://richmondconfidential.org/2009/10/13/green -collar-jobs-give-richmond-residents-hope/.

12. "RichmondBUILD Academy," City of Richmond, August 27, 2024, https://www .ci.richmond.ca.us/1243/RichmondBUILD.

13. Karina Ioffee, "New Businesses Put Richmond on the Food Map," *East Bay Times*, August 12, 2016, https://www.eastbaytimes.com/2015/08/21/new-businesses -put-richmond-on-the-food-map/.

14. Patricia Leigh Brown, "How a Forlorn Playground Became One of America's Most Innovative Public Spaces," *Christian Science Monitor*, May 24, 2017, https://www .csmonitor.com/World/Making-a-difference/2017/0524/How-a-forlorn-playground -became-one-of-America-s-most-innovative-public-spaces.

15. Amy Maxmen, "Stress: The Privilege of Health," *Nature* 531, no. 7594 (March 2016): S58–S59, https://doi.org/10.1038/531S58a.

16. "Building Healthy Communities: A Decade in Review," California Endowment, November 2020, https://www.calendow.org/learning/executive-summary/.

17. "Welcome to RYSE!," RYSE, accessed January 3, 2025, https://rysecenter.org.

18. "Welcome to RYSE!," RYSE.

19. Jason Corburn, Shasa Curl, and Gabino Arredondo, "A Health-in-All-Policies Approach Addresses Many of Richmond, California's Place-Based Hazards, Stressors," *Health Affairs* 33, no. 11 (November 2014): 1905–1913, https://doi.org/10.1377 /hlthaff.2014.0652.

20. "Health in All Policies," City of Richmond, July 27, 2024, https://www.ci
.richmond.ca.us/2575/Health-in-All-Policies.

CHAPTER 10

1. "President Joe Biden to Establish First-Ever White House Office of Gun Violence
Prevention, to Be Overseen by Vice President Kamala Harris," White House, September 21, 2023, https://www.whitehouse.gov/briefing-room/statements-releases/2023
/09/21/president-joe-biden-to-establish-first-ever-white-house-office-of-gun-violence
-prevention-to-be-overseen-by-vice-president-kamala-harris/ (emphasis added).

2. Scott E. Wolfe and Justin Nix, "The Alleged 'Ferguson Effect' and Police Willingness to Engage in Community Partnership," *Law and Human Behavior* 40, no. 1
(2016): 1–10, https://doi.org/10.1037/lhb0000164.

3. Rashawn Ray, "What Does 'Defund the Police' Mean and Does It Have Merit?,"
Brookings, June 19, 2020, https://www.brookings.edu/articles/what-does-defund-the
-police-mean-and-does-it-have-merit/.

4. "National Offices of Violence Prevention Network—Landscape Scan," National
Institute for Criminal Justice Reform, April 2022, https://nicjr.org/wp-content
/uploads/2016/01/National-OVP-Landscape-Scan-April-2022.pdf.

5. Jacob Charles, "The Dead Hand of a Silent Past: Bruen, Gun Rights, and the
Shackles of History," *Duke Law Journal* 73, no. 1 (September 19, 2023): 67–155.

6. Everytown Research & Policy, "Gun Laws in California," Everytown for Gun Safety
Support Fund, January 2024, https://everytownresearch.org/rankings/state/california/.

7. Rob Bonta, "Homicide in California, 2022," California Department of Justice,
California Justice Information Services Division, 2023, https://data-openjustice.doj
.ca.gov/sites/default/files/2023-06/Homicide%20In%20CA%202022f.pdf.

8. Mike McLively and Brittany Nieto, "A Case Study in Hope: Lessons from Oakland's Remarkable Reduction in Gun Violence," Giffords Law Center to Prevent Gun
Violence, April 23, 2019, https://giffords.org/lawcenter/report/a-case-study-in-hope
-lessons-from-oaklands-remarkable-reduction-in-gun-violence/.

9. Rocco Pallin, Julia P. Schleimer, Veronica A. Pear, and Garen J. Wintemute,
"Assessment of Extreme Risk Protection Order Use in California from 2016 to 2019,"
JAMA Network Open 3, no. 6 (June 18, 2020): e207735, https://doi.org/10.1001
/jamanetworkopen.2020.7735.

10. Elizabeth A. Tomsich, Veronica A. Pear, Julia P. Schleimer, and Garen J. Win-
temute, "The Origins of California's Gun Violence Restraining Order Law: A Case
Study Using Kingdon's Multiple Streams Framework," *BMC Public Health* 23, no. 1
(June 30, 2023): 1275, https://doi.org/10.1186/s12889-023-16043-6.

11. Veronica A. Pear, Rocco Pallin, Julia P. Schleimer, Elizabeth Tomsich, Nicole
Kravitz-Wirtz, Aaron B. Shev, Christopher E. Knoepke, and Garen J. Wintemute,
"Gun Violence Restraining Orders in California, 2016–2018: Case Details and
Respondent Mortality," *Injury Prevention* 28, no. 5 (October 2022): 465–471, https://
doi.org/10.1136/injuryprev-2022-044544.

12. "Healing Systemic and Interpersonal Violence," HAVI: Health Alliance for Violence Intervention, accessed November 1, 2024, https://www.thehavi.org; "Proven Strategies for Safer Communities," Cure Violence Global, accessed June 1, 2024, https://cvg.org/; "What Is Community-Based Public Safety?," CBPS Collective, accessed March 1, 2024, https://www.cbpscollective.org; Aqeela Sherrills, "Newark Community Street Team," NCST, accessed July 11, 2024, https://www .newarkcommunitystreetteam.org/; Aquil Basheer, "The Build Program," Build Program, accessed August 22, 2024, https://buildprogram.org/; "Who We Work With," Roca, accessed September 2, 2024, https://rocainc.org/.

13. "Community Violence Intervention: A Summer Toolkit," Cities United, CBPS Collective, HAVI, and NICJR, 2022, https://cdn.prod.website-files.com/62757217 c0cf1df1b1fbd310/646e2e2b3b332b1c02f4c953_Summer%20Tool%20Kit-1.pdf.

14. John Jay College Research Advisory Group on Preventing and Reducing Community Violence, *Reducing Violence Without Police: A Review of Research Evidence* (New York: Research and Evaluation Center, John Jay College of Criminal Justice, City University of New York, 2020), https://johnjayrec.nyc/2020/11/09/av2020/.

15. Ryan Zhang and Swathi Srinivasan, "Successful Reentry: A Community-Level Analysis," Harvard University Institute of Politics Criminal Justice Policy Group, December 2019, https://iop.harvard.edu/sites/default/files/2023-02/IOP_Policy_Pro gram_2019_Reentry_Policy.pdf.

16. David M. Hureau, Theodore Wilson, Hilary M. Jackl, Jalon Arthur, Christopher Patterson, and Andrew V. Papachristos, "Exposure to Gun Violence Among the Population of Chicago Community Violence Interventionists," *Science Advances* 8, no. 51 (December 23, 2022): eabq7027, https://doi.org/10.1126/sciadv.abq7027.

17. "In Historic Win for Gun Safety, Build Back Better Act Passes the House, Including $5 Billion Investment in Community Violence Intervention," Everytown for Gun Safety, accessed November 1, 2024, https://www.everytown.org/press/in-historic -win-for-gun-safety-build-back-better-act-passes-the-house-including-5-billion -investment-in-community-violence-intervention/.

18. Hanna Love and Glencora Haskins, "As Local Governments Look for Solutions to Gun Violence, Pandemic Funding Is an Under-Tapped Resource," Brookings, June 28, 2023, https://www.brookings.edu/articles/as-local-governments-look-for-solutions-to -gun-violence-pandemic-funding-is-an-under-tapped-resource/.

19. "Fact Sheet: Highlights from the Biden Administration's Historic Efforts to Reduce Gun Violence," White House, December 14, 2021, https://www.whitehouse .gov/briefing-room/statements-releases/2021/12/14/fact-sheet-highlights-from-the -biden-administrations-historic-efforts-to-reduce-gun-violence/.

20. "FY 2023 Office of Justice Programs Community Based Violence Intervention and Prevention Initiative," Bureau of Justice Assistance, May 25, 2023, https://bja .ojp.gov/funding/opportunities/o-bja-2023-171647.

21. "California Violence Intervention and Prevention—CalVIP," BSCC California, accessed November 1, 2024, https://www.bscc.ca.gov/s_cpgpcalvipgrant/.

22. Steve Gorman, "California Enacts First State Tax on Guns, Ammunition in US," Reuters, September 23, 2023, https://www.reuters.com/world/us/california-enacts -first-state-tax-guns-ammunition-us-2023-09-27/.

23. Anne Marks, "Getting Paid for Treatment to Prevent Homicides: A Practical Guide and Call to Action for Providers to Leverage the New Medi-Cal Benefit for Violence Prevention," Giffords Law Center to Prevent Gun Violence, November 15, 2023, https://giffords.org/lawcenter/report/getting-paid-for-treatment-to-prevent -homicides/; "Governor Hochul Signs Legislation Permitting Medicaid Reimbursement for Violence Prevention Programs," New York State, Governor Kathy Hochul, October 18, 2023, https://www.governor.ny.gov/news/governor-hochul-signs-legislation -permitting-medicaid-reimbursement-violence-prevention.

INDEX

Urban and Industrial Environments

Series editors: Robert Gottlieb, Professor of Urban and Environmental Policy, Emeritus, Occidental College

Bhavna Shamasunder, Mellichamp Chair in Racially Just, Resilient and Sustainable City Futures, University of California, Santa Barbara

Maureen Smith, *The U.S. Paper Industry and Sustainable Production: An Argument for Restructuring*

Keith Pezzoli, *Human Settlements and Planning for Ecological Sustainability: The Case of Mexico City*

Sarah Hammond Creighton, *Greening the Ivory Tower: Improving the Environmental Track Record of Universities, Colleges, and Other Institutions*

Jan Mazurek, *Making Microchips: Policy, Globalization, and Economic Restructuring in the Semiconductor Industry*

William A. Shutkin, *The Land That Could Be: Environmentalism and Democracy in the Twenty-First Century*

Richard Hofrichter, ed., *Reclaiming the Environmental Debate: The Politics of Health in a Toxic Culture*

Robert Gottlieb, *Environmentalism Unbound: Exploring New Pathways for Change*

Kenneth Geiser, *Materials Matter: Toward a Sustainable Materials Policy*

Thomas D. Beamish, *Silent Spill: The Organization of an Industrial Crisis*

Matthew Gandy, *Concrete and Clay: Reworking Nature in New York City*

David Naguib Pellow, *Garbage Wars: The Struggle for Environmental Justice in Chicago*

Julian Agyeman, Robert D. Bullard, and Bob Evans, eds., *Just Sustainabilities: Development in an Unequal World*

Barbara L. Allen, *Uneasy Alchemy: Citizens and Experts in Louisiana's Chemical Corridor Disputes*

Dara O'Rourke, *Community-Driven Regulation: Balancing Development and the Environment in Vietnam*

Brian K. Obach, *Labor and the Environmental Movement: The Quest for Common Ground*

Peggy F. Barlett and Geoffrey W. Chase, eds., *Sustainability on Campus: Stories and Strategies for Change*

Steve Lerner, *Diamond: A Struggle for Environmental Justice in Louisiana's Chemical Corridor*

Jason Corburn, *Street Science: Community Knowledge and Environmental Health Justice*

Peggy F. Barlett, ed., *Urban Place: Reconnecting with the Natural World*

David Naguib Pellow and Robert J. Brulle, eds., *Power, Justice, and the Environment: A Critical Appraisal of the Environmental Justice Movement*

Eran Ben-Joseph, *The Code of the City: Standards and the Hidden Language of Place Making*

Nancy J. Myers and Carolyn Raffensperger, eds., *Precautionary Tools for Reshaping Environmental Policy*

Kelly Sims Gallagher, *China Shifts Gears: Automakers, Oil, Pollution, and Development*

Kerry H. Whiteside, *Precautionary Politics: Principle and Practice in Confronting Environmental Risk*

Ronald Sandler and Phaedra C. Pezzullo, eds., *Environmental Justice and Environmentalism: The Social Justice Challenge to the Environmental Movement*

Julie Sze, *Noxious New York: The Racial Politics of Urban Health and Environmental Justice*

Robert D. Bullard, ed., *Growing Smarter: Achieving Livable Communities, Environmental Justice, and Regional Equity*

Ann Rappaport and Sarah Hammond Creighton, *Degrees That Matter: Climate Change and the University*

Michael Egan, *Barry Commoner and the Science of Survival: The Remaking of American Environmentalism*

David J. Hess, *Alternative Pathways in Science and Industry: Activism, Innovation, and the Environment in an Era of Globalization*

Peter F. Cannavò, *The Working Landscape: Founding, Preservation, and the Politics of Place*

Paul Stanton Kibel, ed., *Rivertown: Rethinking Urban Rivers*

Kevin P. Gallagher and Lyuba Zarsky, *The Enclave Economy: Foreign Investment and Sustainable Development in Mexico's Silicon Valley*

David N. Pellow, *Resisting Global Toxics: Transnational Movements for Environmental Justice*

Robert Gottlieb, *Reinventing Los Angeles: Nature and Community in the Global City*

David V. Carruthers, ed., *Environmental Justice in Latin America: Problems, Promise, and Practice*

Tom Angotti, *New York for Sale: Community Planning Confronts Global Real Estate*

Paloma Pavel, ed., *Breakthrough Communities: Sustainability and Justice in the Next American Metropolis*

Anastasia Loukaitou-Sideris and Renia Ehrenfeucht, *Sidewalks: Conflict and Negotiation over Public Space*

David J. Hess, *Localist Movements in a Global Economy: Sustainability, Justice, and Urban Development in the United States*

Julian Agyeman and Yelena Ogneva-Himmelberger, eds., *Environmental Justice and Sustainability in the Former Soviet Union*

Jason Corburn, *Toward the Healthy City: People, Places, and the Politics of Urban Planning*

JoAnn Carmin and Julian Agyeman, eds., *Environmental Inequalities Beyond Borders: Local Perspectives on Global Injustices*

Louise Mozingo, *Pastoral Capitalism: A History of Suburban Corporate Landscapes*

Gwen Ottinger and Benjamin Cohen, eds., *Technoscience and Environmental Justice: Expert Cultures in a Grassroots Movement*

Samantha MacBride, *Recycling Reconsidered: The Present Failure and Future Promise of Environmental Action in the United States*

Andrew Karvonen, *Politics of Urban Runoff: Nature, Technology, and the Sustainable City*

Daniel Schneider, *Hybrid Nature: Sewage Treatment and the Contradictions of the Industrial Ecosystem*

Catherine Tumber, *Small, Gritty, and Green: The Promise of America's Smaller Industrial Cities in a Low-Carbon World*

Sam Bass Warner and Andrew H. Whittemore, *American Urban Form: A Representative History*

John Pucher and Ralph Buehler, eds., *City Cycling*

Stephanie Foote and Elizabeth Mazzolini, eds., *Histories of the Dustheap: Waste, Material Cultures, Social Justice*

David J. Hess, *Good Green Jobs in a Global Economy: Making and Keeping New Industries in the United States*

Joseph F. C. DiMento and Clifford Ellis, *Changing Lanes: Visions and Histories of Urban Freeways*

Joanna Robinson, *Contested Water: The Struggle Against Water Privatization in the United States and Canada*

William B. Meyer, *The Environmental Advantages of Cities: Countering Commonsense Antiurbanism*

Rebecca L. Henn and Andrew J. Hoffman, eds., *Constructing Green: The Social Structures of Sustainability*

Peggy F. Barlett and Geoffrey W. Chase, eds., *Sustainability in Higher Education: Stories and Strategies for Transformation*

Isabelle Anguelovski, *Neighborhood as Refuge: Community Reconstruction, Place Remaking, and Environmental Justice in the City*

Kelly Sims Gallagher, *The Globalization of Clean Energy Technology: Lessons from China*

Vinit Mukhija and Anastasia Loukaitou-Sideris, eds., *The Informal American City: Beyond Taco Trucks and Day Labor*

Roxanne Warren, *Rail and the City: Shrinking Our Carbon Footprint While Reimagining Urban Space*

Marianne E. Krasny and Keith G. Tidball, *Civic Ecology: Adaptation and Transformation from the Ground Up*

Erik Swyngedouw, *Liquid Power: Contested Hydro-Modernities in Twentieth-Century Spain*

Ken Geiser, *Chemicals Without Harm: Policies for a Sustainable World*

Duncan McLaren and Julian Agyeman, *Sharing Cities: A Case for Truly Smart and Sustainable Cities*

Jessica Smartt Gullion, *Fracking the Neighborhood: Reluctant Activists and Natural Gas Drilling*

Nicholas A. Phelps, *Sequel to Suburbia: Glimpses of America's Post-Suburban Future*

Shannon Elizabeth Bell, *Fighting King Coal: The Challenges to Micromobilization in Central Appalachia*

Theresa Enright, *The Making of Grand Paris: Metropolitan Urbanism in the Twenty-First Century*

Robert Gottlieb and Simon Ng, *Global Cities: Urban Environments in Los Angeles, Hong Kong, and China*

Anna Lora-Wainwright, *Resigned Activism: Living with Pollution in Rural China*

Scott L. Cummings, *Blue and Green: The Drive for Justice at America's Port*

David Bissell, *Transit Life: Cities, Commuting, and the Politics of Everyday Mobilities*

Javiera Barandiarán, *Science and the Environment in Chile: The Politics of Expert Advice in a Neoliberal Democracy*

Benjamin Pauli, *Flint Fights Back: Environmental Justice and Democracy in the Flint Water Crisis*

Karen Chapple and Anastasia Loukaitou-Sideris, *Transit-Oriented Displacement or Community Dividends? Understanding the Effects of Smarter Growth on Communities*

Henrik Ernstson and Sverker Sörlin, eds., *Grounding Urban Natures: Histories and Futures of Urban Ecologies*

Katrina Smith Korfmacher, *Bridging the Silos: Collaborating for Environment, Health, and Justice in Urban Communities*

Jill Lindsey Harrison, *From the Inside Out: The Fight for Environmental Justice Within Government Agencies*

Anastasia Loukaitou-Sideris, Dana Cuff, Todd Presner, Maite Zubiaurre, and Jonathan Jae-an Crisman, *Urban Humanities: New Practices for Reimagining the City*

Govind Gopakumar, *Installing Automobility: Emerging Politics of Mobility and Streets in Indian Cities*

Amelia Thorpe, *Everyday Ownership: PARK(ing) Day and the Practice of Property*

Tridib Banerjee, *In the Images of Development: City Design in the Global South*

Ralph Buehler and John Pucher, eds., *Cycling for Sustainable Cities*

Casey J. Dawkins, *Just Housing: The Moral Foundations of American Housing Policy*

Kian Goh, *Form and Flow: The Spatial Politics of Urban Resilience and Climate Justice*

Kian Goh, Anastasia Loukaitou-Sideris, and Vinit Mukhija, eds., *Just Urban Design: The Struggle for a Public City*

Sheila R. Foster and Christian Iaione, *Co-Cities: Innovative Transitions Toward Just and Self-Sustaining Communities*

Vinit Mukhija, *Remaking the American Dream: The Informal and Formal Transformation of Single-Family Housing Cities*

Cindy McCulligh, *Sewer of Progress: Corporations, Institutionalized Corruption, and the Struggle for the Santiago River*

Susan Handy, *Shifting Gears: The History and Future of American Transportation*

Manisha Anantharaman, *Communal Sustainability: Gleaning Justice in Bengaluru's Discards*

Zachary B. Lamb and Lawrence J. Vale, *The Equitably Resilient City: Struggles and Solidarities in the Face of Climate Crisis*

J. Mijin Cha, *A Just Transition for All: Workers, Communities, and a Carbon-Free Future*

Jamie Wang, *Reimagining the More-Than-Human City: Stories from Singapore*

Jason Corburn and DeVone Boggan, *Advancing Peace: Ending Urban Gun Violence Through the Power of Redemptive Love*

Publisher contact:
The MIT Press
Massachusetts Institute of Technology
77 Massachusetts Avenue, Cambridge, MA 02139
mitpress.mit.edu

EU Authorised Representative:
Easy Access System Europe, Mustamäe tee 50,
10621 Tallinn, Estonia
gpsr.requests@easproject.com

Printed by Integrated Books International,
United States of America